THE

CRITICAL

MYTHOLOGY

OF IRONY

Joseph A. Dane

The University of
Georgia Press
Athens and London

© 1991 by the University of Georgia Press
Athens, Georgia 30602
Designed by Mary Mendell
Set in Perpetua
The paper in this book meets the guidelines
for permanence and durability of the Committee on
Production Guidelines for Book Longevity of the
Council on Library Resources.
Printed in the United States of America
95 94 93 92 91   5 4 3 2 1
Library of Congress Cataloging in Publication Data

Dane, Joseph A.
   The critical mythology of irony / Joseph A. Dane.
      p.   cm.
   Includes bibliographical references (p.   ) and index.
   ISBN 0-8203-1309-2 (alk. paper)
   1. Irony in literature.   I. Title.
PN56.I65D36   1991
809'.918—dc20   90-11235
                                              CIP

British Library Cataloging in Publication Data available

Barbarous Monster!
how have I deserved
that my Passion
should be *resulted* and
treated with *Ironing*?
—Henry Fielding
Joseph Andrews

CONTENTS

ACKNOWLEDGMENTS

I had help from many family members, friends, colleagues, and students during the course of this project, and I thank in particular John Benton, Jackson Cope, Theresia de Vroom, David Fox, Thomas Gustafson, Seth Lerer, Howard McMaster, Josef Raab, Jo Sarzotti, Marc Schoenfield, and Max Schulz. Others who read portions of this in manuscript will know, even without this reference, that I am grateful to them as well. To Marvin Morillo and Leslie Whitbread, I owe more general thanks, somewhat past due. And it is perhaps too late to note that some twenty years ago I learned all I know about work from one who was incapable of getting anything in return except for this late and grudging acknowledgment. Finally, without the support of Lawrence and Susan Green, I might not have been in a position to begin this project and I certainly would have had little interest in completing it; I dedicate everything of value here to them.

INTRODUCTION

Johnson's *Dictionary* contains an interesting misprint under the entry "Irony"; the Greek origin for the word is given not as *eirōneia* but as *ierōneia*. *Eirōneia* (irony), *eirōn* (commonly defined as a dissembler), *eirō* (to speak) are displaced by a nonsense word that could be construed as a nominal form of the adjective *hieros* (holy; hallowed). Irony is transformed from a manner of dissembling in speech, particularly in questioning, into something characteristic of holy men.[1]

The transposition of the two letters results in an inadvertent sketch of the history of the word. Two forces are in opposition within its semantic history, and it is the balancing of these two poles that results in the modern understanding of irony. The word irony has long been associated with Socrates, and the meaning of the word has depended largely on the reception of Socrates. To his opponents, Socrates was a liar, a dissembler (*eirōn*). In the Middle Ages, Socrates was simply an exemplar of ordinary moral or philosophic virtue, exhibited in his patience with his wife Xanthippe. With the reestablishment of Plato's texts in the canon and the subsequent redefinition of Socrates, first in the Renaissance and then in the romantic period, came a new understanding of irony. *Eirōneia*, Socrates' characteristic manner of speech, becomes what I will call **ierōneia*—something undefined and undefinable, but something deserving veneration. When, in the language of New Criticism, irony becomes something threatened by so-called heresy, the eighteenth-century printer's error proves prophetic: "To pursue the ironic and tensional theories in the way most likely to avoid the Manichaean heresy will require a certain caution in the use of the solemn and tragic emphasis. Dark feelings, painful feelings, dismal feelings, even tender feelings move reality toward the worship of evil." [2]

The participants in this transformation of irony include philosophers, writers, critics, poets, aristocrats and would-be aristocrats. Lord Shaftesbury sees the proper use of irony as a mark of "good-breeding"; Hegel attacks Friedrich Schlegel's supposed theory of irony in the same breath as he attacks Schlegel's claim to nobility.[3] And postromantic critics find in the word irony a convenient evaluative term for what is interesting, moral, or worth study in literature.

The following study is an examination of the history of the word implied by the printer's error in Johnson's *Dictionary*. That the understanding of irony has changed and is still changing has been well documented. But what has been the function of these changes? What particular advantages have there been for the philosopher, the poet, or the critic in invoking irony? And why privilege a term that in some of its early uses is clearly meant as a form of abuse?

A study on irony does not need a statement pleading for the centrality of the topic in literary studies. Most literary scholars in the United States are associated in some way with New Criticism, either directly as a result of their education or through their working association with colleagues. Despite our critical sympathies, the language we speak is heavily indebted to New Criticism, even as we try to mask that debt or change the meaning of that language. In the most influential statements of New Criticism, the word irony designates not a special technique or literary phenomenon but rather what might be called literariness itself—whatever makes literature worthy of critical attention. Cleanth Brooks's *Well-Wrought Urn* states this directly:

> If the structure of poetry is a structure of the order described, that fact may explain (if not justify) the frequency with which I have had to have recourse, in the foregoing chapters, to terms like "irony" and "paradox." By using the term irony one risks, of course, making the poem seem arch and self-conscious, since irony, for most readers of poetry, is associated with satire, *vers de société,* and other "intellectual" poetries. Yet, the necessity for some such term ought to be apparent; and irony is the most general term that we have for the kind of qualification which the various elements in a context receive from the context.[4]

Irony is defined as that on which the critic's eye falls.

The fluidity of critical language in this statement by Brooks is fascinating: irony is first a word; it becomes a concept, something readers imagine; finally it is a thing (external to language) that the critic can define at will. There are certain intellectual matters which are not really intellectual at all and must be referred to in inverted commas, indistinguishable in print from quotation marks. Other critics' words? Other readers' errors? And can New Criticism correct the vague concepts associated with these readers' thinking?

According to Brooks, the term irony is arbitrary; other terms would do as well. But it is also characterized as necessary. Some choice must be made; there has to be some consensus as to what is important in literature: "The necessity for some such term ought to be apparent." And in the next sentence, "what is important" is not to be entrusted to a reader's caprice, nor is it something requiring a certain productive blindness or arbitrary bracketing of peripheral material. Rather, the particular critical choices (those of Brooks) are universalized: the critic's focus organizes all significant literary phenomena. The focal point itself (something perceived in a poem) exists in a context, and the relation of that point to its context is called irony. If we accept Brooks's definition, we must consequently view anyone who does not deal with irony as overly specialized, narrow, pedantic. Irony becomes the subject matter of any serious literary scholar within the liberal tradition.

The critic's eye lends legitimacy to its objects, and it is not uncommon for literary scholars and critics to describe their subject matter, however specialized, in the same terms used by Brooks for irony.[5] Critics can focus on minutia, but (given the realities of modern academia) it is not in their interest for such minutia to remain minutia. Whether the object of attention is a pun, a slip of the pen, a minor poem, a neglected genre, or even an eighteenth-century misprint—that object can be seen as representative of the entire field of literature. The detail tends toward the universal. There are clearly scholarly examples of such a technique that most of us would regard as abuses. But would we consider Derrida's *Éperons,* based on a personal note by Nietzsche ("I have lost my umbrella"), to be such an example?[6]

The present study of irony is not immune from these criticisms. My history of a particular word will imply to some extent a skeletal history of Western literature and its critical reception. I will be challenging many of the ahistorical notions that have developed in the history of irony; the familiar critical notions of dramatic irony and romantic irony in particular seem to rest on very shaky ground when their origins are considered. But I obviously do not consider these matters of interest solely to a handbook on irony or to histories of irony. The problems I encounter in this history are problems that affect the history of criticism generally; the word irony itself will unavoidably tend toward a universal ahistorical meaning even in my discussion of those particular meanings I wish to discredit.

I have made one methodological assumption that will distinguish this study from others on irony, and this assumption, I believe, has also determined many of my conclusions. I consider irony not a literary or philosophical phenomenon that has been received by criticism. That is, irony is not something created by writers, readers, and their related institutions and subsequently studied by critics and historians. Rather, irony is a word or complex of words made up of its cognates in various European languages; it is of interest only insofar as it is invoked by critics and historians to explain or to define certain literary phenomena (I am using the term literary in a broad sense). From the point of view of this study, Socratic irony is not something exemplified by the Socrates of Plato (or the somewhat different Socrates of Aristophanes or Xenophon); it is rather something Socrates is said to have exemplified. Socratic irony, in this sense, does not exist for Plato (or his Socrates) at all, since there is no term for such a phenomenon in Plato. Socratic irony is a later phenomenon; in the rhetorical tradition, it is what in Latin comes to be known as *urbana dissimulatio*—that irony related to Socrates, or to a particular version of Socrates. Nevertheless, the irony *of* Socrates can be studied in the texts of Plato, Aristophanes, and later writers—for example, in the *Symposium* where Alcibiades specifically refers to Socrates as ironic; in Aristophanes' *Clouds* where again the word appears in association with Socrates (albeit a very different Socrates).

Because I focus on critical language rather than the objects of that language, I am not concerned with the existence or nonexistence of Socratic irony or of the irony of Socrates. I am concerned only with the invocation of such things by scholars who have studied Socrates, and with that curious certainty of scholars who, while shrewd enough to know that no single definition is possible, do not consider this much more than an inadequacy of language. J. A. K. Thomson's opening statement is exemplary: "Irony, which is a criticism of life, is as hard to define as poetry. On the other hand, it is perhaps no harder to recognize. I hold it therefore the wiser course to treat it as one treats poetry, content in the main to know it when one meets it." [7] My approach to various types of irony—Socratic irony, romantic irony, rhetorical irony, dramatic irony—contrasts sharply with such approaches. These phrases do not necessarily refer to preexistent literary or philosophical phenomena; ironies are not embedded in texts awaiting discovery and classification by me or by any other critic. These phrases are, rather, part of the language of criticism; and it might be useful, although typographically unsightly, to mark them with brackets, inverted commas, or quotation marks throughout. [8]

The qualification is an important one, for it will determine the questions this study can legitimately ask. Who announced the existence of romantic irony? Why, when Schlegel uses the word irony, is it assumed he is thinking of romantic irony rather than, say, Socratic irony? And what happens to Schlegel when we assume a total coherence for his statements on irony? How is a medieval writer such as Chaucer transformed when described by nineteenth- and twentieth-century critics as ironic? When we find Socrates, Plato, Chaucer, or Schlegel referred to as ironic over centuries, do we have a continuous critical tradition? or is that tradition better regarded as discontinuous—a series of revisions disguised through specious verbal repetitions? The qualification will similarly exclude a number of familiar and not uninteresting questions: what are the precedents for romantic irony? what tradition of irony can be found in the history of the novel?

This work studies the critical mythology of irony and its origins. By the mythology of irony, I mean the assumptions and accepted beliefs (often contradictory) that control our reception of irony, and I am concerned with how that mythology directs both my own thinking and that of my reader. My characterization of the critical discourse of irony as mythology does not mean that its objects (ironies) are necessarily nonexistent, nor that such mythology is invalid as an intellectual system. Creation myths may or may not be true, yet their mythic nature is indifferent to their truth. Similarly, there are innumerable myths that in ordinary literary-critical discussions might not be worth disputing—for example, that Shakespeare is a great poet. I am not certain what greatness means; but I can learn much about Shakespeare (and about Shakespeareans) by ignoring the problems the concept of poetic greatness raises. It is possible to consider the implications of that myth (the notion of poetic greatness) without denying the possible truth of the myth. And even if I deal critically with the notion of greatness—perhaps it is something created by the economics of publishing or academia—I do not deny the history of that greatness (the sales figures, the number of critical studies, even their interest). Irony is another such critical myth. My own examination is not intended to eliminate or to transform that myth, but it should, for my readers, expose some of the assumptions underlying the myth and perhaps lessen its influence over critical thinking.

The skeptical tone and language I have adopted are the results of methodological considerations. Since my object of study is the critical institution, I have looked with suspicion on the critical pronouncements contained within the received language of irony. I do not accept the statement that Socrates is ironic because the statement that Socrates is ironic is the object of my study; I do not accept the notion that romantic irony is an invention of the early romantics because that myth is also the object of my study.

The danger in any discussion of irony is the assumption that the word must have a coherent and universal referent in the objects to which it is applied. According to the assumptions of this study, the word is better understood in terms of origins and motivations. What it means, what it refers to, cannot be articulated without reference to these origins, whether critical, literary, or institutional, and the entire referential function of irony may well be critical mystification. The lure of the referent is powerful: it is the invitation to go beyond Alcibiades' description of Socrates into the mind of Socrates itself—the question (which I will excise here) as to how Diotima's speech is itself an example of the irony spoken of by Alcibiades. Diotima's speech will not be at issue here; my question concerns only the often less appealing critical discourse that has received that speech. I have worked within the strictures of this assumption as much as possible, and it will be easy enough to see where I have violated them.

The questions asked throughout this study deal with the critical functions of irony: why invoke it? what is the critic attempting to do? The specific answers to such questions may well be of less critical interest than the discussion those questions provoke. My study will attempt to show in what way irony is and always has been a critical weapon—one deployed in the struggle between the critic and his object. That Socrates is called ironic says little about Socrates but much about the reception of Socrates. If we wish to refocus on Socrates, while retaining the assumptions of this study, we can say that irony refers to the situation of the critic as defined by Socrates and the texts about Socrates. The question of Plato's ironic Socrates then becomes a question of the Socrates of Platonists, and Socrates himself once more proves elusive.

The view adopted here is double, or parallactic.[9] A description of irony is the product of two critical points of view—one directed toward the literature and its history (the words of Socrates as recorded by Plato, the words of Schlegel, Thomas Mann, Kafka) the other toward the critical reception of that literature (Cicero, Haym, Brooks). Irony lies at the intersection of those views. Even more strongly, irony may well be created by that intersection. The critical tradition brings its objects into being by invoking them. I balance the two views and their corresponding objects (literary and critical) only by pretending I can exclude one of them.

The subject headings I will use below are familiar to anyone who has dealt with irony and its history: Socratic irony, dramatic irony, Chaucerian irony, romantic irony, New Critical irony. By stretching, and in some cases ignoring, the limits of my competence, I could add many more: German scholars might define a special irony to describe the work of Mann; French scholars might define one for Flaubert or Proust. The difference between an English and a German scholar's views of romantic irony is substantial, and each may deserve its own chapter.

My chapter divisions thus are not exhaustive. I have chosen particular topics defined in the critical tradition of irony, topics that I believe are representative. Each has a history and in all cases those histories intertwine. An adequate twentieth-century discussion of Socratic irony must entail a discussion of romantic irony. The particular evasions used by critics of medieval irony cannot be understood fully without an understanding of the history of dramatic irony. Dramatic irony must be understood within the context of the institutions that defined Socratic irony. A literary history is essentially anachronistic, not accidentally so. A phrase such as "medieval irony" is essentially ambiguous, meaning either "irony characteristic of the medieval period" or "irony described by medievalists" (the phrase "medieval scholar" describes Anselm, Thomas, and many of my friends as well). Medieval irony thus is both a variant of rhetorical irony and a product of romantic irony; its history is one that necessarily involves gaps, repetitions, and discontinuities, and the same could be said of any of the topics I have defined below.

Some of those discontinuities and gaps result from the literary tradition itself. A history of the ironic novel (a topic only touched on in this study) is necessarily discontinuous, with its chief examples including most probably Cervantes, Sterne, Flaubert, Stendhal, Mann, Kafka, the French New Novelists. But which Cervantes? A Spanish Cervantes? or, in relation to irony, the Cervantes as received by Schlegel and Tieck? In addition to the discontinuities of national traditions, there are from a critical perspective the even more striking discontinuities between historical theory and practice. Such discontinuity between the theory and practice of irony has been noted by Paul de Man, but the discontinuity is not strictly a failure of nineteenth-century theory to coordinate with nineteenth-century literary practice, as de Man implies; not the failure of German novelists to produce an ironic novel and the failure of French critics to produce a theory for Flaubert and Stendhal.[10] The discontinuity is more basic: it is the result of arbitrary scholarly definitions overlaid on an evolving tradition. To ask whether Flaubert is more ironic than Stendhal, or to claim flatly, as does de Man, that Wordsworth, Hölderlin, and Rousseau are never ironic, whereas the fully developed ironic consciousness is to be found in Schlegel, Kierkegaard, and Nietzsche, is to deny the very evolution in the critical term that makes discussions of irony within historical contexts at all meaningful. Irony must necessarily mean different things to readers of Cervantes, Flaubert, Musil, and Mann. The fluid terminology of the early romantics, which I will have occasion to criticize, had the particular advantage of its own deficiencies: it failed to provide a theory that made *Don Quixote* and *Wilhelm Meisters Lehrjahre* the same thing. Critical definitions evolve just as does literature, and those evolutions are not necessarily parallel.

I have chosen the subject of irony in part because I have used that word to describe my own approach to literature, in teaching and in scholarship. Although I am perfectly convinced of my ability to recognize my own irony, I am equally convinced, as a scholar, that what I recognize is not something that really exists at all except in my own claim that it does. I am ironic; you are; scholarship is: in one sense, these are empty claims; they do not provide ironclad or even coherent definitions. But they are not without their implications—literary, philosophical, critical. They set an activity within a particular institutional context. And it is the implication of that context that I will be studying below.

Studies of irony are of various types: what I call meditative studies, inspired often by Kierkegaard's *Concept of Irony;* rhetorical and stylistic studies; structural and practical studies; and finally general histories of irony. Most studies combine aspects of different types; for example, Wayne Booth's *Rhetoric of Irony* is as much a meditation (a polemical one) as it is a rhetoric; historical studies involve practical concerns in their actual and implied readings as well as structural concerns in their very organization.[11] My own work is one I am clearly trying to situate in the last category, although no history of irony is even thinkable without the limits established by alternate approaches.

Kierkegaard's *Concept of Irony* has served as a starting point, or at least as an inspiration, for many twentieth-century studies of irony. For various reasons, some of them linguistic, I have relegated this work largely to my notes.[12] In French, Vladimir Jankélévitch's *Ironie* is clearly inspired by Kierkegaard; yet Jankélévitch's refusal to state or to follow a method has resulted in a book that is often praised but seldom used as a basis for further studies.[13] For Jankélévitch, irony is not something to be defined; it is rather the subject of what for medieval writers might be called a meditation. Jankélévitch follows Kierkegaard, but a different Kierkegaard from the dissertation writer of 1841; Jankélévitch seems to imagine a later Kierkegaard—one who might have written about irony had the earlier Kierkegaard not already done so. Irony is a philosophical and moral problem, and it is to these ends that Jankélévitch employs his chapter headings: "Le Mouvement de conscience ironique"; "La Pseudologie ironique; et de la feinte"; "Des pièges de l'ironie." Jankélévitch is often given credit for defining irony in existentialist terms as "la bonne conscience," but his headings imply a movement away from such an understanding of irony to a more negative one involving the dangers and traps of irony. These headings are themselves traps, often introducing unexpected content. Chapter 1 deals with Socrates and the moral dimensions of irony. But chapter 2 ("Pseudologie") introduces the romantic notion of self-reflection. And chapter 3 is less a warning about the dangers of irony than a reveling in those dangers: "confusion," "vertige et ennui," "probabilisme," "l'ironie humoresque," "jeux de l'amour et de l'humour"—dangers that lead to Jankélévitch's final quotation, from Proudhon: "Ironie, vraie liberté!"

Kierkegaard's study has also been the inspiration for recent structural studies of irony—studies that attempt to define irony (or types of irony) by opposing it to another term or terms. Such studies differ from mine in that they originate in or seek a universal definition of irony, a definition that serves as the basis for mapping oppositions involving irony onto other oppositions. The problematic history of the word can be ignored, and often to great advantage. In Alan Wilde's *Horizons of Assent: Modernism, Postmodernism, and the Ironic Imagination,* irony has no history, either as a word or as a concept.[14] Wilde raises the same questions in this study as in his earlier study of Forster, questions focusing on the difference between modernism and postmodernism. For scholars of twentieth-century literature, such questions are important; to those who specialize in other fields, however, the nuances of a new study of these questions are lost. The word irony is only artificially linked to such questions. And the supposed forms of irony that result ("mediate irony," "disjunctive irony," "suspensive irony") are simply the product of the dichotomy modern/postmodern. The controlling dichotomy and its relation to irony are assumed: "If . . . the defining feature of modernism is its ironic vision of disconnection and disjunction, postmodernism, more radical in its perceptions, derives instead from a vision of randomness, multiplicity, and contingency" (131). And critics who do not share such an assumption are disparaged: "But the tendency of most critics [despite Kierkegaard] is still, I believe, to regard irony as little more than a series of techniques and strategies" (3). Irony is not a word with a history, but a modern way of thinking: a "mode of consciousness, a perceptual response to a world without unity or cohesion" (2). It seems to have a life of its own: "Somehow irony manages again and again to escape its association with this or that school and to recast itself constantly into new and unpredictable modes" (1).[15]

I have spent some time with this work because it seems to me to represent a number of studies of irony, and to represent as well the way irony has been used as a critical topic. Irony is extremely ill defined, even for those critics who would not admit a direct lineage to a New Critic such as Brooks. It can be made to cover almost any literary topic imaginable and, furthermore, it can provide an audience for that topic. I would be very unlikely to read a book describing the difference between modernism and postmodernism. I did, however, read this one, and not without profit.

My own study is situated among the inevitably partial and often biased histories of irony. Most have their roots in classical meanings of irony, others have their roots in romanticism.[16] I have used these often, as I have used another book I came to quite late in my research, one that is arguably the single best history of irony: Uwe Japp's *Theorie der Ironie*.[17] The history these studies describe is a flexible one, and chronological categories can be mapped only loosely onto structural ones. Ernst Behler's diachronic categories (classical, modern, tragic) are similar to categories described by Japp as historical "dominants"—categories that could also be analyzed as particular elements of irony: *dissimilatio, assimilatio,* and *reservatio,* or *Verstellung, Anverwandlung,* and *Vorbehalt.* But neither triad is purely historical: as noted by both Japp and Behler, the words tragic and classical do not define irony in the same way. Historical, or diachronic, categories blur into synchronic ones. Furthermore, categories developed in the context of one national literature, German romantic irony, for example, cannot be as casually transferred to another as some scholars imply.[18]

My own categories respond to the same problems considered by Behler and by Japp—the difficulty of setting forth a universal definition, and the further futility of attempting to determine historical categories on rational and logical grounds. The context in which I write is, however, a distinctly American one. I differ from both Behler and Japp in terms of the direction in which my critical history leads. To Behler and Japp, the endpoint of the history of irony is a literary one—the modern novel, with its representatives in the work of Musil and Mann. To an American, the endpoint will be a critical one—the New Critical understanding of irony and its sometimes unwitting reception.

I will be presenting no universal definition of irony here, only a series of traditional definitions. Some are useful as objects of criticism; others provide convenient polemical standpoints. When we hear definitions or understandings of irony derided by critics as "too narrow," we might ask "too narrow for what?" and the answer to that question is obvious: too narrow for the critic to discuss what happens to be a favorite topic or, less kindly, a critical hobbyhorse.

The condemnation of limited definitions of the word irony has many variants. In a recent study by Gary Handwerk, irony is used to organize a number of what at first glance seem unrelated topics on Schlegel, Meredith, and Lacan.[19] Irony is defined in radically ahistorical, Lacanian terms: "Irony is . . . a question of the human subject, of how and where that subject emerges into language" (viii). And even Schlegel's own use of the word is suspect: "To trace the word *irony* alone through [Schlegel's] writings is to fall prey to the terminological fixity against which the entire force of his own reflections was directed" (20).

I will have occasion to discuss these questions again in my chapters on romantic irony. But here it is enough to note Handwerk's clear and direct statement of the problem and the issues involved. To proceed by following the word alone is to read Schlegel as he does not wish to be read. To read Schlegel as Schlegel wishes to be read (Handwerk does this extremely well) is to transcend the level of language itself.

And I do not wish to read Schlegel this way.

The following chapters are organized around five main topics: the question of beginnings (Socrates, dictionaries); rhetorical irony; romantic irony; nineteenth-century developments; American New Criticism and its aftermath. Irony, however defined, always suggests an authority. The history of irony outlined here will show a shift in that authority: from the domination of spoken statements by intended meanings, to the usurping of that linguistic authority by the romantic writer, to the final usurping of that authority by the postromantic critic. This final move entails the reconception of the ironist, who becomes associated more with the critic than with the poet. The evaluative force of the word seen in the quotation above by Brooks (irony is what is valuable in literature) becomes transformed into an implied evaluation of critics.[20]

This is the basis of a polemic that will be developed through this study. Stated more strongly, critics use the term irony in a self-serving manner and often in bad faith. In its history, irony generally involves an authority (for example, the authority of meaning over statement in rhetorical irony). In deriding such an authority or claiming to eliminate it altogether, critics only relocate that authority in themselves. The history that results is a mythic history legitimizing their own privileged positions, and it contains many of the features of an ancestral history: the noble origins in Socrates;

the various taxonomies that oppose a higher and more noble form of irony to a vulgar one. The association of the term in the United States with New Criticism has led to a further complication: how to retain one's noble lineage without admitting kinship to this suddenly disreputable forebear? I hope that the present study can provide at least a starting point for the more thorough critique of modern and contemporary criticism that remains largely implicit here.

PART ONE

BEGINNINGS

I

Socrates

∎

In this first section, I will set up two approaches to the problem of irony, both of which are essential to a history of irony. The two following chapters—the first on Socrates, the second on lexicons—should be regarded as charting limits for the chapters that follow.

Chapter 1 introduces Socratic irony, or what Japp might call a version of it—an irony that I will discuss with primary reference to Plato and with particular reference to the *Symposium*. How are we to discuss the problem of irony in Plato? in Socrates? And whose irony is this? How do we discuss these figures that survive the entire history of irony? To presume, as I do in my introduction, that a history of irony, however defined, can be constructed by limiting discussion to passages where the word irony itself appears is to imagine that a history can be produced in disregard of many of the most significant figures in that history, such as Socrates. The chapter is thus a deliberate violation of some of the principles established in my introduction and defines an upper limit for my discussion of irony.

Chapter 2 takes up a different problem, that of the lexicon. In my earlier study on parody, these lexicons proved to be the controlling force in the history of the word.[1] In regard to irony, the function of the lexicons is quite different. They are belated, conservative, uncritical. And yet it is from the lexicons that we derive much of our vocabulary and consequently our thinking about irony, and it is in the lexicons that we see many of our clichés recorded. Last, and perhaps most important, a lexicon is to a large extent a synchronization of the diachronic processes of language, an attempt to make wholly present the history of language. In the history of lexicons themselves, these synchronic tendencies are epitomized by the historical lexicon, a genre with its origin in works such as Junius's seventeenth-century English lexicon and what may be its endpoint in the *Oxford English Dictionary*.

The following section thus sets forth two traditional starting points in histories of irony: the image of the ironist in Socrates and the regulation of the word in the lexicons. On the surface, these two beginnings are opposed in the same way a concept is opposed to the words that correspond to it. The material word is the physical constraint on the abstract theory—as I have pointed out in my introduction, a check on the type of speculation made attractive by our own cultural situation.

Despite these apparent differences, these two beginnings lead to similar results or, more accurately, similar problems. For the word is as much conditioned by unchecked speculation on its supposed philosophical origins as is a history of those origins by the constraints of language. The figure of Socrates is rarely absent from modern discussions of irony, but the nature of this figure is shaped by romantic and postromantic views both of Socrates and of Plato. Historical origins (philosophical and political) blur quickly into modern prejudices concerning those origins—prejudices that not only are interesting in and of themselves but, considered strictly in relation to irony, condition what we imagine irony to be. Concentration on lexical definitions of irony yields similar results but through a completely different path. The conventional plan of the lexicon, even one with historical concerns such as the *Oxford English Dictionary,* is a denial of historicity. Meanings are listed by number, not by date, not by culture. A lexicon necessarily depends on a myth of universality.

The following section establishes these two divergent beginnings; a mediate approach will be the rhetorical tradition discussed in chapters 3 and 4.

Alcibiades and the Silenus

Alcibiades' drunken appearance at the end of the *Symposium* provided later writers with what was to be a characteristic description of Socrates. Socrates is a Silenus, whose external appearance contrasts with the "treasures" (*agalmata*) within. He is a Marsyas (a satyr), whose ugliness contrasts with the beauty and charm of his music: "And now I shall praise Socrates through figures (*di eikonōn*). And perhaps he will think this done for fun, but the icon will be used for truth, not for laughter. I say he is most like those sileni in statuary shops, which the craftsmen make to hold flutes and pipes, and they open up and have valuable images (*agalmata*) of the Gods inside" (215a–b).[2] Alcibiades' speech is the last in a series of speeches and is the only speech to praise love through praise of a particular beloved; Socrates himself characterizes it as a "satyr play" (223d). Forms of the word irony appear twice in this section, once in the simile of the Silenus and later in one of

Socrates' reported responses. Both times it is a word used by Alcibiades of Socrates, and it is intended to describe his usual manner.

Alcibiades tells of his attempted seduction of Socrates. But it is Alcibiades, not Socrates, who is charmed with Alcibiades' beauty, and Alcibiades who is seduced into doing whatever his lover desires:

> But having opened and examined him, I don't know if anyone has seen the beautiful treasures within. But I once saw them, and they seemed to me so divine and golden and beautiful and marvelous that I would have instantly done (*poiēton einai embrakhu*) whatever Socrates commanded. Imagining him to be enamored of my youth, I thought a most wonderful piece of luck had befallen me. It would be possible for me, having granted Socrates my favors, to hear him tell what he knew. For I thought highly of my youth. To carry out this plan, I sent away my servant so that we could be alone. (216e–217a)

Furthermore, Socrates' seduction of Alcibiades is nonsexual. As Alcibiades lies down with Socrates, he feels a "sting"—one higher than the sting of sexual love:

> Moreover, I have suffered the sting of the serpent. And they say that he who has suffered this does not wish to speak of it except to those who have also been bitten, since only they will understand and have compassion no matter what I was driven to do and to say because of the pain. For I have been bitten by a more painful bite than anyone can suffer, in the most painful place—I have felt in the heart or soul or whatever else it can be called the blows and bites of the words of philosophy, which are more painful than those given by any snake. (217e–218a)

Alcibiades then resolves to speak freely to Socrates (*eleutherōs*) and not to use fancy language (*khrēnai mēden poikillein;* 218c), but Socrates responds to this openness in another register—ironically (*eirōnikōs*):

> [Alcibiades:] "I believe you are the only lover worthy of me, and you seem too modest to speak. I think it would be very foolish of me not to grant this and anything else you might ask of me or my friends. For nothing is more noble for me than that I should become as good as possible, and I think there is no better help that could be chosen than you. Indeed I would be much more ashamed before wise men not to have favored a man such as you, than before all other ordinary men (*aphronous*) if I did favor you." And having heard, he answered in

his ironical manner that is so characteristic of him (*mala eirōnikas kai sphodra heautou te kai eithotōs*). (218c–d)

Socrates' following speech, then, is ironic. Or is it?

My dear Alcibiades, in fact, you risk being not ignoble, if what you say about me happens to be true, and if there is any power in me through which you might be better. You must see an irresistible beauty in me very different from any well-formedness in yourself. And indeed if having seen this you wish to share it with me and to exchange beauty for beauty, you must be thinking to take advantage of me not a little; for in place of the appearance, you are trying to possess the truth of beauty, and in fact you think to exchange brass for gold. But, o noble one, look better, lest I trick you, being nothing. The sight of the mind begins to see more sharply when that of the eyes begins to lose its acuity. And you have a long time ahead of you before this happens. (218e–219a)

The response that Socrates offers is a reversal of Alcibiades' praise. What does it mean that this response is ironical? in Socrates' customary manner? Does the irony lie in the content of this speech (which the text records)? or in a Socratic manner to which the text itself can only allude? Socrates claims he is nothing (*ouden*). The beauty of Socrates perceived by Alcibiades is chimerical. Not only is Alcibiades too smitten to recognize physical beauty (Socrates is ugly), he is also too young to recognize true beauty. Socrates' "usual ironical manner" as conceived by Alcibiades seems to be a logical manner of denial and rejection: he rejects Alcibiades' sexual advances; he rejects the implications of those advances (he will not exchange his own beauty for Alcibiades'); and he denies the premise of Alcibiades' proposition (it is not true that Alcibiades judges value correctly). This is, at least, how Alcibiades (in retrospect) seems to characterize Socrates' ironical manner. Socrates devalues what others value.

The same implications (with the same erotic overtones) are associated with the image of the Silenus—the "icon" through which Alcibiades describes Socrates:[3]

For you see that Socrates is enamored of beautiful men and is always around them and smitten by them and in turn is ignorant of everything and knows nothing. Isn't this form of his like a Silenus? Indeed. This is his outside appearance, like the carved Silenus. Inside, when he is opened, you know, my fellow drinkers, what temperance is within. You know that he does not care if anyone is beautiful, but despises it more than anyone could imagine, nor if a man is wealthy, or if he has any other honor valued by the many. He thinks that all such posses- sions are worth nothing and that we ourselves are nothing; I tell you, he spends his whole life ironizing (*eirōneuomenos*) and despising such things. (216d–e)

Socrates thus ironizes and toys with (*eirōneuomenos, paizōn*) all that other men find valuable.

Socrates' irony, as characterized here, is a reaction to what other men find important—whether that be an argument or a seduction. He is dan- gerous because of this, but also fascinating. He is the Marsyas who seduces with his music, like the sirens who attempt to seduce Odysseus (216a). He is also a Silenus, whose charms are hidden rather than open. But Alcibiades' apparent humiliation before Socrates has its own irony (or hypocrisy): his recognition of Socrates' secret charms is a sign of his superiority to the many. The distinction between the Marsyas (whose music is immediately charming) and the Silenus (whose charms are hidden) is a distinction be- tween two different audiences. Alcibiades' praise of Socrates is thus also Alcibiades' praise of himself and his own powers of perception.[4] Yet can Alcibiades' description be valid? If the Silenus contains images of the gods that only Alcibiades finds attractive and only Alcibiades can appreciate, then how can such an image be intelligible to Alcibiades' hearers or to Plato's readers? If we comprehend Alcibiades' image, the hidden charms are no longer hidden. The Silenus is then a deception that has no real victims but only imagined victims, just as Socrates' ironical manner flatters its audience by creating a class of fictitious hearers who cannot understand it.[5]

Socrates as Eirōn

The modern notion of the ironic Socrates depends on a number of factors, among them the reception of Plato and, as we shall see, the revision of the images that Plato leaves us (in this case that of the Silenus). The verbal basis of this notion, however, is weaker than might be supposed. Although Socrates becomes the exemplary ironist to later writers, the word *eirōn* and its derivatives are not often used of him by Plato and other contempo- raries. The word does not appear in reference to Socrates in Xenophon's *Memorabilia, Apology,* or *Banquet,* although some scholars note that Xeno- phon describes Socrates in terms that conform to some definitions of irony.[6] Aristophanes uses the word in *Clouds* (line 449) with reference to Socrates' "think tank" (*phrontisterion*), but not with reference to Socrates himself.[7]

The description in *Clouds* was stereotypical enough for Socrates (or Plato's version of him) to cite it in the *Apology*. In the *Apology*, Socrates refers to a "certain comic poet" who has slandered him (18c–d), and identifies this poet as Aristophanes (19c) while paraphrasing *Clouds:* "aerobatō kai periphronō ton hēlion" (line 225) ["I wander in the air and contemplate the sun"]. In *Clouds, eirōn* appears as a term of abuse in a lyric passage spoken by Strepsiades: "masthlēs eirōn gloios alazōn" (line 449) ["a slippery, oily knave, an *eirōn,* a braggart"]—an *eirōn* is one of the disreputable types Strepsiades hopes to become by associating himself with Socrates' think tank. But despite the stereotypical comic description of Socrates earlier in the play, the word *eirōn* itself is not here applied to him. To Socrates' contemporaries, the word irony is a term of abuse, but one with only a casual association with Socrates himself.[8]

I will be examining this early history and the development of the rhetorical meanings of the word in more detail in a later chapter; here, I will look briefly at Plato's use of it. Plato uses the word irony and its derivatives sparingly, generally, but not exclusively of Socrates.[9] In the *Apology,* the use of the word by Socrates implies that irony is characteristic of him. He claims that it is most difficult for him to respond to the suggestion that he flee Athens: "For if I tell you that this would be to disobey the god, you would not be persuaded by me [whom you imagine to be] ironic (*ou peisesthe moi hōs eirōneuomenō)*" (38a). Apparently, to imagine that Socrates was not serious was easy for his audience to do, and that lack of seriousness could be characterized as an example of his irony.

In the *Sophist,* the word appears several times, always associated with sophists, among whom Socrates appears to be included. The stranger identifies two types of ironists, public and private. The public ironist (a demagogue) "ironizes" in long speeches before crowds; the private ironist uses brief statements to force an opponent into contradictions (*Soph.* 268a–b). The word appears at the end of the stranger's speech, and if his purpose is to identify Socrates with the sophists, the use of a word characteristic of Socrates would certainly be useful in doing so.[10]

But even by the time of Plato's later work, the association of irony with Socrates is not fixed. Socrates uses the word in the *Laws,* referring to the hypocrisy of the atheist who pretends to religion (908e; and there seems nothing in this passage to justify calling it self-consciously ironic). In an earlier dialogue, the *Euthydemus,* the word is also used without direct reference to Socrates. Here, Socrates (reporting the dialogue) is being questioned by Dionysodorus: "Then, after an ironic pause [*eironikōs*], in which he seemed to be thinking of something great, he said: 'Tell me, Socrates, have you an ancestral Zeus?' Here, suspecting that the argument was about to reach a conclusion, I tried to escape; I gave a desperate twist as if caught in a net and said: 'No, Dionysodorus, I have not' " (302b). Socrates later describes himself as "struck dumb" in this dispute and defeated to "universal applause and laughing" (303a–b). But there is no suggestion that we should be, nor is Crito, to whom Socrates is reporting the dialogue. Nonetheless, the "ironical pause" is said by Socrates to be part of his opponent's weaponry.

In the *Republic,* the word is used by Thrasymachus simply in exasperation: what annoys Socrates' opponents in dialectic is his irony; irony is his usual manner (1, 337a). The use is reminiscent of Alcibiades' use of the word in the *Symposium,* but only these two texts suggest the stereotypical association with Socrates. The association of irony with Socrates may originate with Plato, but its persistence is largely a product of the later rhetorical tradition I will consider in chapter 3.

Erasmus and Rabelais

The image of the Silenus and the word irony provide later writers with fixed and stereotypical descriptions of Socrates, even though both the image and the word may be radically reinterpreted. The importance of the texts by Erasmus and Rabelais does not lie in the definitions of irony they provide; nothing particularly new or interesting is added to the rhetorical tradition here. Rather it lies in their association of the Silenus image (and consequently the ironic Socrates linked to it) with general problems of interpretation. The Silenus becomes proverbial in the Renaissance, and, as a proverb, it becomes extremely flexible in meaning and potential application. The Silenus is explicitly taken as a proverb as early as 1485; Pico della Mirandola uses the image to defend medieval theology: "Ita extrinsecus si aspexeris, feram videas, si introspexeris, numen agnoscas" [11] ["Thus, if you look at the outside, you will see a beast; if you look within, you will recognize the divine"]. Subsequently, it is used by Erasmus in several works and from there it makes its way into Rabelais's prologue to book 1 of *Gargantua and Pantagruel.*

Erasmus includes a short essay on the Silenus in the 1508 Aldine version of his *Adages.* This short essay was expanded to become the longest essay included in the 1515 edition. For Erasmus, as for Pico, the Silenus image contrasts an external husk with an internal meaning. It is used of two referents, a thing and a person:

Silēnoi Alkibiadou, id est *Sileni Alcibiadis,* apud eruditos in prouerbium abiisse videntur, certe in collectaneis Graecorum prouerbii vice referuntur, quo licebit vti vel de re, quae cum in specium et prima, quod aiunt, fronte vilis ac ridicula videatur, tamen interius ac propius contemplanti sit admirabilis, vel de homine, qui habitu vultuque longe minus prae se ferat, quam in animo claudat. (159–60, LB 2:770)[12]
[In learned writers, *Alcibiades' Sileni* seem to have been changed into a proverb—at least, it appears in the place of a proverb in Greek collections, where it can be used either of a thing (one that on the surface and, as they say, at first glance, seems vile and ridiculous but is admirable to one who observes it more deeply within and more closely) or of a man, who in his dress and face bears much less before him than he encloses in his soul.]

The contrast between body and soul allows Erasmus to define various types of Sileni—Diogenes, Antisthenes, Epictetus, and finally Christ: "An non mirificus quidam Silenus fuit Christus?" (164, LB 771). Christ bears an abject appearance and humble home. From there, Erasmus adds the prophets, martyrs, hermits, the apostles, paupers, the unlettered, the ignoble, and abject imbeciles. In addition to these, there are also what Erasmus calls "inuersi Sileni" (168, LB 2:773–74), by which he means those ecclesiastics with a beautiful exterior and corrupt interior.[13]

A similar description of Sileni occurs in *Praise of Folly,* with the emphasis less on the contrast between internal and external than on the potential reversal of all oppositions:

Principio constat res omneis humanas, velut Alcibiadis Silenos, binas habere facies nimium inter sese dissimiles. Adeo ut quod prima, ut ajunt, fronte mors est, si interius inspicias, vita fit: contra quod vita, mors: quod formosum, deforme: quod opulentum, id pauperrimum: . . . breviter, omnia repente versa reperies, si Silenum aperueris. (LB 4:428a–b)
[First, all human affairs, like the Sileni of Alcibiades, have two aspects that are very dissimilar. So that, as they say, what at first glance is death, becomes life if you look inside; and what seems life is death; what appears beautiful is ugly; what rich, the most poor: . . . in brief, if you open the Silenus, you will find everything suddenly reversed.]

The life of man is a play (428c), one that depends on the masks of the actors staying in place: "Adumbrata quidem omnia, sed haec fabula non aliter agitur" (428d) ["Everything is masked, but this play could not be performed otherwise"]. Life, thus, depends on pretence—but these are Folly's words.

Perhaps the most pointed reference to the Silenus is one of Erasmus's earliest, in the *Enchiridion* (1503). The description here is similar to that in Pico; the Silenus is related directly to problems of interpretation:

> Idem observandum in omnibus litteris, quae ex simplici sensu & mysterio, tanquam corpore atque animo constant, ut contempta littera, ad mysterium potissimum spectes: cujusmodi sunt litterae Poetarum omnium, & ex Philosophis Platonicorum: maxime vero Scripturae divinae, que fere Silenis illis Alcibiadeis similes, sub tectorio sordido ac pene ridiculo, merum Numen claudunt. Alioqui si sine allegoria legeris . . . (LB 5:29b)
>
> [So you must consider in all writing what rests on the simple sense and what on the allegorical (*mysterio*), as on the body and soul, so that having left the literal meaning you can most easily look to the allegorical. This applies to all the writings of the poets, as well as to Platonic philosophers: but especially to the Holy Scriptures, which like those Sileni of Alcibiades, enclose the pure divinity within, under a sordid and ridiculous cover. Now if you read without allegory . . .]

Alcibiades' Sileni (plural here, as in *Praise of Folly*) function both as an icon of the holiest type of writing (Scripture) as well as a signal as to how that writing is to be interpreted—allegorically. Erasmus may be extending a classification found in traditional rhetorical manuals, where *ironia* (as a verbal trope) is classed as a species of *allegoria*.[14]

Erasmus's texts become the *loci classici* for the image of the Silenus, and Rabelais's editors generally cite the *Adages* as Rabelais's source.[15] Yet whereas Erasmus in the *Adages* concentrates on the moral aspects of the image and follows Plato (perhaps unwittingly) in linking the image to praise and blame, Rabelais seems to follow Pico and Erasmus's brief reference in the *Enchiridion,* associating the image with problems of interpretation. Pico wished to save medieval theology from neglect; Rabelais wishes to pose the problem of the arbitrariness of any type of interpretation:

> Illustrious drinkers, and you, precious syphilitics—because my writings are dedicated to you and to no others—Alcibiades, in Plato's dialogue entitled the *Symposium,* praising his teacher Socrates, without doubt prince of the philosophers, among other words says he is like the Sileni. Sileni were once little boxes such as now we see in the stores of apothecaries, painted on the outside with joyous and frivolous figures, like harpies, satyrs, tamed birds, horned rabbits, saddled dogs,

flying bulls, harnessed deer and other such fantastic paintings made to make the world laugh (such was Silenus, master of Bacchus); but inside are contained fine drugs like balm, ambergris, *amomon,* musk, *zivette,* jewels and other precious objects. So Socrates is said to be, because seeing him from the outside and judging him by his external appearance, you wouldn't have given a slice of onion for him, so ugly was he of his body and ridiculous of manner, his nose pointed, with the look of a bull, the face of a fool, simple in manners, rustic in clothes, poor of fortune, unfortunate in women, inept for all duties of the republic, always laughing, always drinking with everyone, always mocking himself, always dissimulating his divine knowledge [*toujours disimulant son divin sçavoir*]; but opening this box, you would have found within a celestial and inappreciable drug—an understanding more than human, marvelous virtues, invincible courage, unequaled sobriety, certain contentment, perfect assurance, unbelievable contempt for all that humans desire and for which they run, work, sail and do battle.

(Prologue, *Gargantua*)

To Rabelais, the contrast between exterior and interior suggests less a difference between ugliness and beauty than one between frivolity and seriousness. The figures painted on the exterior of the apothecary boxes are not ugly at all, but rather "joyeux et frivoles."

Rabelais refashions the image of the Silenus as an icon for his own work: it bears on problems of interpretation of the superficially frivolous text. And if we consider Rabelais's "matieres assez joyeuses" as something we find on the literal level (corresponding, he tells us somewhat enigmatically, to the sweet sound of the Sirens), there will be a higher sense corresponding to the internal beauty of the Silenus. But Rabelais then adds a second interpretative icon. Haven't you ever seen a dog attacking a bone? What the dog is after is the "substantific marrow," or, for the exegete, the inner meaning of abstruse symbols: "la sustantifique mouelle, c'est à dire ce que j'entends par ces symboles Pythagoricques" ["the substantific marrow, or that which I understand by these Pythagorean symbols"]. Presumably, *Gargantua* is itself a Silenus, with treasures within; or a bone, whose surface (hard? or tasty?) hides nourishing marrow. The reader should penetrate the exterior fiction for the interior meanings . . . Or perhaps not:

Do you believe truly that Homer, writing the *Iliad* and *Odyssey,* ever thought of the allegories which have been attributed to him by Plutarch, Heraclides Ponticus, Eustathius, Phornutius, and that which Politian has stolen from them? If you believe it, you don't come close

to my opinion, which is that such things were as little dreamed of by
Homer as the sacraments of the Gospel by Ovid in his *Metamorphoses*—
which a certain Brother Lubin, a true cracker [*vray croque lardon*], tried
to prove, if by chance he found any as foolish as himself and (as the
proverb says), a cover worthy of the pot. (Prologue, *Gargantua*)

So we are not to read *Gargantua* for hidden meanings—precisely the opposite of what we were told to do earlier.

Rabelais reads the Silenus as an image of allegory. The rhetorician coats
words in sweetness to make the substance more palatable. Just so, the Silenus has appealing images on the exterior. A bone is like the medicine (the
drug), with a healthy inside and a useless exterior. But the appeal of the
bone is the same as its nourishment—the wise dog does not chew the bone
for the exterior shell.

So how are we to read Rabelais's "matieres assez joyeuses"? Rabelais
merely lists the two alternatives. We can believe that there is a "sustantifique mouelle," although no more hidden from us than the marrow of
the bone is hidden from a dog; in this case, his books are allegories. Or
we admit that Rabelais, as he claims, never imagined an allegory, any more
than did Homer or Ovid; in which case the work is not allegorical. Or is it?
Rabelais never says that, because Homer and Ovid did not dream of their
allegories, they were not there. That Virgil did not know of Christ did not
mean, according to many readers, that his fourth *Eclogue* did not predict
the birth of Christ. The image of the Silenus, then, poses the problem of
allegorical interpretations without solving it.[16]

The image of the Silenus in Rabelais is a revision of Erasmus, based in
part on a reading of the *Symposium*. It is associated with allegory (as the two
words are associated in rhetorical manuals), and contains the customary
language that in Latin describes Socrates' irony ("disimulant . . ."). [17] But it
leads only to a choice presented to the reader. The image of the Socrates
offered by Alcibiades, a Socrates twice labeled ironic, remains only an image
of authority closely linked to the notion of interpretation. As Rabelais suggests, it provides no guidance for interpretation. Rather, it posits a split
between the text and its interpretation. It is a sign not of an ironic spirit
(Socrates), but rather of a binary situation in which the text must be read
and perhaps transformed (legitimately?) in ways the author never imagined.

Modern Scholars and the Ironic Socrates

The use of the word irony by modern classicists with reference to Plato or
to Socrates has little support in sources contemporary with Socrates. It is

based rather on an understanding of Socrates, Plato, and irony conditioned in part by the Renaissance reception of Socrates and Plato and in part by romanticism (in the latter case, that relation often betrays itself as polemic against romanticism). Again, to discuss such irony in strictly chronological terms is impossible. Is Socratic irony as we know it preromantic? or post-romantic? The reception history outlined in this chapter can only allude to a major component of that history, which will receive more extensive treatment in chapters 5 through 7. The following section is intended only to sketch some of the options presented by classicists and to suggest the necessary anachronisms involved in them.

Two traditional and opposing approaches to Socratic irony are represented by Paul Friedländer and W. K. C. Guthrie.[18] Each begins by rejecting a particular version or definition of irony, characterized either as over-simplified or anachronistic. The rejected form of irony will yield to true irony. But this resulting true irony never seems freed of the assumptions associated with the rejected form. As we shall see in subsequent chapters, the strategies of such arguments, as well as their unintended results, have centuries of precedent.

Friedländer clearly states his debt to romanticism. There are various types of irony that exist in a hierarchy; Platonic irony, properly understood, is a higher form of irony than ordinary irony: "If irony were nothing but 'a mere swapping of a Yes for a No'—to put it into the jocularly polemical definition of Jean Paul—then we would be at the end of our discussion even before we had started it" (137). According to Friedländer, we must learn about irony from Thomas Mann.[19] The paragraph ends with another reference to Jean Paul, a quotation from his *Vorschule der Ästhetik:* "Plato's irony . . . could, if there is such a thing as world humor, be called world irony, swinging and hovering playfully not only over human errors (as humor hovers not only over human folly), but over all human knowledge, free as a flame that devours, delights, moves with ease, yet aspires only toward heaven."[20]

Friedländer, taking his lead from the romantics, rejects what we will define as rhetorical irony and seeks a higher form of irony:

> The form this ironic discourse takes is that Socrates places himself side by side and on the same level with the young men, though, ac-cording to common opinion and the actual practice of the Sophists, he, as teacher, should hold them at a distance. . . . Irony is particu-larly prominent at the conclusion of the aporetic dialogues. To admit

ignorance—this experience, this confession, forced upon us by logical reasoning, brings about a humbling of the self. (140–41)

Irony is part of Socratic eroticism: "Thus eroticism, not as a mask, but permeated with irony . . ." (142). Socrates is misunderstood by those who misunderstand irony: "Thrasymachos, on the other hand, fails to understand why it is impossible. He regards it as arbitrary dissimulation, as 'irony' in the ordinary sense of the word. 'I knew you would not answer, but play hide and seek' (eirōneusoio, [Rep. 1] 337a). He would have to grow beyond his own nature if he were to understand that this irony is not willful, but necessary" (143).

Friedländer's distinction between Socrates and Plato further supports his hierarchy: "Even those features of Socrates which we have so far seen—however much they were part of the life of the son of Sophroniskos—required Plato's hand in order to become as visible as they are. But gradually we ascend to forms of irony for which Plato, the artist and thinker, alone is responsible" (145). This ascent leads finally to the "last manifestation of ironic play: wordless irony consisting in the fact that Socrates, by virtue of his silent presence, represents ironic tensions—unspoken yet felt" (152).

The phrase "Plato, the artist and thinker" has its own implications. The dichotomy between Socrates and Plato is more than strictly historical. It is also no longer one between the teacher and pupil. Rather, Socrates is reduced in this formula to an object—the object of Plato's art and thought. And thus Socrates becomes something created by Plato (his art) and furthermore, something interpreted by Plato (his thought). Socrates is reduced to a text, or fixed as a text, which in turn must be viewed through Plato's eyes alone. Plato first creates the text, then interprets it. To imagine there is a Socrates here that can be extracted by Plato is only to fall prey to Plato's art. By attempting to isolate and strip away Plato's thinking, we are left with what we have defined as his art.

The hierarchy, then, is both historical (privileging later periods, renouncing origins) and interpretive (privileging the critic over the text). Friedländer's deceptively simple hierarchy defines us as participating in a power struggle between artist and exegete. As readers, we must necessarily privilege the reader-critic and thus logically the very text we are confronting.

Friedländer's hierarchy is itself an icon of the history of irony—the gradual accrual of definitions, implications, connotations, and the layering of those definitions over a substrate of some kind (a word with its imagined historical definition). This hierarchy is simply constructed. There are at least two basic forms (or understandings) of irony: the true form (undefined and perhaps undefinable), and a false form to which it is opposed. This second form is inauthentic, simple, trivial, vulgar, accessible; and true irony becomes defined through a *via negativa*. In combination with other problematic structures (the opposition between Socrates and Plato, for example), such a characterization of irony proves to be extremely productive. Both Plato and Socrates move through history: Plato's own views develop and evolve from Socrates' views; Socrates (or Plato's Socrates) develops and evolves toward a more Platonic philosophy as he is viewed by later philosophers through Plato's eyes. It is possible to imagine that either has an ironic relation to the other; does Plato ironize Socrates? or does the later, ahistorical Socrates ironize Plato? Over both Plato and Socrates hovers the philosopher-critic who addresses such questions. What, in the quotation from Jean Paul, is finally the source of Plato's "world irony"? Plato? or a Platonist?

Guthrie, following in the tradition of Wilomowitz, takes a much harder line on romanticism.[21] But this antipathy to romantic excesses does not free him from romantic assumptions and associations.

Guthrie dismisses what he calls the "attractive" (and thus false) interpretations by Friedländer and Kierkegaard in favor of the "more strictly scholarly" account of Eduard Zeller. Guthrie demands a strong sense of the word (presumably the "scholarly" one):

> This is the *eirōneia* which makes Thrasymachus so angry (*Rep.* 337a), and if we translate it "irony" we water it down unduly. In the fifth century it was a term of abuse meaning plainly deceit or swindling as in . . . Aristophanes. . . . In Plato it retains its bad sense. . . . It is not used for the gentle irony which [Socrates] employs with his young friends when he puts himself on a level with them and says "Come now, let's look into this, you and I, for I don't know any more about it than you do." (*The Fifth-Century Enlightenment,* 446)

According to Guthrie, we must give up our romantic inclinations and accept the scholarly facts—a "hard" sense of the word irony. Despite these admonitions, Guthrie himself cannot or will not maintain this hard sense in reference to Socrates. On the next page Guthrie defends Socrates as follows: "But the accusation of *eirōneia* in the full sense, involving deliberate deceit, can scarcely be maintained." Guthrie seems to be defending Socrates against his own philological accusations.

Zeller's notes, the basis for Guthrie's discussion, show a similar reaction against romanticism. Zeller's limited definition of irony is an attempt to foreclose the influence of romantics, specifically Hegel and Kierkegaard:

[Socrates] appears to establish himself as ignorant and seeking knowledge only to let others realize their own ignorance. In truth, the situation is quite different. We must understand under Socratic irony not merely a manner of conversation, nor worse that comic condescension and contrived ingenuousness that leads others to the ice only in order to laugh at their fall, or that absolute subjectivity and that denial of all general truth, which was for so long called by the name of irony in the romantic school.[22]

Zeller reintroduces some of the romantic language he explicitly rejects by considering Socrates' irony itself part of his dialectical method. Socrates confesses ignorance, but only to expose another's ignorance; this results in a dialectic in which knowledge is possible. Although Zeller rejects the common Hegelian definition of irony as "absolute subjectivity," his analysis of irony seems quite compatible with Hegel's own interpretation of irony in Solger, whereby negativity is a *Moment* in the dialectical development of the Idea.[23] Zeller has stripped away what he feels are the extravagances of romanticism only to retain its philosophical result.

Both Zeller and Guthrie see irony as having the same function—a function that is best revealed in the *Meno;* Socrates' admission of ignorance is a means whereby knowledge can emerge from the slave (Guthrie, *The Fifth-Century Enlightenment,* 447). Zeller and Guthrie thus begin with a notion of what irony is (a notion unavoidably influenced by romanticism) and apply that notion to Plato's texts. The *Meno* may well offer a clear model for Socratic dialectic. But the *Meno* never associates this method with the word irony, and the claim that the *Meno* is a model of irony (a claim found also in Hegel) is as anachronistic as the supposedly romantic notions of irony both Zeller and Guthrie reject.

The fortunes of the word irony and its derivatives follow the fortunes of Socrates himself. As long as he is regarded as suspect, the negative connotations of the word are brought out, as in *Clouds.* When Socrates becomes the exemplary philosopher, the word itself is subject to reevaluation, as we find in Aristotle's *Nicomachean Ethics.* At best, the association of irony with Socrates by his contemporaries is similar to his characterization of himself as a gadfly. When Alcibiades accuses Socrates of irony, he does so both in the context of praise and as a rejected lover. When Socrates refers to himself as ironical, he is doing so in a passage where he is mouthing a possible accusation. The stranger in the *Sophist* uses the word almost to mark his victory over Socrates. To the stranger, the use of the word irony should have the same function as does the "ironical pause" of Dionysodorus in the *Euthydemus*.

Let us look again at the *Symposium* text. Alcibiades' objection to Socrates is bound up in the question of *erōs,* and Friedländer is right to discuss irony in those terms. But Alcibiades' accusation also bears simply on the problem of irony. His objection to Socrates is not necessarily one directed at his emotions or his control—how can a man reject me? Nor is it necessarily resentment of the strength of the public man, that is, the warrior Socrates who fulfills a role to which Alcibiades the future general aspires. (Either interpretation would surely be legitimate.) In terms of irony, and in terms of the Silenus icon Alcibiades offers, Socrates is involved in a duplicity that itself involves victims. The images of strength and weakness (Socrates' indifference to physical pain, his courage) also relate to the image of power. Alcibiades constructs himself as a text, with a clear intention of seduction. Socrates not only rejects the seduction; he ignores the text, or misreads it. When Alcibiades offers himself, Socrates simply misreads the evidence (or so Alcibiades thinks): Alcibiades wants to exchange brass for gold. But which, in the example, is the brass? and which the gold? That is something that can only be decided by the Silenus-like figure of Socrates, whose decision can turn inside into outside, who can turn questions of the body into questions of the soul, and who can turn rhetorical exercises into discussions of their objects. A contest of speeches on love is transformed by Socrates into an inquiry into the nature of love, and finally into a demonstration of its expression—an expression which turns out to be the reverse of what is expected. True love, as manifested by Socrates toward Alcibiades, requires the absence of its own expression.

Alcibiades objects to Socrates for the same reason that Thrasymachus does in the *Republic.* Socrates reacts in a predictable and evasive manner, which both Alcibiades and Thrasymachus associate with the word irony. Socrates refuses to answer as the text dictates. Of course he does not refuse to answer Thrasymachus, any more than he rejects the advances of Alcibiades (Alcibiades admits that his attraction to Socrates is not physical; the bite he has suffered is the bite of philosophy). He simply proves to be the recalcitrant exegete—the exegete who refuses the artist's intentions and constructs an exegetical version of a text. Socrates and Alcibiades/Thrasymachus thus are engaged in the same struggle that will find its counterpart in Plato's own exegetes—the struggle of the reader against the text. And such a reading will result often in a rejection—the rejection of the political Plato (Karl Popper);[24] the rejection of a historical Socrates, the son of Sophronistos (Friedländer); the rejection of the rhetorical view of Socrates (the romantics); and the rejection of the extravagant Socrates of the romantics (Zeller, Guthrie). Irony, thus, is not this action itself, but rather a word that becomes associated with such a struggle; if not a sign of that struggle, the word at least indicates its existence. When a reader, critic, or exegete speaks of irony, that reader is invoking a struggle between reader and text, and likewise the struggle of the reader, not for understanding, but rather for mastery.

It should be clear throughout this discussion that even as I seek what could be called a central meaning for irony (or some general propositions associated with the word irony), I do not wish to characterize this meaning as an original meaning. We cannot hope to uncover such a meaning by stripping away centuries of exegetical excrescences, since these are part of whatever meaning the term may have. In Japp's terms, history provides various versions of Socratic irony, but each new version affects a previous one, and they cannot be separated by a strict chronology. If there is a central meaning for the word irony, it is one that is central only from the standpoint of the twentieth-century context in which I write.

My characterization of Socratic irony, thus, looks ahead to rhetorical irony (what Friedländer qualifies with the word "mere"); it looks ahead as well to romantic irony (dismissed by other classicists as anachronistic). We cannot leave the problem of Socrates here. We will find that problem subject to reanalysis within each area of irony we define, from its apparent suppression in the rhetorical tradition through the reduction of Socrates to a teachable exemplum, to its elaboration in world-historical terms by the romantics and their successors.

2

Lexicography

■

The previous chapter points out the impossibility of isolating a historical Socrates, or a historical Socratic irony. The apparent chronology, Plato to modern, is belied by the nature of our thinking about chronology. One historical Socrates died in 399 B.C., but another equally historical Socrates continues to develop. The lexical tradition—with Socrates, the second standard beginning for inquiries into irony—reveals the same problems. Two histories are conflated in this tradition: that of the lexicon itself and that of its subject matter. I will be dealing below with a series of lexicons: the medieval lexicons of Godefroy and Du Cange; classical lexicons (the French lexicons of Richelet, Furetière, and the Académie française); and the *Oxford English Dictionary*. The relations among these are so close that even the most basic distinctions, such as French vs. English or medieval vs. modern, are misleading. Medieval dictionaries often use definitions from modern dictionaries to provide what will seem to be historical precedent for those definitions.

The lexicographical definitions to be discussed here were themselves based on definitions already current in rhetoric manuals of the type to be discussed in chapter 3. They are clearly reductive, but that very reductiveness has had a productive effect on the history of irony in criticism. Lexical definitions can of course provide specious authority for various practical literary readings (with predictable results), but they can also provide a negative basis for revision of terminology. The dictionaries of the seventeenth and eighteenth centuries refined the classificatory schemata and standard definitions developed in the field of rhetoric, particularly in the schools and in the handbooks in which that tradition is recorded. The lexicon thus freed irony from its rhetorical context, allowing romantic and postromantic writers greater freedom to reevaluate the word based on the positive associations (with Socrates for example), while considering the basic definition of irony a convenient object of polemic.

The chronological problems of the lexical tradition can be seen by referring quickly to the definition of irony given by Godefroy in *Dictionnaire de l'ancienne langue française*.[1] The date of the following entry is 1902: "Ironie. s.f. raillerie particulière par laquelle on dit le contraire de ce que l'on veut faire entendre" ["a particular kind of raillery through which one says the contrary of what one wishes to be understood"]. Anyone familiar with the history of the word irony will recognize immediately the bases of this definition. It is neither a definition pertaining directly to Old French (as it claims), nor one expansive enough to contain the connotations of the word at the beginning of the twentieth century. It has its origins not in its subject matter (the word irony and its history) but rather in its own form: it is a product of the tradition of French lexicons. I will return to Godefroy's complete definition later. But first, let us look at the origins of his language.

Three dictionaries were produced almost simultaneously in France, by Richelet, by Furetière, and by the Académie française. Relations between these lexicons are close—so close, that Furetière was expelled from the Academy for presumed plagiarism. The later editions of these, especially the later editions of the Academy dictionary, are particularly valuable in tracing the received history of the word.[2]

Richelet's 1680 dictionary gives a simple definition that owes much to the rhetorical tradition (the lineage of Godefroy's definition is instantly apparent): "ironie. s.f. Raillerie fine. Figure qui consiste à se moquer avec esprit. L'ironie étoit la figure favorite de Socrate. *Cost.* Il a une facilité merveilleuse à manier l'ironie. *Dépreux, Longin* c. 28" ["Fine raillery. A figure that consists of humorous mockery. 'Irony was the favorite figure of Socrates'; 'He has a marvelous facility of using irony' "].[3] Richelet also recognizes the adjective: "ironique, adj. Qui tient d'ironie (ton ironique)" ["that which has irony, as 'ironic tone' "]. As we shall see in a subsequent chapter, Richelet's two definitions (raillery; a rhetorical figure) are variations of those developed in the earlier rhetorical tradition. The dictionary of Furetière is also in this tradition:

> ironie, subst. fem. Figure dont se sert l'Orateur pour insulter à son adversaire, le railler, & le blasmer, en faisant semblant de loüer. L'*ironie* consiste dans le ton, aussi-bien que dans les paroles. Les contre-verités sont les plus fortes *ironies*. Ce mot vient de Grec *eirōneia; dissimulation. feinture*, du verbe *eirōneuomai, dissimulo, je dissimule*.

[A figure used by the orator to insult his adversary, to rail at him and blame him, while pretending to offer praise. Irony consists in the tone as well as in the words. The strongest ironies are counter-truths. The word comes from the Greek *eirōneia*, meaning dissimulation, or feigning, from the verb meaning to dissimulate.]

Furetière also recognizes both an adjective and adverb. The adverb is glossed only as "in an ironic manner"; "ironic" is the opposite of "serious": "Cet Auteur n'a pas dit cela serieusement mais *ironiquement*" ["That author did not say that seriously, but ironically"]. The adjective is associated with satire and burlesque: "Les termes *ironiques* conviennent fort à la satyre, au burlesque" ["Ironic terms are well suited to satire and burlesque"].

The 1694 Academy dictionary is slightly more expansive, and later editions will show the general movement in the meaning of the word:

ironie. s.f. Figure de Rhetorique par laquelle on veut faire entendre le contraire de ce qu'on dit, & qui consiste presque toute dans le ton de la voix & dans la maniere de pronouncer. *Tout ce discours n'est q'une ironie. l'ironie estoit la figure de Socrate. il dit cela par ironie.*

[Rhetorical figure through which one says the contrary of what one wishes to be understood, and which consists almost entirely in the tone of voice and the manner of pronunciation. "This entire discourse is nothing but irony; irony was the figure of Socrates; he says that through irony."]

The adjective and adverb recognized by the dictionary add little to this. Irony is primarily a figure of rhetoric, and the dictionary essentially translates the Latin definitions found in rhetorical manuals.[4]

There is no significant change in these definitions until the editions of the nineteenth century.[5] The sixth edition (1835), despite the potential influence of the romantic conception of the word, alters only the citation section, where the distinction between two types of irony is recognized— one "fine," the other "cruel":

ironie. s.f. Figure de rhétorique, par laquelle on dit le contraire de ce qu'on veut faire entendre. *Ce compliment n'est q'une ironie. L'ironie était la figure favorite de Socrate. Il dit cela par ironie. Ironie fine. Ironie amère, cruelle.*[6]

[Rhetorical figure through which one says the contrary of what one wishes to be understood. "This compliment is nothing but an irony. Irony was the favorite figure of Socrates. He says that through irony. Fine irony. Bitter, cruel irony."]

The seventh edition (1879) adds a single citation ("Il mit dans ses paroles une nuance d'ironie") and for the first time what is called a "figurative" meaning:

> Fig. *Ironie du sort*. Accident qui arrive à quelqu'un si à contretemps, qu'il paraît une moquerie du sort; ou encore, Contraste étrange que présentent deux faits historique rapprochés par quelque côté. C'est comme par une Ironie du sort que le dernier empereur d'Occident s'appella Romulus Auguste.
> [Figuratively, "irony of fate." An accident that happens to someone so unexpectedly that it seems a mockery of fate; or a strange contrast presented by two historical facts that are somehow connected. It is by an irony of fate that the last Western emperor was called Romulus Augustus.]

This definition is also recognized in the nearly contemporary dictionary by Littré (1863).

Interestingly, in 1862, Firmin-Didot published a *Complément* to the 1835 Academy dictionary which included additions that did not appear in the later edition, of 1879.[7] For *ironie* the dictionary adds the obvious Socratic irony:

> ironie. s.f. *Ironie socratique* (phil.) se dit, particulièrement, de la méthode qu'employait Socrate lorsqu'il questionnait ses disciples avec une feinte ignorance, pour les conduire à reconnaître la vérité ou à rejeter l'absurde. *Ironie,* d'après sa racine, signifiait primitivement, *Interrogation.*
> [Socratic irony (philosophy) is said particularly of the method employed by Socrates when he questioned his disciples while feigning ignorance, to lead them to recognize truth or to reject the absurd. According to its root, irony signifies originally "interrogation."]

This is the first indication in the Academy's definitions that the meaning of the word, even a figurative meaning, can be determined by etymological considerations. The additions also include a verb, and here the traditional rhetorical meanings are set in a social context: "Railler avec politesse, en feignant de louer" ["To rail politely, while feigning to praise"]. Irony is a socially acceptable form of raillery; irony seems limited to the "ironie fine" of the 1835 edition, as opposed to its "ironie amère."[8]

In the edition of 1935, the basic meaning is unchanged, and the figurative definition "Ironie du sort" remains the same as in the seventh edition:

Ironie. n.f. Figure de rhétorique par laquelle on dit le contraire de ce qu'on veut faire entendre. *Ce compliment n'est qu'une ironie. L'ironie abonde dans les* Lettres provinciales, *dans les* Lettres persanes. *Il a une grande facilité à manier l'ironie.*

Par extension, Ironie signifie plus ordinairement Moquerie sarcastique dans le ton ou dans l'attitude. *Il intimidait par son ironie continuelle. Il y avait de l'ironie dans sa façon de le regarder. Il dit cela par ironie. Ironie fine. Ironie amère, cruelle. Il mit dans ses paroles une nuance d'ironie.*

Ironie socratique, se dit des Interrogations par lesquelle Socrate, discutant avec les sophistes, les amenait peu à peu à se contredire.

[Rhetorical figure through which one says the contrary of what one wishes to be understood. "That compliment is nothing but an irony"; "irony abounds in *The Provincial Letters,* and in *The Persian Letters.*" "He has a great talent for irony."

By extension, irony signifies generally a sarcastic mockery in tone or attitude. "He intimidates through his continual irony." "There was irony in his look." "He says that through irony." "Fine irony." "Cruel, bitter irony." "He puts a nuance of irony in his words."

Socratic irony refers to the interrogations through which Socrates, disputing with the sophists, led them little by little to contradict themselves.]

The edition adds a definition for *Ironiste:* "Celui qui affecte l'ironie, soit en écrivant, soit en parlant" ["He who affects irony, either in writing or speaking"]. There is also a change in the meaning of Socratic irony, perhaps made to retain the earlier notion that irony is a form of abuse. Socratic irony as defined here is directed at Socrates' opponents rather than toward his students.

The 1863 dictionary by Littré adds little to the basic definitions, but seems to have had some influence, as we will see, on the *Oxford English Dictionary:* "ironie. 1. Proprement, ignorance simulée . . . 2. Par extension, raillerie particulière par laquelle on dit le contraire de ce que l'on veut faire entendre" ["1. properly, simulated ignorance . . . 2. By extension, particular raillery through which one says the contrary of what one wishes to be understood"]. Under this extended meaning, however, Littré lists Pascal for the notion of "God's irony."[9]

The citations in the Academy dictionary indicate an extremely conservative tradition in France. Pascal's statement concerning irony of fate finds no correspondent in the early editions of the dictionary, in which irony is a product of human expression. Reading these dictionaries, one could miss two important developments in the history of the word: the notions of romantic irony (of particular importance in Germany) and dramatic irony (associated primarily with English classicists).

The lexicographical tradition is a conservative force: the definitions developed in the seventeenth century remain at the core of later dictionaries, which respond to their predecessors rather than to contemporary developments in the meaning of a word. If we look again at Godefroy's definitions, intended to apply to medieval uses of the word, we can see the force of this tradition: "Ironie. s.f. raillerie particulière par laquelle on dit le contraire de ce que l'on veut faire entendre. Il li dist tels paroles ausi come par *yronie* (Chron. de S. Den. ms. Ste-Gen. fo. 58d)" ["Particular raillery through which one says the contrary of what one wishes to make understood. 'He said such words to him as if through irony'"]. Godefroy's definition is a combination of the typical elements of the earlier lexicons: raillery and the rhetorical figure. And it is not clear which applies to his citation. The reference to the adjective is to the rhetorical figure; but how Godefroy would define that figure is unclear: "Ironique. adj. qui a de l'ironie. Figure *yronique* (Fabri. Rhetor. fo. 7v)." [10]

Godefroy's definitions are not incompatible with those of standard Latin dictionaries, Du Cange's *Glossarium* and the continuing *Thesaurus Linguae Latinae*.[11] But the history of irony suggested by these lexicons is a distorted one. Old French borrowed (or transliterated) a word barely domesticated into Latin, as Godefroy's citations prove. In modern French, the word is again referred back to its supposedly academic origins in rhetoric manuals.

The lexicons, based as they are on a rhetorical tradition whereby irony is something definable and classifiable, provide both a check on the extravagant metaphoric or philosophical uses and a means for such uses to come into being through a *via negativa*. But these definitions are bound inextricably to the anachronisms of the history that produced them, and the foundation they seem to provide for inquiry into the word is illusory.

The Oxford English Dictionary

French lexicons record French usage. But the influence of the resultant definitions extends beyond national boundaries. Even English lexicons, responding to some distinctly English uses of the word, draw on French sources. The *Oxford English Dictionary*, despite its historical claims, provides, like the French dictionaries, a synchronic view of irony. Definitions are not presented as resulting from continuous evolution; rather, they are hierarchized as discrete, synchronic meanings. The chronological continuum underlying the history of the word is reduced to a binary distinction between active and obsolete meanings.

The English use of the word irony during the eighteenth century has been well studied by Knox; the definitions are conservative and familiar. Johnson's definitions are representative:

> Irony, n.f. [*ironie*, Fr. *ierōneia* (*sic*)] A mode of speech in which the meaning is contrary to the words: as, *Bolingbroke was a holy man.*
>
> So grave a body, upon so solemn an occasion, should not deal in *irony,* or explain their meaning by contraries. *Swift.*

The citation of Swift is appropriate, since Swift claimed to have introduced irony into England:

> Arbuthnot is no more my Friend,
> Who dares to Irony pretend;
> Which I was born to introduce,
> Refin'd it first, and shew'd its Use.
> ("Verses on the Death of Dr. Swift," lines 55–59)

The *Oxford English Dictionary,* like Godefroy's medieval dictionary, and in this case like Johnson's dictionary, builds on the basic definitions provided by the French dictionaries. There are three definitions: the first, or presumably proper, definition, then what is called a "figurative" meaning, and finally an "etymological" one. The proper meaning is given as follows: "1. A figure of speech in which the intended meaning is the opposite of that expressed by the words used; usually taking the form of sarcasm or ridicule in which laudatory expressions are used to imply condemnation or contempt." This seems to combine two definitions that appear in French lexicons: the rhetorical meaning and the meaning "raillery." The 1533 quotation from More is exemplary: "When he calleth one self noughty lad, both a shreud boy & a good sonne, the tone in [th]e proper simple spech, the tother by the fygure of ironye or antiphrasis." The most familiar translation of this form of irony into English is from Puttenham's *Arte of English Poesie,* also quoted—"*Ironia,* which we call the *drye mock.*" [12]

Definition 2 is figurative: "2. *fig.* A condition of affairs or events of a character opposite to what was, or might naturally be expected; a contradictory outcome of events as if in mockery of the promise and fitness of things (In F. *ironie du sort*)." The earliest citation (1649) is roughly contemporary with Pascal. "Yet here: (and 'tis the Ironie of Warre Where Arrowes forme the Argument) he best Acquitts himselfe, who doth a Horse praefer To his proud Rider" (reference given as "G. Daniel, *Trinarch., Hen. V,* cxcviii").

The citation is problematic, and G. G. Sedgewick claims (correctly I think) that the dictionary editors completely misread it.[13] The second and more convincing citation is to Connop Thirlwall's 1833 essay on Sophocles, the subject of chapter 8 below. The point here is not whether the 1649 citation provides direct support for this definition (and I agree with Sedgewick that it does not), but rather that this definition has for whatever reasons become a standard definition, and that a history (probably an illegitimate one) has been written for it.

The final definition is the presumed etymological one, and what the dictionary says is an interesting indication of the conception of historical origins: "3. In etymological sense: Dissimulation, pretence; esp. in reference to the dissimulation of ignorance practised by Socrates as a means of confuting an adversary (*Socratic irony*)." Reference is given to "Wynken de Worde, 1506, *Ord. Crysten Men* iv, xxii, 293": "To say of hym selfe ony thynge of his feblenesses & necessytes, or of his synnes . . . to the end that a man be renowmed & reputed humble abiect & grete thynge in merytes & deuocyons before god . . . such synne is named yronye, not that the whiche is of grammare, by the whiche a man sayth one & gyueth to understande the contrarye." The next citation (1655) seems to come straight from Quintilian: "Stanley, *Hist. Philos.* III (1701) 76/1: The whole confirmation of the Cause, even the whole Life seems to carry an Irony, as was the Life of Socrates, who was for that reason called *eirōn;* that is, one that personates an unlearned Man, and is an admirer of others as Wise." This clearly refers back to the history of the word that heads the entry: "[ad. L. *ironia* (Cicero), a. Gr. *eirōneia* 'dissimulation, ignorance purposely affected.' Cf. F. *ironie* (*yronie, Oresme,* 14th c.). In early use often in Lat. form *ironia.*]." The reference to Oresme appears to be taken from Littré.[14] Although the editors may find this the etymological sense (and in this they again seem to be following the lead suggested in Littré), it is clear that de Worde does not. Rather, his use of the word is simply an extension of what he calls its grammatical meaning. He may well be reintroducing into the word the moral implications associated with it through Socrates, but this seems entirely accidental.

By the time the Greek word *eirōneia* is recorded (the first use I know of is in Plato), the association of Socrates with an ironic manner is fixed. The history of the word *eirōneia* appears to have a limit, and this distinguishes it from the word *eirōn,* the earliest uses of which are problematic enough to suggest a rich etymological history (see the following chapter). It is possible to define *eirōneia* in accordance with the *OED* as "dissimulation, ignorance purposely affected." But this meaning is itself the result of development in the complex of words whose history shows clear traces of earlier meanings, such as the Aristophanic sense of *eirōn*. What is given as an etymological meaning by the *OED* is not an original meaning but an early association (with Socrates), combined with an interpretation of that association.

The rhetorical definition of the word is a later one only insofar as it was developed after the word already was associated with Socrates. Yet the notion of Socratic irony (one assumed by the *Dictionary* and by its contemporary readers) is more likely to postdate than to predate this rhetorical definition. In English history, this association is as bookish as is the rhetorical meaning.[15] The *Dictionary*'s etymologies, intended to record a history, create that history.[16]

The sketch of the lexical history of the word shows a marked conservatism in the reception of the word in France and England. This conservatism is in part a simple function of the lexicon itself. For what constitutes conservatism in the history of this particular word is in its packaged and analyzable meanings. The language of the rhetorical meanings is easily translatable and dominates the lexicons into the twentieth century.

Paradoxically, the lexical tradition also indicates the possibility of breaking through its own conservatism. For the meaning of the word, however restricted, is freed from its context of lists of tropes and figures, the context that controls it in works such as Puttenham's *Arte*. Socratic irony is a discrete category of irony; so is irony of fate; each begins to exist independently. In the 1935 Academy dictionary, irony is a "façon de le regarder," and can exist in an attitude as well as in speech. The privileged status enjoyed by irony in twentieth-century literary criticism is in part a result of the derhetoricization of the word—its removal from its rhetorical context. And this the lexical tradition inadvertently facilitated.

PART TWO

RHETORICAL

IRONY

3

The
Development of
a Definition

■

In the history of irony, Socrates becomes the exemplary ironic man. While based on the historical Socrates and on the representation of that Socrates in Plato, this particular Socrates gradually loses its foundation in classical texts. Aristophanes' portrait of Socrates in *Clouds*, the presumed self-portrait of Socrates in Plato's *Apology*, Alcibiades' and Thrasymachus's characterizations of Socrates as ironic, the Socratic method as represented by Plato—these assume no more direct importance for the exemplary Socrates than do zoological descriptions of animals for the writer of a bestiary. What is Socratic may have little to do with the historical being of Socrates; what is ironic can be defined apart from any description or example of that irony. In the fourteenth century, Chaucer speaks of Plato as an abstruse philosopher:

> Eek Plato seith, whoso kan hym rede,
> The wordes moote be cosyn to the dede.
> *(Canterbury Tales,* General Prologue, 741–42) [1]

Socrates, on the other hand, has an exemplary moral function. He is the model of patience:

> Remembre yow of Socrates,
> For he ne counted nat thre strees
> Of noght that Fortune koude doo.
> *(Book of the Duchess,* 717–19)

A more specific example of Socrates' patience is found in the Wife of Bath's paraphrase of Jerome:

> No thyng forgat he the care and the wo
> That Socrates hadde with his wyves two,
> How Xantippa caste pisse upon his heed.

> This sely man sat stille as he were deed;
> He wiped his heed, namoore dorste he seyn,
> But "Er that thonder stynte, comth a reyn!"
> (*Wife of Bath's Prologue*, 727–32)[2]

The transformation of Socrates into an example of patience and the reduction of Plato to an exemplary philosopher continues a process that had
begun far earlier—the same process that led to the development of short
and memorable definitions of irony. This transformation was in part a function of education. Knowledge had to be packaged into manageable units
capable of being taught; the treatment of Plato and Socrates is one instance;
another is the reduction of moral wisdom to the simple couplets of Cato's
distiches (a source of moral authority referred to by several of Chaucer's
less learned characters, such as the carpenter in the *Miller's Tale,* and the
hen Pertelote in the *Nun's Priest's Tale*).[3]

The brief definitions of irony and the reductive descriptions of Socrates
available in the Middle Ages are convenient, elegant, and economical. They
are useful for rhetorical handbooks, and, in later centuries, they form the
basis of lexical definitions.[4] These rhetorical definitions acquire authority
even as expanded definitions such as those associated with romantic irony
act to challenge that authority. In *Theorie der Ironie* (1983), Uwe Japp can
claim with some conviction that the rhetorical definition underlies all definitions of irony and that the more extravagant and complex ironies are
mere variants (*Anwendungen*).[5]

Japp's statement has merit. It is helpful to imagine a rubric under which
various rhetorical and philosophical techniques and various literary and historical periods can be organized. But this rubric itself is a ruse, and in
discussing the variants of irony (in Plato, Kierkegaard, Hegel, and Mann)
Japp ignores its restrictions; I cannot imagine a reader of Japp who would
wish it otherwise.

The definition of rhetorical irony below serves similar functions: it is
deliberately reductive and (perhaps deceptively) simplistic. What I will call
rhetorical irony is irony as defined in rhetorical manuals, an irony called
"verbal" irony by Japp and Lausberg. It should not be considered historically
or logically prior to other types. Rhetorical irony is rather an organizing
frame for discussing various statements and traditions involving irony. It is
not the beginning of a tradition, but rather one of many attempts in the
history of irony to define an endpoint. For our purposes, the history of
rhetorical irony begins where the history of Platonic and Socratic irony
leaves off; rhetorical irony develops as a response to the threat of abstract

and unmethodical speculation. Rhetorical irony is a theme alluded to in the incomplete and often evasive history of the word found in the lexicons.

The following chapters deal with two aspects of rhetorical irony. Chapter 3 deals with the development of definitions. Chapter 4 deals with the modern reception of those definitions, the first by Lausberg and the second by overzealous medievalists.

The Early Reevaluation of Irony:
Aristotle, Theophrastus

The process by which the word *eirōn* is transformed from Aristotle to Theophrastus was traced a century ago by Otto Ribbeck, and his basic outline of that history, although challenged, has not been overturned.[6] Aristotle uses the word in two important contexts, one in the *Rhetoric* and the other in the *Nicomachean Ethics*.[7] In the *Rhetoric*, the word appears first in a context where Aristotle is discussing the belittling of an opponent. Irony is a form of showing contempt, and can be used to mock what an opponent presents as serious ("kai tois eirōneuomenois pros spoudazontas"); for irony is disdainful ("kataphronētikon gar hē eirōneia"; 1379b). Aristotle classifies ironists with other wretches (*panourgoi*) who are to be feared because of their dissembling nature; they are more dangerous than those who speak passionately and freely (1382b). Irony thus is a form of dangerous deception.

None of these uses of the word is inconsistent with the negative connotations that it has in Aristophanes. Such uses are the basis for Ribbeck's widely accepted notion that *eirōn* is originally a common term of abuse (*ein Schimpfwort*); they also support the history outlined by Leif Bergson, for whom the original negative connotations of the word rest on its association with sophistry.[8] But the final appearances of the word in the *Rhetoric* imply a reevaluation. Aristotle claims that with irony, a speaker contrasts himself with a rival; "he said *X*, whereas I say *Y*," or "what does he mean by indicating *X* but not *Y*?" (1420a). There is thus an ironic contrast between the speaker and rival, and an ironic contrast (or contradiction) within the rival's speech. A few lines earlier, this contrast between persons is expressed as a contrast between social positions. Gorgias says that seriousness can be used to destroy humor, as humor can be used to destroy seriousness. Irony is one of the forms of humor befitting (*harmottein*) a free man. It is opposed to *bōmolokhia* (vulgar buffoonery). Irony is freer (and thus more noble) than *bōmolokhia*, for it creates laughter for its own sake and not for something else (1419b).

Irony, thus, is not only a descriptive term but an evaluative one. The ironist is socially superior to a buffoon, and uses complex forms of humor (irony among them) which are better suited to a free man (thus an educated man) than direct speech (such as *bōmolokhia*). Deception is accorded a higher social status than truth.

The *Rhetoric* suggests a possible change in the meaning of the word; the negative connotations in earlier uses (however they are defined) seem to be disappearing. But a profound change in the meaning of the word occurs as a result of Aristotle's ethical writings, where he contrasts *eirōn* with *alazōn* (a contrast revived by Northrop Frye in the twentieth century) and firmly associates irony with Socrates. According to some scholars, prior to these writings the relation between Socrates and the word *eirōn* had been merely casual.[9]

In the *Nicomachean Ethics, eirōn* is contrasted with *alazōn* (1127b)—a word that appears with *eirōn* (without apparent contrast) in *Clouds* (line 449). According to Aristotle, an *eirōn* is a "self-deprecator"; a man who uses such irony is better than a boaster (*alazōn*): "Those who use irony moderately, and those who are ironic openly and not excessive in their use of it seem gracious." In other words, while a moderate use of irony is not in and of itself a virtue, it is at least socially appealing.[10] But more important than Aristotle's definition is his association of such irony with Socrates, the man who makes himself appear worse than he is.

The definition from the *Nicomachean Ethics* has assumed a great deal of importance in recent histories of irony. Nonetheless, Aristotle does no more than pair the word with *alazōn* and associate the word with Socrates, and this much is already implied in *Clouds*. Aristotle's recommendation of irony in moderation is not in itself surprising, since the ethical value is attributed less to irony itself than to moderation.[11] Aristotle's specific comments on irony are not in and of themselves enough to change the meaning of the word significantly. What changes the word is rather the association with Socrates and the later reception of Socrates, and these are matters for which Aristotle is only partially responsible.

The earliest extant handbook sketches of irony are found in Theophrastus's *Characters* and in the fourth-century *Rhetoric to Alexander,* once attributed to Aristotle. The sketch by Theophrastus suggests that the *eirōn* is a comic stereotype, but Theophrastus's description has no reference to Socrates. The direct influence of Theophrastus's *Characters* on the history of the word is not great; it serves, rather, as an indication of a possible history—the direction that the meaning of the word irony could have taken were it not for the association with Socrates.[12]

Theophrastus's dedication claims that he is setting forth models of béhavior, and that he will begin with the worst sort of man, the ironist (the only character mentioned in the preface). According to Theophrastus, irony involves affecting to be worse than one is, in actions and words. The ironist will not reveal hatred to an enemy, but would rather go to an enemy and talk, "pretending to be worse (or less) in both actions and words" ("prospoiēsis epi to kheiron praxeōn kai logōn").

To Theophrastus, the ironist is simply a liar. He laughs when he is insulted, delays those who wish to see him, arrives late with poor excuses, refuses to contribute money for friends, forgets inconvenient facts, and forever professes surprise and amazement. Theophrastus's ironist is distinct from Aristophanes' implied ironist in that he does all this for personal gain; he is motivated.[13]

If there is a relation between Socrates and the comic villain described by Theophrastus, it can only be that Socrates himself puts on the role of the buffoon described by Theophrastus. Under such an explanation, Theophrastus's description does not constitute any serious revision of the negative connotations of the word.[14] Both Aristotle and Theophrastus are attempting to stereotype the ironist; their efforts are symptomatic of the contradictions and confusions in the history of a word that became accidentally attached to the Silenus-like figure of Socrates. To Theophrastus, the ironist is a recognizable type that a writer or dramatist may wish to use; it is also a social type that we can all use to categorize others. For Aristotle, it is an intelligible schema which the rhetorician can use to select and evaluate rhetorical tactics. Such attempts to define and stereotype the ironist lead to later rhetorical classifications of corresponding ironies.

Rhetorical Formulae

The rhetorical formulae begin to be fixed in the fourth-century *Letter to Alexander* (once attributed to Aristotle, now attributed to Anaximenes).[15] The *Letter to Alexander* analyzes irony in terms of the traditional branches of rhetoric. Irony is a type of dissimulation related to demonstrative rhetoric: "Irony is to say something while pretending not to say it, or to propose some action in the opposite words." The example used by Anaximenes supports later definitions of irony as praise by apparent blame: "On the one hand, those who do evil to our allies seem very worthy, while we, who are the cause of many benefits, seem to be wretches." Anaximenes goes on to include within irony devices that later become known as *preteritio*, or *occupatio* (the speaker claims to pass over certain details that are then listed).

The association of praise and blame with irony repeats in a somewhat sanitized form the connotation of insult associated with the earlier uses of the word. In Aristophanes, *eirōn* is a term of abuse as is *alazōn;* in Aristotle and in Theophrastus, the *eirōn* is a man who pretends to less than he is, or who understates his case. A simple extension of this leads to Anaximenes' notion: one damns through praise, that is, one understates one's contempt.

Cicero and Quintilian

The most important discussions of the word irony are those by Cicero and Quintilian. Their statements fix the language in which irony would be discussed in western Europe and further strengthen the crucial association of the word with Socrates.

Both Cicero and Quintilian create hierarchies of irony through simple linguistic classifications: irony of words vs. irony of manner; simple vs. complex irony; trope vs. schema. Cicero discusses irony briefly in book 1 of *De Officiis.* Here he distinguishes two types of jokes: one "vulgar (*inliberale*), petulant, biting, obscene," a type of joke characteristic of Greek Old Comedy and Plautus, the other "elegant, urbane, ingenious and witty (*facetum*)," as in the elder Cato's *Apophthegmata* (1.29.104). The distinction, as in the *Nicomachean Ethics,* corresponds to social rank: only one type is "worthy of a free man." [16] There are two types of human characteristics, general and particular. General characteristics (such as reason) separate us from beasts; particular characteristics are both physical (speed, beauty, etc.) and spiritual. Personal characteristics are not the product of particular historical contexts nor of particular cultures, since at each historical period and in every nation, we can find many types of men—men of great wit (*lepos*) as well as those of great severity. Among the Greeks, Cicero contrasts Socrates with Pericles and Pythagoras, and this introduces his comments on irony:

> de Graecis autem dulcem et facetum festivique sermonis, atque in omni oratione simulatorem, quem *eirōna* Graeci nominarunt, Socratem accepimus, contra Pythagoram et Periclem summam auctoritatem consecutos sine ulla hilaritate. (1.30.108)
> [Among the Greeks, however, we take Socrates to be charming and witty, of pleasant speech, and in all speaking a simulator, which the Greeks called an *eirōn;* on the other hand, Pythagoras and Pericles, having attained highest authority, were without any wit.]

The notion of wit as deception (*eirōn* = *simulator*) is further supported by the examples of political wit that follow; Cicero names Hannibal and Q. Maximus, both of whom, one a Carthaginian, the other a Roman, were known for their deception: "facile celare, tacere, dissimulare, insidiari, praeripere hostium consilium."

Cicero defines irony again in *De Oratore,* and the language is very similar; the phrase *urbana dissimulatio* would become standard in descriptions of irony:

> Urbana etiam dissimulatio est, cum alia dicunter ac sentias, non illo genere, de quo ante dixi, cum contraria dicas . . . sed cum toto genere orationis severe ludas, cum aliter sentias ac loquare; . . . hoc in genere Fannius in annalibus suis Africanum hunc Aemilianum dicit fuisse et Graeco eum verbo appellat *eirōna;* sed, uti ferunt, qui melius haec norunt Socraten opinor in hac *eirōneia* dissimulantiaque longe lepore et humanitate omnibus praestitisse. (2.67.269–70)[17]
>
> [Urbane dissimulation is when you understand something other than what is said; not in the way I spoke of earlier, when you say the contrary . . . but when you are mocking when the entire speech itself is serious, when you understand and say diverse things; . . . Fannius in his *Annals* says Aemilian Africanus was of this manner, and in Greek he calls him an *eirōn;* but, as those who know these things better claim, I believe Socrates to have far surpassed all others in wit and humanity in this irony and dissimulation.]

To Cicero, irony is a form of humor involving some degree of simulation. Socrates is clearly an exemplary ironist, but it is not clear that Cicero imagines this to be an adequate description of Socrates; that is, the word irony does not seem in Cicero to widen its definition solely on the basis of Socrates.[18]

Quintilian extends Cicero's definition in a way that provides literary scholars with an authority for even wider applications of the word, to such matters as point of view in the modern novel.[19] Quintilian's discussion of rhetorical figures is based on a distinction between tropes and figures. The trope irony is simply defined; it is a species of the genus *allegoria:*

> Allegoria, quam inuersionem interpretantur, aut aliud uerbis, aliud sensu ostendit, aut etiam interim contrarium. . . . In eo uero genere quo contraria ostenduntur ironia est (inlusionem uocant): quae aut pronuntiatione intellegitur aut persona aut rei natura; nam si qua earum uerbis dissentit, apparet diuersam esse orationi uoluntatem. (8.6.44–54)[20]
>
> [Allegory (which in Latin they call *inversio*) shows one thing in words and another in its sense, or even the contrary. . . . In that type where contraries are shown, we have irony (called *illusio*). And that is under-

stood either in the pronunciation or by the speaker or by the nature of the case; for if in any way one of these is in conflict with the words, clearly the meaning is different from the speech.]

An example to become familiar in the rhetorical tradition is praise by apparent blame and blame by apparent praise.[21]

Quintilian uses the Latin word *ironia* here; later, when speaking of the figure (or schema) irony, he uses the Greek word: "*Eirōneian* inueni qui dissimulationem uocaret: quo nomine quia parum totius huius figurae uires uidentur ostendi, nimirum sicut in plerisque erimus Graeca appellatione contenti" (9.2.44) ["I have found some who define *eirōneia* as dissimulation. But since the Latin word does not cover the whole range of this figure, we will be content as elsewhere to use the Greek word"]. To Quintilian, the distinction between a trope and a schema is first of all one of grades: a trope involves the shift in meaning of a word; a schema (further subdivided into figures of words and figures of thought) can involve phrases and entire sentences in which each individual word retains its proper meaning.[22] This distinction also involves matters of clarity. A trope is supposed to be readily understood; a schema is more complex, and can be misinterpreted.

Igitur *eirōneia* quae est schema ab illa quae est tropos genere ipso nihil admodum distat (in utroque enim contrarium ei quod dicitur intellegendum est), species uero prudentius intuenti diuersas esse facile est deprehendere. Primum, quod tropos apertior est et, quanquam aliud dicit ac sentit, non aliud tamen simulat. (9.2.44)
[As far as the genus is concerned, the trope and figure do not differ, inasmuch as each says the contrary of what is to be understood. But it is easy for a prudent viewer to distinguish their diverse species. First, because a trope is clearer, and although it says one thing and means something else, it does not pretend to do anything else.]

Quintilian then cites an example from Cicero's *In Catilinam* of an irony consisting of two words, which, because it is both clear and brief, should be considered a trope rather than a figure.[23]

Quintilian continues on to his much cited discussions of the figure and of Socrates: "At in figura totius uoluntatis fictio est apparens magis quam confessa, ut illic uerba sint uerbis diuersa, hic sensus [sermoni et uoci] et tota interim causae conformatio" (9.2.46) ["But in the figure, the counterfeiting of the entire will is apparent rather than admitted. Just as in the trope, where words are diverse from other words, here the sense opposes the speech and expression as can the entire conformation of the case"].[24]

With this, Quintilian has progressed to a higher grade of irony, one that transcends the linguistic levels of words and thoughts. In the trope and in most figures of thought, the conflicting meanings that constitute irony can be articulated; Cicero's phrase "ad virum optimum," for example, means "ad virum pessimum." But irony also includes cases where meanings are not articulable. Socrates' whole life (*uita uniuersa*) is an example of irony:

> . . . cum etiam uita uniuersa ironiam habere uideatur, qualis est uisa Socratis (nam ideo dictus *eirōn,* agens imperitum et admiratorem aliorum tanquam sapientium), ut, quemadmodum *allēgorian* facit continua *metaphora,* sic hoc schema faciat tropos ille contextus. (9.2.46)[25]
>
> [. . . as when even an entire life seems to have irony, as seemed to be the case of Socrates. For he was called an *eirōn* because he pretended to be ignorant and an admirer of others as if they were wise. And just as a continuous metaphor results in allegory, so does the development of the trope result in this schema.]

Quintilian creates a hierarchy of ironies with reference both to the verbal construction of irony and to actual audiences. The relative complexity of the verbal construction (word vs. phrase) correlates with the relative complexity of audience reactions and interpretations. The ironic trope is understood by all, and Quintilian does not even admit the possibility of misconstruing Cicero's *vir optimus* as meaning the "best of men." He is not concerned with theoretical audiences but with real ones. Real audiences can, however, misconstrue figures of thought; as for the irony of a whole life, Athens provides classic examples of those who failed to understand Socrates. And those who do misunderstand such higher ironies place themselves below those who interpret them correctly. The irony of an entire life is a dangerous challenge to those forced to judge it.

Quintilian's precise distinctions are less important than his manner of creating those distinctions. He begins with a fundamental definition of verbal irony, and from this he constructs a hierarchy of further meanings. Once the precedent of a hierarchical irony is set, there is no upper limit for irony: local, general, personal, universal, cosmological. Quintilian's discussion provides ample precedent for even the most enthusiastic modern theories of irony.

For Quintilian as for Cicero, Socrates enjoys exemplary status as an ironist. But there are various ways of taking this. To assume that Socrates is a useful exemplum of irony could be construed as defining both Socrates and irony. But the meaning of each term is not necessarily exhausted in such an identification (a dog can likewise be a convenient example of fidelity). Quintilian's interpretation is an open one: we discover the meaning of irony through our understanding of Socrates.

Quintilian, at the beginning of the *Institutio oratoria,* insists on the relation between oratory and the entire moral being of a man: "Oratorem autem instituimus illum perfectum, qui esse nisi uir bonus non potest, ideoque non dicendi modo eximiam in eo facultatem sed omnes animi uirtutes exigimus" (1.pr.9–10) ["The orator we are instructing cannot be perfect unless he is also a good man; and therefore, we require in him not only the faculty of speaking well but also all spiritual virtues"]. Morality and rhetorical skill, albeit on different levels, are intimately related. And since Socrates' rhetorical devices and moral being are inseparable, it is a short step to seeing irony as a mark not only of literary quality but of moral quality as well.

The potential reevaluation of the word would not be soon realized. Quintilian's text was not available in the Middle Ages, and in medieval Latin rhetorics what we find is less an expansion along the lines suggested by Quintilian (irony as a form of life) than a reduction to definitions. These find their way into the lexicographical tradition and are often repeated verbatim, as shown, for example, by Norman Knox's extensive references from the English neoclassical period. The potential of Quintilian's conception of irony would not be realized until the romantic period.[26]

Isidore of Seville

The typical medieval understanding of irony can be seen in various school texts and in encyclopedic works such as the *Etymologiae* of Isidore of Seville. Arnulf of Orleans uses the word in his glosses on Lucan, a school text. The works of Donatus and his commentators are basic grammar texts. The rarity of the word in medieval vernacular languages and its marginal domestication in Latin thus reflect the artificial nature of the academic dialect in which it survived.[27] When medieval vernacular texts such as the early romances and the later works of Chaucer are discussed by modern scholars as examples of medieval irony, they are being transferred to a context (an academic one) to which their audiences (which included women) did not have access.

Medieval rhetoricians reduce the word irony to its most easily handled and intelligible forms. Its association with allegory, which has been denounced by modern scholars as an oversimplification, becomes widespread.[28] A rhetorical manual cannot classify a personal attitude, a tone, much less a dialectical method or a way of life. But it can classify statements and their relation to articulable meanings.

Isidore, like Quintilian, considers irony both a trope and a figure.[29] In book 1, it is discussed under the heading "De Tropis": "Tropos Graeco nomine Grammatici vocant, qui Latine modi locutionum interpretantur. Fiunt autem a propria significatione ad non propriam similitudinem" (1.37.1) ["What grammarians call tropes in Greek are called in Latin modes of speech; they consist of a change from proper to improper signification"]. *Ironia* as a trope is a subcategory of *allegoria:*[30]

> Allegoria est alieniloquium. Aliud enim sonat, et aliud intellegitur, ut (Virg. *Aen.* 1.184): "Tres litore cervos / conspicit errantes." Vbi tres duces belli Punici, vel tria bella Punica significantur. . . . Huius tropi plures sunt species, ex quibus eminent septem: ironia, antiphrasis, aenigma, charientismos, paroemia, sarcasmos, astysmos. Ironia est sententia per pronuntiationem contrarium habens intellectum. Hoc enim tropo callide aut per accusationem, aut per insultationem aliquid dicitur, ut est illud (Virg. *Aen.* 1.140):
>> Vestras, Eure, domos; illa se iactet in aula
>> Aeolus, et clauso ventorum carcere regnet.
> Et quomodo aula, si carcer est? Solvitur enim pronuntiatione. Nam carcer pronuntiatio est: iactet et aula ironia est; et totum per contrariam pronuntiationem adnuntiatur per ironiae speciem, quae laudando deridet. (1.37.22–23)

[Allegory is "other-speech." One thing is said, another is meant. As in Virgil: "He saw three stags running on the shore," where he means the leaders of the three Punic wars or the three Punic wars. There are many types of this trope, of which seven are eminent: irony, antiphrasis, enigma, *charientismos, paroemia,* sarcasm, *astysmos.* Irony is a statement that has a contrary meaning because of its pronunciation. Something can be said by means of this trope most craftily for accusation or insult, as in Virgil: "Let Aeolus rule your domains, Eurus, in the closed prison of winds, and boast in that court." And why the word "court" if it is a prison? This is answered through pronunciation. For the pronunciation indicates that what is meant is "prison"; the words "boast" and "court" are examples of irony. And the whole thing is indicated with contrary pronunciation by means of a kind of irony, which derides by praising.]

Because they occur in a written text, Isidore's distinctions are not as clear as they might be. We cannot hear the pronunciation of Virgil, but only imagine what Isidore thinks it must be. In other manuals, these difficulties are even more obvious (see the section in chapter 4 on Donatus).

The second time Isidore discusses irony is in book 2, under the category "De Figuris verborum et sententiarum." These figures are considered ways of "augmenting" and "adorning" a speech, and they involve not only words but the "contexio verborum" (2.21.4):

> Ironia est, cum per simulationem diversum quam dicit intellegi cupit. Fit autem aut cum laudamus eum quem vituperare volumus, auc vituperamus quem laudare volumus. Vtriusque exemplum erit, si dicas amatorem reipublicae Catilinam, hostem reipublicae Scipionem. (2.21.41)
>
> [Irony is when the speaker, through simulation, wishes something diverse from what is said to be understood. It occurs when we praise someone we wish to vituperate, or vituperate someone we wish to praise. An example of each will be if you call Catiline a lover of the commonwealth and Scipio an enemy of the commonwealth.]

The same hierarchical gradation seen in Quintilian appears here. The classification moves from tropes to figures of words to figures of thought, and within the various definitions are hierarchies of authority: the speaker's *will* ("volumus," "cupit") and what that speaker wishes to be known ("intellegi") have authority over what that speaker says ("dicit").[31]

The apparently innocent association of the word with allegory in Isidore is significant. Irony, even as its definitions are radically simplified and made more academic, shifts from a word dealing with literary production to one dealing with literary reception. In medieval glosses, the invocation of irony is a mark of the exegete's reevaluation: the text deemed ironic means something other than what it says. In the twelfth-century glosses on Lucan's *Pharsalia* by Arnulf of Orleans, the word *yronice* appears several times; each time, Arnulf is referring to a situation where the text provides two possible interpretations and where one interpretation is clearly higher, or preferred. The ironic meaning opposes and cancels the literal meaning. Lucan's phrase "O bona libertas" is either serious or ironical: "vel yronice *O bona libertas* quasi diceret: hec libertas non est libertas" ["Or perhaps we should take this ironically: 'O wonderful liberty!' as if he were saying 'this so-called liberty is not liberty'"].[32] Once invoked by exegetes such as Arnulf, irony becomes a powerful interpretive tool; it enables them to manipulate the meanings of texts in the same way that certain notions of allegory permit the reinterpretation of both the Old Testament and various classical texts as Christian.[33] It also entails a refocusing of the question of irony onto the reader-exegete: Thrasymachus's accusation "You are being ironical" is a critical interpretation of Socrates' speech, not a description of it. The association of irony with allegory as seen in Isidore is reductive only in a certain sense. For this simplification of definitions grants irony almost unlimited power to interpret and to transform texts.

4

The Modern
Reception: Lausberg;
Medieval Misprisions
1 and 2

■

Heinrich Lausberg

I have defined rhetorical irony as "something is said; something else is meant" ("aliud dicitur, aliud significatur"). This is a useful standpoint from which to critique other definitions of irony as well as a useful base on which to organize a theory of irony. But the rhetorical tradition within which that definition exists is no more neutral than are the ironies it supposedly describes.

The most important modern contributions to the tradition outlined in the preceding chapter are two works by Heinrich Lausberg: *Elemente der literarischen Rhetorik* (1949) and *Handbuch der literarischen Rhetorik* (1960).[1] Each provides a schematic discussion of the various parts of classical rhetoric, including extensive lists of tropes and figures. Although the two works provide excellent records of the history of the word, together they act through their assumptions to dehistoricize it. They exemplify a dilemma experienced by many historical scholars, whose dual roles as historians and teachers are perhaps incompatible; for this reason, I will discuss them in some detail.

In the preface to the 1967 edition of *Elemente,* Lausberg claims to have organized his material as a "rhetorical analogue to school grammars" (9). He concedes that his traditional terminology and organization can give neither a knowledge of the thing itself (rhetoric and the rhetorical use of language) nor a microscopic measure for judging individual cases; at best, they provide the frame for viewing analogous phenomena in different cultures (9). Despite these caveats, Lausberg does suggest how a classical device such as irony has been received and indicates as well the nature of some of the assumptions involved (and resultant distortions) in assuming a continuity between ancient and modern uses and claims of irony.

The discussions in *Elemente* and in *Handbuch* differ in two principal ways. Lausberg adds Greek authorities in *Handbuch* (most of the authorities in

Elemente are in Latin, with many of the examples taken from the vernacular), and includes also the level of irony that Quintilian suggests applies to Socrates—an irony of life.

Lausberg distinguishes verbal irony from the figure of thought (dissimulation and simulation), as do classical rhetorics (*Elemente* 232–34, 426–30; *Handbuch* 582–85, 902–4). What Lausberg calls rhetorical irony is the first of two "evidence-grades" of the figure of thought; it is an irony that is intended to be understood by the hearer. A second grade, "handlungs-taktische Ironie," is the opposite of sincerity and uses *dissimulatio* and *simulatio* as "weapons" of deception (*Elemente* 430). There is an implied hierarchy of complexity, and the final forms of irony (or its limits) are those forms that cease to be verbal. Lausberg's "handlungs-taktische Ironie" involves extralinguistic actions, either real or dramatic (*Elemente* 430); in *Handbuch*, these final forms of irony will be suggested by Quintilian's "totius voluntatis fictio" (*Handbuch* 904).

Lausberg follows Quintilian in coordinating his distinctions between various levels of irony with levels of understanding. According to Quintilian, the lowest level of irony (involving single words) is immediately intelligible, the higher levels less so. Lausberg seems to agree, but notes the possibility of multiple audiences at all levels, even on the level of the trope: "As a verbal trope, *ironia* is the use of the biased language of an opponent in full confidence that the public recognizes its lack of credibility, through which the credible nature of one's own cause is established to the extent that the ironic words are ultimately understood in a sense opposed to their proper sense" (*Elemente* 232). The relative complexity of ironic forms, then, is not to be confused with the complexity of the situations in which those forms can be used. Here, Lausberg distinguishes two audiences—an audience that acts as a judge and an implied audience that acts as a legal opponent—and these audiences need not interpret irony in the same way.[2] The very existence of Lausberg's commentary, of course, implies a third audience—the literary or legal critic of the rhetor. Lausberg's examples of the trope lead to further complexities: he quotes Marc Antony's "And Brutus is an honorable man" as an example of the trope; the word "honorable" is changed in meaning (*Elemente* 233 and n. 1). This is a long process, as Lausberg notes: the word is changed in meaning only gradually through context and through repetition; its first appearance will be taken at face value. But even this is an oversimplification, since Marc Antony's irony involves at least three audiences: Brutus, the crowd, and the theater audience. Similarly, the example points out the difficulty of assuming that victims of irony are those who do not understand it. The crowd may or may not understand the irony of the word "honorable," but they are nonetheless victims of that irony unless they resist Marc Antony's demagoguery and stubbornly maintain the belief that Brutus is in fact honorable.

The figure of thought (*Gedanken-Tropus*) is defined simply in *Elemente:* "Irony as a figure of thought . . . consists in replacing the intended thought with another thought that is opposed to it; [the thought that is substituted] corresponds to the thought of the opponent" (*Elemente* 426). There are two basic types: *dissimulatio* and *simulatio*. *Dissimulatio* consists of hiding one's meaning; one form is Socratic irony defined in what some might feel is a limited sense as "an art of questioning that hides one's proper meaning." Other forms of *dissimulatio* are various tropes such as emphasis, litotes, periphrasis, synecdoche, allegory. *Simulatio* consists of the affectation of agreement with one's opponent. Examples include *Aeneid* 4.93–95 (a *locus classicus*, cited also by Donatus), Marc Antony's speech in *Julius Caesar,* and *Andromache,* act 5, scene 5: "Grâce aux dieux! Mon malheur passe mon espérance! / Oui, je te loue, ô Ciel, de ta persévérance" ["The gods be thanked! My grief passes my hope. Yes, I praise you, of heaven, for your perseverance"]. According to Lausberg, *dissimulatio* and *simulatio* are part of a larger phenomenon, and it is necessary to distinguish two "evidence-grades" (430). These are not necessarily higher forms of irony; they provide rather some sort of measure indicating the limits of irony.

The first grade is rhetorical irony, and Lausberg's immediate reference to sections 423 through 429 suggests that rhetorical irony is what he means by the figure of thought: "Die 'rhetorische Ironie' will, daß die Ironie vom Hörenden als Ironie, also als gegensätzlicher Sinn, verstanden wird" (430) ["Rhetorical irony wishes that the listener understand it as irony, that is, in its opposed sense"]. Rhetorical irony is intended to be understood. Lausberg does not identify the source of this understanding or of the intent (in his own statement, rhetorical irony is itself credited with intention: "Die 'rhetorische Ironie' will . . ."); but clearly, several potential audiences are involved.

The second grade is "handlungs-taktische Ironie," an irony that "uses dissimulation and simulation as weapons of deception (*Täuschung*)" (430.2). Under this final form of irony Lausberg includes what I have called extralinguistic considerations; the speaker or protagonist incorporates deceptive words as part of a larger plot or scheme. Lausberg notes that this is common in drama, but it is clear from his examples that he is not considering here or elsewhere what has come to be known as dramatic irony: "d'un voile d'amitié j'ai couvert mon amour" (*Bérénice,* act 1, scene 2, line 26) ["I covered my love with a veil of friendship"]). Indeed, Lausberg limits irony by positing its opposite: "confession, sincerity" (430.3). Again, the determining ground of irony is the speaker's intention, an intention occasionally transferred to the figure of speech itself. Lausberg's implied audiences are always seen as functions of, rather than determinants of, a speaker's intent. Hierarchies of audience thus correspond to hierarchies of words and intended meanings. There are ambiguities in matters of interpretation and analysis (Lausberg's examples appear both as figures of words and as figures of thought), but there are no ambiguities about the ironies themselves: a competent reader will not think that Marc Antony's statements mean that Brutus is honorable nor that Andromache praises heaven.

Lausberg's *Handbuch* differs slightly in subject matter and in detail. First of all, it is concerned more with the historical foundations of rhetorical categories, particularly those in Greek rhetorics. And secondly, as far as irony is concerned, Lausberg now includes the notion of a "life of irony" implied by Quintilian.

The definitions in *Handbuch* are more closely related to the language of Lausberg's sources. The word-figure is defined as follows: "Die Ironie ist der Ausdruck einer Sache durch ein deren Gegenteil bezeichnendes Wort" ["Irony is the expression of a thing through a word that indicates its contrary"]. And here, rather than examples, Lausberg cites authorities, Tryphon and Isidore.[3]

Lausberg also adds types of irony—for example, Bede's notion of antiphrasis:

> antifrasis est unius verbi ironia: inter ironiam autem et antifrasim hoc distat, quod ironia pronuntiatione sola indicat quod intellegi vult, antifrasis vero non voce pronuntiationis significat contrarium, sed suis tantum verbis quorum est origo contraria.[4]
>
> [Antiphrasis is irony involving a single word. There is this difference between irony and antiphrasis, however, that irony indicates what it wishes to be known in the pronunciation alone, whereas antiphrasis signifies its contrary not in the manner of pronunciation, but rather signifies contrary things in the words alone that give rise to it.]

In addition, he expands distinctions made earlier with respect to figures of thought: "Die Ironie als Gedankenfigur . . . ist ethische ein *vitium* gegen die Wahrhaftigheit" ["Considered ethically, irony as a figure of thought is a crime against truth"]. Lausberg considers as well the supposed dialectic between the *alazōn* and the *eirōn*. And, as in *Elemente,* irony is "a weapon of dialectic" (*Handbuch* 902–4). The hierarchical relation between the two basic forms of irony is now more apparent and involves matters of philosophy, politics, and ethics.

To a somewhat different end, Lausberg repeats his earlier distinction between grades of evidence, based on the will (*voluntas*) of the speaker. As in *Elemente,* Lausberg concludes with a suggestion as to the limits of irony. But here, he cites Quintilian's distinction between the schema and the trope and the extension of this, the notion of a global irony—*totius voluntatis fictio*—one that in the case of Socrates involves an entire life. Again, a hierarchy emerges that ends in extralinguistic considerations. In *Elemente,* the endpoint was the speaker's actions, plots, schemes; in *Handbuch,* it is Socrates' life. Both of these move beyond the bounds of rhetoric.

Lausberg's invaluable *Handbuch* contains extensive evidence on the early history of irony. But his work is less a history of the tradition of irony than an example of that history—it is *in* history rather than *of* it, and in this sense, it is radically different from the works of Ribbeck, Büchner, and Bergson, all of whom cover much of the same ground. What Ribbeck and his followers organize along diachronic lines, Lausberg organizes synchronically. The implication (and Lausberg himself clearly recognizes the problems with such an implication) is that irony and the categories by which it can be defined are universals. Even where differences exist due to cultural and national differences (Lausberg acknowledges these in the preface to *Elemente*), there remain intercultural analogies; that is, rhetorical categories point to higher categories that transcend cultural differences.

Lausberg's field is literary rhetoric, but it is clear that what is literary is being drawn into a specific cultural and political history. Rhetorical language developed in a political and judicial context that imposed legal sanctions against victims. By keeping this context in view (in part because of the necessary assumption of universality), he seems to preclude many common understandings of irony: the notions of irony as a purely poetic ornament or a simple game, the romantic notion of irony as dealing with poetic self-consciousness.

Lausberg clearly acknowledges the difference between Greek and Roman historical contexts, and also the difference between the classical context for rhetoric and the medieval one through which rhetoric was reduced to a grammatical function. He is also aware of the constraints within which his own work functions: *Elemente* is intended to make rhetoric teachable; *Handbuch* organizes historical sources around the teachable categories developed in his first book. But the literary history that emerges from this attempt at schematization has large gaps.

Lausberg is ambivalent about modern history. If Shakespeare and French classical dramatists offer authoritative examples of irony, then there is no reason that modern lexicons and handbooks cannot offer similarly authoritative definitions of irony. But there is no reference to such authorities, either in *Elemente* or in *Handbuch*. Lausberg's methods require a distinction between those who produce irony and those who discuss it—a distinction we could define as one between artist and scholar, rhetor and rhetorician, or (in literary terms) poet and critic. And the evidence that Lausberg is willing to admit is different in each of the two categories: the artistic tradition is both classical and modern (examples of irony can be found in Racine as easily as in Cicero). But the scholarly tradition is something else; it is confined to Greek and Latin and extends only through the Middle Ages. Lausberg cites no Renaissance rhetoricians and no modern ones.

Under this view, ancient scholarship, although dealing with universals, is itself confined to history; the artist and ironist, by contrast, are universals. This universalizing of the artist and ironist yields another result: art is translatable, and can be understood according to anachronistic categories defined by classical rhetoricians or by a modern scholar. Lausberg's apparent conservatism creates a literary world that is timeless but a scholarly world that excludes Renaissance and post-Renaissance traditions of scholarship. Modern readers of Lausberg find themselves in a peculiar situation. Unlike previous scholars, who are within time, we stand outside of time on the same implied level as the artist-ironist.

I must emphasize that it is not my intention to judge Lausberg's strategy as correct or incorrect, legitimate or flawed. Lausberg has set himself a task, a task which becomes two tasks: to provide a teachable system of rhetorical language and to expose its historical basis. These two aims, realized in two different books, may well be incompatible. The teachability of a subject is constantly challenged by its historical incoherence: Socrates breaks free of synchronic categories with each new version of Socrates that is created. The surreptitious introduction of literary universals only masks this incoherence.

The rhetorical definition of irony developed within educational institutions and due to educational constraints. Its utility, as well as its limitations, are linked to questions of teachability and in some cases intelligibility. In a later chapter, I will use a basic definition of rhetorical irony to critique later notions of irony such as romantic irony. But Lausberg's work makes clear that convenient distinctions based on such definitions are themselves arbitrary. For we can define rhetorical irony in various ways. A common definition such as "a statement that has a meaning contrary to its expression" has become ingrained in modern Western academic institutions, where the distinction between words and concepts, signs and referents, is a perennial object of revival, among both linguists and critics of various political, philosophical, or whimsical persuasions. This form of irony is also analyzable—it consists of a statement that can be written down, and the equally articulable meaning of that statement.

The utility of such a definition can be easily seen in Wayne Booth's *A Rhetoric of Irony,* a meditation on irony in the form of a stylistics.[5] Booth relies on the model of rhetorical irony to study how readers reach agreement, how they establish or reestablish the basis for communication that irony seems to subvert: "Ironic reconstructions depend on an appeal to assumptions, often unstated, that ironists and readers share. In this they resemble—and can help to illuminate—all other forms of verbal communication" (33). To analyze this process, Booth builds on the notion of what he calls "stable ironies." These are simply ironies that could be described in terms of the rhetorical trope (the author says X but means Y).[6] The process outlined by Booth involves four steps: the rejection of the literal meaning because of something the reader knows; the testing of alternative interpretations; the making of decisions about the author's knowledge or beliefs; the selection of "a new meaning or cluster of meanings with which we can rest secure" (10–12). In a clearly polemical move, Booth labels this process "reconstruction," a process that results not only in assent among readers but also in a meaning "in harmony with the unspoken beliefs that the reader has decided to attribute to [the author]" (12). The dominance of statement by meaning, knowledge, belief runs throughout this description. And the rhetorical model at the heart of this four-step process reappears later in Booth's description of parody, itself a form of irony where "the surface meaning must be rejected, and another, incongruous, and 'higher' meaning must be found by reconstruction" (72).

The meanings Booth claims to find are intended and thus authoritative; alternate readings are the products of a reader's bias and self-interest: "For the time being, we are seeking a kind of hard knowledge about 'meanings,' and we are relegating to 'significance' all of the indefinitely extendable interpretations that any work might be given by individuals or societies pursuing their own interests unchecked by intentions" (19). Focusing discussion on stable ironies limits the literary tradition he wishes to include to a stable tradition. Truth, for Booth, is what is teachable, and he has stated this directly more recently in *Critical Understanding:* "Having done what you want to do, can you teach it to me, or to anyone? If not, whom do you really liberate?"[7] According to Booth, there is something wrong with those who discount such authority; after a witty misreading of Barthes as pro-bourgeois, he adds: "Either my imagined first reader knows how to read or he does not; and he does not. One must simply question the good faith of anyone who really disagreed with this view" (231). Booth's literary universe, like that of Jonathan Culler in *Structuralist Poetics*, is one in which what is true is what can be taught; that is, it is one where the hierarchy of professors and students is unchallenged.[8] The assumptions Lausberg's work requires us to make as we use it are very similar.

Medieval Misprisions 1: Pompeius on Donatus

Rhetorical irony in a general sense (and not the special sense of Lausberg) can be defined as follows: something is said; something else is meant. This model of rhetorical irony is a variation of the classical model of linguistics opposing words to things, or signs to their referents.[9] For convenience, I have stated this definition in terms of a speaker and that speaker's intentions, but "what is meant" can easily be seen as a shortened version of "what is imagined to be meant." Rhetorical irony opposes an expression (or statement) to its meaning. The source of that meaning (the speaker, the audience, the context) is a decision determined by a linguistic or poetic theory.

The literal and ironic meanings of a statement do not exist in a state of equilibrium: to the rhetoricians, irony is not a matter of ambiguity, as it would become to twentieth-century poetic theorists. It is a situation in which a superficial meaning is dominated by a different one—according to Isidore, what the speaker wishes to be understood: "diversum quam dicit intelligi cupit" (*Etym.* 2.21.41). It is a situation in which a sophisticated reader (or listener) is superior to an unsophisticated one, who may not understand the higher, intended meaning.

These and similar definitions were the only ones to which medieval writers had access; even Quintilian's brief notes on Socrates were not available. The medieval period thus provides an excellent ground for examining critical misprisions. Later historical developments (in this case, the evolution in the word irony) are read back into the medieval period, and medieval writings are interpreted by means of these critically redefined terms. I should note that my criticism of these misprisions is not intended to be harsh or even corrective. Medieval texts are misread productively, just as Socrates has been transformed into more interesting and useful versions and just as Greek rhetoric was transferred by medieval academics from a then-obsolete legal context to a broader educational and aesthetic one.

Let us consider a modern interpretation of the brief comments on irony by the grammarians Donatus and Pompeius. Donatus is cited even in vernacular works as an exemplary grammarian,[10] and his definition of irony (or a close variant of it) was probably the basis for Isidore's definition, cited earlier.[11] Of particular note is the role played by pronunciation in Donatus's definition and the interpretation of that role by later commentators.

Donatus classifies *ironia* as one of seven species of *allegoria:* "allegoria est tropus, quo aliud significatur quam dicitur; . . . ironia est tropus per contrarium quod conatur ostendens" (*Ars Grammatica,* 401) ["allegory is a trope whereby something is signified other than what is said; . . . irony is a trope showing what is intended through its contrary"]. (This is a traditional classification and the same one appears later in Isidore.) Donatus then quotes Virgil: "egregiam vero laudem et spolia ampla refertis / tuque puerque tuus" (*Aen.* 4.93–94; *Ars Grammatica,* 401–2)[12] ["Indeed, you and your boy win great praise and much plunder"]. Juno, who is speaking here, means that Venus and Cupid can hardly take pride in their manipulation of one woman, Dido. Donatus notes that such irony depends on the pronunciation: "hanc nisi gravitas pronuntiationis adiuverit, confiteri videbitur quod negare contendit" (402) ["this will seem to confirm what it wishes to deny, unless, that is, a gravity of pronunciation supports it"].

Donatus is clear. But his commentator Pompeius elaborates; and his comments are occasionally cited as evidence that medieval irony, like New Critical irony, is equivocal, and that the grammarians recognized a form of irony in which no single meaning dominates the statement in the text. Pompeius glosses Donatus as follows: "ironia est, quotienscumque re vera aliud loquimur et aliud significamus in verbis; . . . sed isdem verbis potes et negare et confirmare; sola autem pronuntiatione discernitur" (*Commentum Artis Donati,* 310)[13] ["Irony is whenever we speak of something in fact and signify something else in words; . . . but you can both deny and confirm with the same words; it is only discerned in the pronunciation"]. Pompeius then cites Donatus's example from Virgil. There are problems with this passage to be sure. At issue below, however, is only the meaning of "to deny and confirm with the same words."

In an excellent book published in 1975 on the reception of Chaucer by English Renaissance readers, Alice Miskimin reads Pompeius's comment as evidence that Pompeius recognizes an irony that affirms and denies *simultaneously.*[14] Initially Miskimin seems to translate the passage as I do: "But you can in the same words both deny and affirm" (83 n. 6). But what she takes the passage to mean becomes clearer on the next page, where Pompeius is quoted and translated again: "Ironic words can both affirm and deny what they state." Miskimin adds: "I suggest that what we frequently find in Chaucer, and find so difficult to describe, is in effect allegorical irony: the literal meaning of words *simultaneously* undermined and affirmed" (85; emphasis added). In other words, Miskimin finds in Pompeius's comments a medieval precedent for what I shall show below is essentially a twentieth-century view of irony—a view of irony dependent largely on the New Critical association of irony with forms of ambiguity. Miskimin's position on the relation between rhetorical and modern irony is by no means unique, but she is the only scholar I know of to have articulated this position in terms of specific texts.

Such a reading depends on a misinterpretation of "sed isdem verbis potes et negare et confirmare"—a misinterpretation, or reinterpretation, conditioned by twentieth-century views of irony. Pompeius is making a parenthetical comment about the nature of words: you can use the same words to deny something and to confirm it; that is what makes irony possible. Words out of context are equivocal, but neither Pompeius nor Donatus suggests that irony itself is equivocal. According to Pompeius, irony is involved with the importation of an authoritative intent—here, an intent signaled by pronunciation—just as Donatus tells us.

Two points need to be made here. The first is that the irony described here involves two statements: one is the statement of the text; the other is the implied statement of meaning. Irony, thus, is the appeal to an authority absent from the text. This is the rhetorical sense of the word irony, and it is a sense respected in most uses of the word until the late eighteenth century.[15] From a twentieth-century perspective, such an understanding of irony is limited; but it is probably close to the understanding of irony typical of medieval writers trained in the rhetorical tradition and with only limited knowledge of Socratic dialogues.

The second point concerns a problem of historical distance, or what is now called "alterity."[16] Modern readers of medieval literature rely on texts, that is to say, written statements. What Isidore and Donatus describe as the authority for irony, pronunciation, is absent. A modern reader faces the situation suggested by Pompeius—words alone are equivocal. Pompeius's example, which must have been very clear to his students, looks to us like the work of Borges's Pierre Menard:

nam ita pronuntia,
> egregiam vero laudem et spolia ampla refertis
> tuque puerque tuus
si ita pronunties, videberis confirmare. aliter vero pronunties:

> egregiam vero laudem et spolia ampla refertis
> tuque puerque tuus.

ergo omnino tunc est ironia. (311)
[Now pronounce it thus: "Indeed, you and your boy win great praise and much plunder." If you pronounce it thus, you will seem to confirm this. However, if you pronounce it properly: "Indeed, you and your boy win great praise and much plunder," then it is entirely ironic.]

Only Pompeius's second quotation from Virgil is ironic. The apparent textual identity of these quotations is purely a function of the absence of pronunciation—the authoritative context—which we must conjecture on the basis of context. When our conjectures are bad or unconvincing, we may be left with an ambiguous statement (we do not know how to interpret it). To claim that such a statement is ironic in any sense of the word is to lend critical authority to our unavoidable critical or historical ignorance.

In Arnulf's gloss of Lucan quoted in chapter 3 above ("vel yronice *O bona libertas* quasi diceret: hec libertas non est libertas"), Arnulf certainly recognizes the ambiguity of the text on which he comments. But the association of the word irony with that ambiguity is accidental. The invocation of the word irony is a way to eliminate the ambiguity from the text. If the text is ironical, then it is no longer ambiguous. The use of the word *yronice* by Arnulf is fully consistent with the use of the word *ironia* by Donatus and Pompeius. There are ambiguous texts, but irony as a critical tool is a way of disambiguating them. Irony is the authoritative solution to the ambiguous text.

The implications of accepting medieval notions of irony are serious. The method of interpreting medieval literature used by D. W. Robertson, Jr., is a notorious example. In general, Robertson uses the word irony in its rhetorical sense; irony is an example of figurative language.[17] How do we know when a passage is ironic? figurative? or allegorical? When it does not conform to what we believe to be the meaning of the medieval text, and to Robertson, the possible meanings of medieval texts are limited: medieval poetry was "by nature allegorical" (286) and its meanings uniform. Robertson's principles are based on Augustine's *De Doctrina Christiana:*

> Demonstrandus est igitur prius modus inveniendae locutionis, propriane an figurata sit. Et iste omnino modus est, ut quidquid in sermone divino neque ad morum honestatem neque ad fidei veritatem proprie referri potest, figuratum esse cognoscas. (3.10.14)[18]
> [Therefore, we must first consider whether a manner of speaking is proper or figurative. And indeed the method is as follows: whatever in

Scripture cannot in its proper sense be referred to honesty of manners nor to the truth of faith, you know to be figurative.]

Whatever verbal statement is not in keeping with our preselected meanings is by definition figurative or ironic. But to accept such a definition would mean to follow literally the advice Robertson gives in the introduction to his *Preface to Chaucer*—to renounce the romantic literary tradition in which we were all trained. And this even Robertson himself is unwilling to do.[19]

Medieval Misprisions 2: Green's
Ironic Romances

To speak of medieval irony without strictly limiting the meaning of such irony is to impose onto the medieval period a modern concept—one foreign to the medieval period. There is nothing illegitimate about such an approach, but it is specious to cite medieval texts in support of a modern notion of irony. All such citations prove is that a medieval cognate for the modern word exists.

I will be discussing Chaucerian irony in chapter 9 below—an irony that owes more to nineteenth-century theories of poetry than to Chaucer's texts. But Chaucerian irony is only one example of an irony that modern critics have created for medieval writers. In the following section, I will consider one of the more interesting and elaborate discussions of so-called medieval irony, D. H. Green's *Irony in the Medieval Romance* (1979).[20]

Skepticism over medieval irony is not new, and Green provides an account of that skepticism, citing in particular Jean Frappier.[21] To Frappier, the word irony is simply a modern critic's desperate means of sweeping aside difficulties of interpretation; it is easier to label a text ironic than to explain precisely what that text means. Green wishes to confront such difficulties directly, and to do so through the use of modern critical terminology. According to Green, the problem is not in the critical terminology itself but rather in shoddy applications of it.

The modern concept of irony, however vaguely defined, can justify its own existence. Green responds to those who object to the vagueness of the word irony with the following statement, in which no attempt is made to disguise the circularity of reasoning: "To this kind of criticism the answer must be to learn the lesson from irony as a questioning mode by not stopping short of such questions as: what precisely do we mean by irony" (2).

Green begins with a brief but clear history of the word in medieval (and modern) texts. That history concludes with a definition: "Irony is a statement, or presentation of an action or situation, in which the real or intended meaning conveyed to the initiated intentionally diverges from, and is incongruous with, the apparent or pretended meaning presented to the uninitiated" (9). This definition lays the groundwork for his study by incorporating specifically the notion of a double audience of initiates and the uninitiated to correspond to the rhetorical definitions of double meanings.[22] Green then uses this double audience as a basis for an analysis of romances. The romance is written for two audiences: a real audience of initiates and a virtual audience of the uninitiated—an audience that will fail to understand the ethics of the romance. All this has precedent, of course; I have mentioned one in Plato. In medieval studies, such an interpretation of the romance has become a staple of romance criticism.[23] But to speak of irony in relation to a courtly society is to move it out of the society in which it seemed to exist for the medieval writer—a clerical one. The word irony, for the medieval writer, is not used to describe the (fictitious) moral superiority of the initiated knight to the churl; its use implies rather the critical superiority of the clerical exegete to a text or to superficial readers of that text (Arnulf's gloss on Lucan is an example). Green's use of the word results in an inadvertent clericalization of medieval courtly romance.

Despite Green's critical consideration of the use of the word by medieval writers, he relies on the later history of the word in his discussion. The phrase "irony of fate" is assumed to refer to a universal: irony of fate has always existed, but it was not discovered and defined until the seventeenth and eighteenth centuries. Dramatic irony as well (an irony I place in the nineteenth century) is equally real, and can even assume metaphoric status. Green's chapter 6 ("Verbal Irony") identifies five categories of irony: verbal irony, irony of the narrator, dramatic irony, irony of values, and structural irony, and each of these has a chapter devoted to it. None of these ironies is simple. Green associates verbal irony with ambiguity, quoting Booth's notion of pluralism in support: "Irony can arise from nothing more than a discrepancy or divergence between two meanings, both of which can be true, but in different ways. . . . Both meanings of the ironic statement are true" (184). Interestingly, neither medieval writers nor I think Booth himself would support the notion that there is an egalitarian relation between meanings. Verbal irony also includes such figures as oxymoron, litotes, hyperbole, and what Green calls "irony of inversion" and "irony of divergence." Thus, within verbal irony, Green includes even extravagant descriptions of the sickness of love.

The next four chapters are equally wide in scope. "Dramatic Irony" includes "irony of events." "Irony of Values" discusses the clash between secular and religious values. "Structural Irony" includes the relation between a character and the poet, or simply the juxtaposition of two fictional characters.[24] Green's final chapter, "The Reasons for Irony in the Medieval Romance," deals with the poet's status as an outsider at court. Green arranges these ironies in a hierarchy from verbal to structural to the actual historical relations of poet and audience. All of these topics are interesting, but to claim that they are all aspects of irony only legitimizes the apparent incoherence of that word's history. Such a strategy assumes that the referents for such terms as irony of fate have always existed. Under such an assumption, the history of criticism and critical language is a history of the discovery of critical universals.

Green ends up with a position similar to that adopted by Brooks thirty years earlier. To Brooks, irony is finally that which is worth discussing in poetry. To Green, irony is equally all-encompassing. Green knows what formal features are worth consideration in romance—those formal features that relate either to features of society or to the way literature was presented in society. These features are then classified under an all-encompassing rubric—irony. We are back to Green's original statement: we must "learn the lesson from irony as a questioning mode by not stopping short of such questions as: what precisely do we mean by irony" (2). But that question is to Green an open one, and his own mode of questioning precludes his stopping at any answers. Green's universal concept precedes and perhaps precludes any inquiry into the history of the word.

Where Green's history matches my own is in a secondary theme that runs through his entire analysis. The social relations between various romance characters and the relations between those characters and the real participants in the production and reception of romance are always at issue in romance. The poet-outsiders are interesting to Green not because they are strange and unknown but rather because their social status is uncertain. What is the social relation between these outsiders and the court?

Written language to Green is necessarily involved in these social hierarchies (216–17). In Green's view, oral poetry includes only verbal and dramatic irony. But this seems based on a nostalgic notion of oral poetry as a "unity of views shared by poet, characters and listeners and ignorant of any distinction between poet and narrator" (217). Once written romances are produced, a new irony is possible, "irony of the narrator." This social consensus ("unity of views") makes possible the kind of irony spoken of by rhetoricians which involves no possibility of misunderstanding. But even this nostalgic view of oral poetry is tenuous: the supposed unity of views exists in a barbaric context; the society that enjoys such unity equates its intelligibility to itself with cultural superiority. The Geats can understand *Beowulf,* but Grendel cannot. The irony of which Green speaks here is an irony whereby the poet and the modern reader can achieve a stance of superiority: "When Chaucer the pilgrim-narrator whitewashes the Prioress and agrees with the Monk, we are led towards the poet's true opinion which we accept as our own" (221).[25] The status we can enjoy here is one of superiority to Chaucer's characters. When the supposed unity of poet, character, and audience is lost (a unity that characterized a society in the past) the resultant hierarchy privileges the poet and modern reader. The myth of unity and the myth of oral poetry, thus, have a function—and an important one—in the history of complex forms of irony. They are the background against which the critic's superiority seems to exist not as an assumption but as a historical conclusion.

The limited definitions of irony known to medieval writers have seemed inadequate to modern critics of medieval literature. But the implications of those definitions have not changed. The reductive definition of rhetorical irony was created by the schools; it is, in Booth's terms, eminently teachable. This definition was perfectly compatible with the schools in a way that Socrates' methods (whatever they might have been) were not. An instructor must determine which meaning is correct. To determine what Lucan means by "libertas" is to distinguish between a sophisticated and a naive reader, and this is what an instructor is paid to do. It is also what a scholar is paid to do. Although Green is openly ahistorical in his use of the word irony, he also most clearly exposes the implications of its history.

PART THREE

ROMANTIC

IRONY

5

Romantic Irony:
Introduction

∎

From a twentieth-century perspective, the most crucial area in the history of irony is that described by the term romantic irony. While it may be possible in modern discussions of irony to bracket such understandings of irony as rhetorical irony or even Socratic irony,[1] the language and theory of romantic irony continue to influence our basic critical vocabulary.[2]

But what is romantic irony? A universal type of irony? the irony used by romantics? or an irony envisioned by the romantics and romanticists? The answer to this question will depend largely on the method used to answer it, or on the texts used to provide a basis for that answer. Included among the common (and contradictory) definitions of romantic irony in modern scholarship are: the self-conscious attitude of the artist toward the artistic work, a dialectical process involving the artist or the artistic work, the destroying of illusion in the artistic work, the endpoint of all art, pure artistic subjectivity (or objectivity), that indeterminacy congenial to deconstruction, romanticism itself. Such definitions can be further linked to a polemic—a polemic the romanticist often adopts from the romantic—for example, the argument that the third definition, concerning the destruction of artistic illusion, is a corruption and vulgarization of the more profound theory stated in the first two definitions (essentially the argument of Alfred Lussky); or that the phrase itself, however defined, is merely an example of romantic extravagance (the argument implied by such common phrases as "so-called romantic irony"). These definitions (as well as their critiques) are actually readings of selected romantic literature and evaluations of that literature. Romantic irony is itself a product of such readings and of associated critical polemic. Many of the most important theoretical statements on romantic irony occur in the form of literary reviews: Solger's review of A. W. Schlegel's lectures on drama; Hegel's review of Solger; Friedrich

Schlegel's review of *Wilhelm Meister* and his response to criticism of the *Athenaeum*.

The romantics themselves rarely used the phrase romantic irony. In 1841, Kierkegaard uses the phrase in dealing with Solger as the "spokesman for romanticism and romantic irony."[3] But Kierkegaard does not privilege this phrase, and regards the two terms that form it as virtually interchangeable: "Throughout this discussion I use the expressions: *irony* and the *ironist*. But I could as easily say *romanticism* and the *romanticist*. Both expressions designate the same thing. The one suggests more the name with which the movement christened itself, the other the name with which Hegel christened it" (292n). Novalis uses the phrase once in an unpublished notebook: "Die Philosophie und Moral des Romans sind *romantisch*. Das Gemeinst wird wie das Wichtigste mit romantischer Ironie angesehn und dargestellt"[4] ["The philosophy and morality of the novel [*Wilhelm Meister*] are romantic. The most common like the most important matter is considered and represented with romantic irony"]. And even Friedrich Schlegel, traditionally considered the father of romantic irony, uses the phrase only in his notebooks.[5] Its use there is enigmatic, and difficult to relate to his contemporary published fragments; the heavily abbreviated and obscure fragment 716 is one example: "[Absolute Sentimentalität] und [absolute Fantasie] führt auch ohne Univ[ersalpoesie] zu R[omantischem], aber doch erst mit dieser durch Trennung und Gegensatz zu [absolut Romantischem] oder zur romant.[ischen] Ironie"[6] ["Absolute sentimentality and absolute fantasy without universal-poetry lead to the romantic; only with it do they lead through division and opposition to the absolute romantic or to romantic irony"]. At best, the notebooks of Novalis and Schlegel provide early experimental contexts for the word *Ironie*. And until recently, they played little part in the traceable reception of romantic irony. The notion of romantic irony was well formed before these notebooks were widely read.

In 1850, the phrase romantic irony appears in Hermann Hettner's *Die romantische Schule*.[7] Hettner glosses the phrase as "fantastic caprice" and implies that it is current: "How was it possible, so soon after the sunlike clarity and plasticity of a Goethe or a Schiller, that we see develop that fantastic caprice of creation that dissolves its own forms, which under the name of romantic irony has become so celebrated and notorious?" (57). Later in the same work, Hettner devotes a chapter to "Die Phantastik und die Ironie" (82–91). Tieck's artistic irony is the practical equivalent of the theories of Solger and Schlegel (something later scholars will dispute). According to Hettner, there is nothing new in the practice of romantic irony; only the name and doctrine are new, both discovered by Friedrich Schlegel:

[As characterized in Schlegel's lectures, 1804–6], irony always means what it means for Solger, the aesthetician of the romantic school—nothing other than the necessary counterpart of artistic enthusiasm (*Begeisterung*), that hovering of the artist over his material (*das Schweben des Künstlers über seinem Stoffe*), and his free play with it; or, as Tieck once expressed it: "that final completion of an artistic work, that ethereal spirit, that free and unfettered hovers over the whole" (*der . . . über dem Ganzen schwebt*).

In a word, irony in and of itself is only a new name, and indeed a very striking one, for an old thing, for the eternal law of free form. (89)[8]

Rudolf Haym's more influential work of the same title, *Die romantische Schule* (1870), does not use the phrase "romantic irony," but his emphasis on irony and the notion of a romantic school did much to legitimize the concept, or problem, of romantic irony.[9] Haym's emphasis is on the philosophical roots of romantic irony:

As far as Schlegel was concerned, in the concept of irony, the transference to art and poetry of the scheme by which Fichte explained the world reached its apex and established itself as a fixed doctrine. It plays such a prominent role that early on it began to be used as the key word for romantic theory, and properly could Novalis say that irony in the *Athenaeum* fragments is the ace of trumps.

Irony! For Schlegel, this was the same as romantic poetry. (257)

Kierkegaard's equation of romantic and ironic is here attributed to Schlegel.

Haym's title repeats that of Hettner; it had been used earlier by Heine in his essay "Die romantische Schule" (1835).[10] The exact characterization of this supposed school in relation to irony varies. Heine associates irony with Tieck and Goethe (324–26) and even with God, but not with the Schlegels (275–78); for Hettner, irony is what distinguished Tieck from Goethe. But the use of such a title is symptomatic of a growing critical myth—a myth of coherence. The romantics are not diverse writers of aphorisms, essays, plays; they become a school. And a school implies an articulable program or doctrine. Attacks such as Heine's on the presumed school are as powerful in its formation as defenses.[11] Hettner would prefer the clarity of Goethe to the repackaging of old material by the Jena romantics. And many of the most forceful scholarly proponents of romantic irony begin by defending Schlegel against the early attacks of Hegel.

A common strategy in the scholarly development of the notion of romantic irony (the doctrine of a supposed school) has been to divide romantic irony into two forms: either a higher and lower form (a scheme from the romantics' own descriptions of irony) or a theoretical and practical form (the approach of Ingrid Strohschneider-Kohrs). Alfred Lussky does both in defining two types of romantic irony: one based on the theories of Friedrich Schlegel, the other based on the practices of Tieck, for which Tieck found precedent in eighteenth-century novels. Tieck's irony, limited by Lussky to a mere "breaking of illusion" or "destroying of objectivity," is thus a "secondary" form:

> Hence a definition of this *spurious* kind of romantic irony (if we re-gard that defined by Friedrich Schlegel as the *genuine* kind) would be somewhat as follows: the secondary kind of romantic irony is (unlike the primary kind as defined by Friedrich Schlegel and found by him in Shakespeare) that irony in a literary work which aims to reveal the sovereign greatness of the author by means of the destruction of the objectivity of the work as seen in personal reflections of the author aimed at the author himself, his poetic creation, his readers, and his literary contemporaries. This kind of romantic irony is to be found in *Don Quixote, Tristram Shandy, Wilhelm Meister,* and many of Tieck's works. . . . [This secondary kind of romantic irony] has usurped the field once held, briefly enough, by the subtle and profound type championed by the originator of the term.[12]

Lussky's distinctions are critically useful in explaining the apparent incon-sistencies in the evidence, such as Heine's association of irony only with Tieck and Goethe. Applying Lussky's argument, we could describe Heine's views on the irony of Tieck as pertaining only to secondary irony, a pos-sible solution, but one that leaves us with the conclusion that the greatest romantic artists were unable to understand the greatest romantic theory. Schlegel considered Tieck a less profound thinker than Schleiermacher, for example, and Lussky simply reads Tieck the way Schlegel demands.[13]

Readings of romantics? Or readings by romantics? Lussky's reading of Tieck is a reading of Tieck's plays through various clichés of German roman-ticism, many of which originate in Schlegel.[14] In Tieck's nondramatic work, however, Tieck himself sets forth some of the categories through which Lussky reads and criticizes him.[15] In Rudolf Köpke's *Erinnerungen,* Tieck is said to define the irony set forth in Solger's *Erwin* as "das Göttliche-Menschliche in der Poesie"; and does anyone who experiences this, he asks, require a further definition? (2:238). Hegel, Tieck claims, was mis-taken in failing to distinguish such irony from ordinary, "prosaic" irony or the "coarse irony of Swift." This higher irony is not negative, as Hegel had claimed, but "thoroughly positive": "Sie ist die Kraft, die dem Dichter die Herrschaft über den Stoff erhält" (2:239) ["It is the power that preserves for the poet the power over the material"].[16]

Tieck's direct comments on irony are clearly indebted, as he states, to Friedrich Schlegel and to Solger. To romanticists such as Joachimi, Lussky, and Strohschneider-Kohrs, this relation has been troublesome. Although Tieck claims to be distinguishing ordinary from higher irony, his statements on irony can all be understood within traditional notions of irony such as Socratic irony (understood by Tieck as Socrates' feigned lack of understanding) and the ironies of character noted in Shakespeare, most of which can be understood as a contrast between a character's appearance and actual being. Brutus seems noble, but is politically blind; Macbeth is originally strong and noble, but is driven by ambition to commit murder. Tieck's direct statements on irony, then, plead for a special sense of irony, but explain irony in traditional ways.[17] For Lussky and Strohschneider-Kohrs, Tieck is less useful as an object of study than as a foil for Friedrich Schlegel.

Subjective vs. Objective Irony

Hegel's definition of irony as "infinite negativity" and "absolute subjectivity" was borrowed directly by Kierkegaard and proved to be a basis for much discussion until well into the twentieth century.[18] Such terminology is extremely flexible, both in and out of the hands of Hegelians. But the association of the two terms, subjective and negative, particularly in a non-philosophical context, leads to a quick condemnation of irony. Defenses of romantic irony in terms of the positive or objective nature of irony are all related directly to Hegel.[19]

But what, to romanticists and to readers of romanticists, is subjective irony? objective irony? And what is the nature of the typology of irony such terms imply?[20] These types of irony have been defined in entirely contradictory ways. Raymond Immerwahr, for example, in an article that has become a near classic on this topic, distinguishes two forms of irony: the self-consciousness of the artist, and the deliberate destruction of poetic illusion.[21] Given these descriptions, it would be reasonable to interpret the first as subjective (since it deals with the subject's self-consciousness) and the second as objective (since it deals with the objective products of art). This is precisely how a similar dichotomy was labeled earlier in Walter Benjamin's influential *Begriff der Kunstkritik in der deutschen Romantik*.[22] To Benjamin, writing in 1919, the *only* form of irony that had been regarded by critics was a subjective irony, defined on the basis of Schlegel's *Athenaeum* fragment 116 as the lawless caprice of the poet. Subjective irony, so understood, is negative and deals only with the *Stoff* of art, not with its form. Positive and objective irony deals with the form of art—a form subject to objective artistic laws, "die objektive Gesetzlichkeit" (83). Irony of form consists of its willful destruction ("freiwillige Zerstörung"), as in Tieck's comedies (84); in these comedies, the particular form is destroyed in order to reveal (as a positive result) the "absolute form" (86). And this is what Benjamin calls the "objective moment of the artwork" (87).

Immerwahr, however, in distinguishing subjective from objective irony, means the exact reverse of this. Subjective irony is the "destroying of illusion" found in Tieck's plays; objective irony is the "self-consciousness of the artist," the artist's "sovereignty of mind" (174), the "intangible reflection of the creator in his work" (190–91). The ground for agreement between Benjamin and Immerwahr is solely in their assumption of the validity of the dichotomy itself (subjective vs. objective) and the necessity of privileging whichever pole is labeled objective. For Benjamin, this privileged form of irony is the destruction of dramatic illusion in Tieck's plays, but for most twentieth-century romanticists, Tieck's plays are just one more form of ordinary irony, or a debased form of irony. Lussky, for example, argues in precisely the manner of Benjamin, criticizing those who consider romantic irony as "merely" subjective (*Tieck's Romantic Irony,* 8). But what Lussky means by subjective irony is Tieck's irony, Benjamin's privileged form.[23]

Romantic Realism

Could a concept such as romantic irony develop apart from coherent critical descriptions of it? Or is the conventional name itself a sign of its creation? Are we to regard romantic irony as a creation of the early romantics such as Friedrich Schlegel? or of the early romanticists such as Hettner? According to Novalis, the precise terminology of the early romantic theorists is unimportant:

> Was Schlegel so scharf, als Ironie, karacterisirt, ist, meinem Bedünken nach, nichts anders—als die Folge, der Caracter der ächten Besonnenheit—der wahrhaften Gegenwart des Geistes. Der Geist erscheint immer nur in *fremder, luftiger* Gestalt. Schlegels Ironie scheint mir echter Humor zu sein. Mehrere Namen sind einer Idee vorteilhaft.[24]
> [What Schlegel so sharply characterized as irony is, in my opinion, nothing other than the product, the character of genuine discretion,

the true presence of the spirit. The spirit appears always only in a foreign, ethereal form. Schlegel's irony seems to me to be genuine humor. Several names are useful for one idea.]

Recent romanticists follow Novalis; I have noted Gary Handwerk's statement of method earlier: "To trace the word *irony* alone through [Schlegel's] writings is to fall prey to the terminological fixity against which the entire force of his own reflections was directed" (*Irony and Ethics in Narrative,* 20). Strohschneider-Kohrs's 1960 study seems based on a similar set of assumptions, although they are never stated this precisely. The following comments on Schleiermacher, Novalis, and Tieck are telling:

> All these statements by Schleiermacher reveal nothing of the high enthusiasm with which the principle of irony was rediscovered in romanticism as the expression of a profoundly spiritual and artistically productive secret and proclaimed as that special possibility of artistic spontaneity and thoughtfulness. (*Die romantische Ironie,* 100)
> Novalis does not often use the word irony, and where he does, it appears for the most part to have no link with the real problems he is considering. It remains to be shown, however, whether there is an analogy to the romantic irony-principle (*zum romantischen Ironie-Prinzip*) in the central problematic of Novalis, even when the word does not appear. (101)
> In Tieck's writings and letters, there are many statements about irony. However, they are for the most part so unclear and self-contradictory that it is almost impossible to derive from them a clear, definite, intelligible content. (128)

Novalis's central problematics may involve irony, even though Novalis does not realize this. The difficulty with Tieck is that his statements on irony are "unscharf und in sich widersprüchlich"; they do not yield what ought to be a clear and distinct idea of romantic irony.

This is what I call a realist solution: language cannot be empty; the language about irony must refer to the phenomenon irony. Under this solution, not only is the modern phrase "romantic irony" assumed to have a historical referent (one that may itself go by different names), but also that counterpart is assumed to be coherent and of a nontrivial nature. Tieck is thus condemned for lack of clarity. But in the case of Schlegel, Strohschneider-Kohrs poses a different set of questions: "The problem indicated by Schlegel through the concept of irony is already visible in the formulations of the Lyceum fragments, and is still relevant in the statements of his late work"

(8). Unlike Tieck, Schlegel need not define this problem. On the next page, the question is raised "whether the principle of irony as proclaimed by Schlegel refers to a principle of subjectivity or objectivity." Is irony a word? a concept? or a principle? The romanticists' claim that the romantics blurred such distinctions allows the romanticists to redraw them or to ignore them altogether. Tieck's explicit statements are thus less important than the potential coherence of Schlegel's enigmas.

Strohschneider-Kohrs's study is without question the most important and influential work to appear on romantic irony in several decades. But it has not necessarily led to a sharpening of focus on romantic irony, as its English reception proves. Strohschneider-Kohrs constructs a theory of romantic irony based on the writings of Schlegel, a theory against which later German writers are read. Anne Mellor, and to a lesser degree Lilian Furst, in transferring the term to English simply find examples. According to Mellor, Byron's *Don Juan* is the "great exemplar of Schlegel's romantic irony," even though there is no evidence that Byron knew Schlegel's work. "The Rime of the Ancient Mariner," also considered relevant by Mellor, was published in 1798, before Schlegel's fragments were available.[25] Under this conception of romantic irony, Schlegel at best discovered the existence of romantic irony. Romantic irony is a thing (a concept, a topic, an idea)— something exemplified by Byron and later English writers. Schlegel cannot under such a notion be the father of romantic irony; he is reduced to a spokesman for it.

A similar reduction occurs in the work of Kathleen Wheeler: "Irony is a structural principle [not] easily acceptable to an English (or American) public, even when it is proposed as a process (such as the reading process), which is less under the conscious control of an artist than 'method' implies."[26] The supposed reluctance of modern critics in English to accept this notion of irony (I assume Wheeler invents such critical reluctance for polemical purposes) "stems from misunderstanding . . . and from a lack of familiarity with the philosophic/aesthetic tradition of Karl Solger, Friedrich Schlegel and Ludwig Tieck, with whom Coleridge had much in common" (59). And although the German writers did not agree, "For our purposes, it will be sufficient to treat their concept of irony in its general aspects *as if they agreed* upon the fundamental issues with which irony grapples" (65; emphasis added). Such an assumption seriously weakens Wheeler's conclusions, as does a later one: "From the preceding chapters it should be apparent that the most important aspect of the concept of irony, that of opposition and reconciliation, was shared by Coleridge and the Germans"

(71)—and, of course, by nearly every other writer. Having begun as a father of irony, Schlegel becomes just another writer who dealt with opposition and reconciliation.

I began this study with a statement of a thesis which I repeat here: the most heated attempts to revise definitions of irony have consistently repeated the assumptions underlying earlier definitions. The negative connotations of irony have never been suppressed. To Aristophanes and Theophrastus, irony was a vice; it then developed (through its association with Socrates) into the symptom or indication of a vice. The ironic man was not himself a vicious man, but a man who noted that others were vicious men; he was not the receiver of an insult but the giver of one. The rhetorical tradition, based in part on Aristotle's positive interpretation of the word, attempted to simplify the meaning of the term, while retaining these earlier connotations in the example of praise and blame. Irony says X and means Y; but this meaning need not always be negative. Romantics such as Schlegel who invoked irony attempted to go beyond what they considered the reductive meanings of rhetorical irony. In addition, the disparaging of rhetorical irony was directed against its associations with an earlier academic tradition seen as artificial, pedantic, and uninspired. Irony was to be something higher.

In the most schematic terms, these various notions of irony can be seen as follows: The earliest meanings of irony established a hierarchy between two persons. One (the *eirōn*) was the subject of criticism. In rhetorical irony, this hierarchy was analyzed as a hierarchy of meanings: the final (hidden) meaning took precedence over the superficial meaning. Romantic irony reevaluated irony to be sure, but in such a way that these hierarchical meanings again became a hierarchy of persons, with those persons defined as the romantic poet and a too often recalcitrant audience. The romantic poet was to exist in relation to an audience in the same way that the two meanings in rhetorical irony were to exist in relation to each other. Thus Tieck's "sovereign greatness of the author."

A writer such as Schlegel would rail most aggressively against a phenomenon such as rhetorical irony because that phenomenon most clearly revealed the assumptions he was attempting to overcome: depending on our view of Schlegel, we can call this overcoming a transcendence, a sublimation, or, more simply and less congenially, a mystification. Each of these various Schlegels may well have his contemporary or his modern reader.

Method

My own method here will be to take what may well seem like the low road. I assume that the implications of romantic irony will appear in those passages by romantics where the word irony appears. In the following section, I will trace the problem of romantic irony backward through the romantics themselves to the supposed father of romantic irony, Friedrich Schlegel. This entails beginning with Hegel, in his review of Solger, and working backward through Solger's writings themselves to those of Friedrich Schlegel.

In a sense, this method is representative of the way we must deal with any concept such as irony. Schlegel has been received through the eyes of Hegel; his detractors often repeat the words of Hegel, his supporters defend him against Hegel (although not, I think, against the real charges of Hegel). Schlegel is thus inseparable from his reception. I have not attempted to solve this problem, but I have attempted to respond to it. The reverse chronology with which I have chosen to frame Schlegel's writings is representative of the chronology that is inevitably involved in any consideration of a critical concept.

In the last century, a flexible canon of romantic ironists and their opponents has been established. Representatives always include Friedrich Schlegel and Solger, and generally such less well-known figures as A. W. Müller. Problematic figures include A. W. Schlegel, Tieck, Novalis. And Kierkegaard and Hegel are now often accused of misunderstanding and misrepresenting romantic irony (although their negative polemic does much to legitimize its own object).[27]

I have not attempted to alter this canon. That there were competing views of irony has been well demonstrated in the second part of Strohschneider-Kohrs's study, which deals with applications of romantic theories and practical alternatives to these theories in the work of Tieck, Brentano, Novalis, and Schlegel himself. I have attempted, rather, to refocus the view of this canon by reorganizing the basic texts. Friedrich Schlegel is clearly central. But to begin with Schlegel inevitably leads to the conclusion that later writers misunderstand or misrepresent him. In the following section, Schlegel will provide only one more version of romantic irony, and perhaps, one more version of himself.

6

Hegel and Solger

■

Hegel, one of the most vehement critics of Friedrich Schlegel's notions of irony, became, somewhat paradoxically, one of the most influential figures in the development of various theories of romantic irony. Kierkegaard's *Concept of Irony,* while overtly attacking Hegel, repeats his basic analysis; the critique of irony in terms of subjectivity and objectivity was to become traditional. Hegel's views on irony were also incorporated quickly into literary history. Hettner's *Die romantische Schule* criticizes Hegel for allowing his personal dislike of Schlegel's "fanaticism" to cloud his interpretation of Schlegel's irony; because of Hegel, Hettner claims, romantic irony (particularly that found in Tieck) has come into undeserved ill repute as an arrogant nihilism, "ein freches Spiel mit den heiligsten Lebensinteressen" (88). To Hettner, romantic irony is purely an aesthetic concept, not, as Hegel and his school understand it, a moral one (88). Although Hegel's condemnation of irony is rejected by many modern romanticists as well, only under the broadest definition of aesthetics could Hettner's particular defense of romantic irony be said to have prevailed.

Hegel reads Schlegel for a referent, a referent Hegel finds not in the content of Schlegel's language but rather, as noted by Hettner, in its moral implications or in its (imagined) social or psychological origins. If, as Hegel implies, Schlegel's language is empty, it becomes nothing more than a reflection of Schlegel himself. In addition, as noted in a preceding chapter, Hegelian terms come with their own moral evaluation and their own implied typology: the objective (however defined) is privileged over the subjective, as is positive over negative.[1]

Hegel's critique responds directly to early critical manifestos, such as those of the *Athenaeum.* Such negative critiques could only increase the vitality of romantic irony, which, however defined, has always been a critical rather than a literary concept. The productivity of such a notion does not depend on supposed literary manifestations, although these can be defined and catalogued by any critic who wishes to do so. Rather, it is found in the polemical tone and verbal structure of its criticism. The notion of romantic irony is based on a series of flexible dichotomies, some with their origins in Schlegel, but many of them staples of idealism in general and Hegel's in particular: subjective/objective, positive/negative, good/bad, illusion/*Zerstörung*, true/false, high/low. The orchestration and reorchestration of these dichotomies, whatever the polemical stance, permits an ever vital reevaluation of the theory.

Words and Referents: Lectures on the History of Philosophy *and the Review of Solger*

Hegel's statements on irony are scattered throughout his work. His views are detailed in his review of Solger's posthumous writings and in his *Lectures on Aesthetics* and placed historically in *Lectures on the History of Philosophy.*[2] In this latter set of lectures, Hegel discusses irony twice, first in relation to Socrates, and second in relation to followers of Fichte, in particular, Friedrich Schlegel.[3] Hegel's starting point is similar to that of Schlegel: a modern (or romantic) irony is intelligible only in relation to historical forms of irony, rhetorical or Socratic. Socratic irony, along with Socrates' midwifery, are the two principle "moments" of the Socratic method, a method, according to Hegel, more properly described as a "manner" (*Weise*). The specific irony of Socrates—Socrates' posture of ignorance and his use of opponents' assumptions to bring out their self-contradictions—is purely subjective (18:60–61). But this irony, however subjective, is not nihilistic; it is to be distinguished from the modern irony of Schlegel and Ast, which Hegel characterizes as follows:

> Die Ironie ist das Spiel mit Allem; dieser Subjektivität ist es mit Nichts mehr Ernst, sie macht Ernst, vernichtet ihn aber wieder, und kann Alles in Schein verwandeln. Alle hohe und göttliche Wahrheit löst sich in Nichtigkeit (Gemeinheit) auf; aller Ernst ist zugleich nur Scherz. (63)
> [Irony (for Ast and Schlegel) is playing with all. To this subjectivity, nothing is serious; it creates the serious, then annihilates it, and can transform all into appearance. All high and divine truth disintegrates into nothingness (or vulgarity); all that is serious is at the same time only a joke.]

Socratic irony is subjective and negative in a dialectical sense; it leads to the creation of new forms. Modern irony is subjective and negative in an evaluative sense; the "pure negativity" of modern irony places the ironist (falsely and illegitimately) as supreme over the objective world.

Hegel repeats this analysis later, in his discussion of the followers of Fichte. Schlegel's irony is a nonphilosophical form of Fichtean thought. Following Fichte, Schlegel considers the *Ich* supreme; such absolute subjectivity, as irony, considers all objectivity as contemptible: "Das Subjekt weiß sich in sich als das Absolute, alles Andere ist ihm eitel; . . . Die Ironie weiß ihre Meisterschaft über alles dieses" (64) ["The subject understands itself as the absolute; all else is contemptible; . . . Irony realizes its own lordship over all this"]. The result is neither fish nor fowl: "weder Fleisch noch Fisch, weder Poesie noch Philosophie" (64).

Hegel seems to define three types of irony here. The "irony of our time" (such as that of Schlegel) is pure negation or "negative dissimulation"; this is the irony of scorn and hypocrisy (*Hohngelächter, Heuchelie*). The irony of Socrates is opposed to this, but it has two forms—the irony specific to Socrates ("bestimmte Ironie"), which is simply "a manner of conversation, social brilliance," and secondly his "tragic irony":

> Aber seine *tragische* Ironie ist sein Gegensatz seines subjektiven Reflektirens gegen die bestehende Sittlichkeit,—nicht ein Selbstbewußtseyn, daß er drüber steht, sondern der unbefangene Zweck, zum *wahren* Guten, zur allgemeinen Idee zu führen. (18:64)
> [But his tragic irony is the opposition of his subjective reflection to established morality—not a self-consciousness of his own superiority to it, but rather the unfettered goal of moving toward *true* good, toward the general idea.]

A more profound irony is always to be found by looking beyond the givens of contemporary history or the given texts of past history. The irony of our time is inferior to past irony, and the irony of the past (Socratic irony) is itself more profound than the irony that presents itself in the most accessible concrete texts. Hegel's implied hierarchy of ironies here will function paradoxically to reinforce the very theories of irony he seems intent on destroying.

Hegel develops a more extensive critique of irony in his review of Solger's posthumous writings, "Über Solgers nachgelassenen Schriften."[4] Because of his admiration for Solger, he is unable to dismiss modern irony unequivocally. The contrast between Socrates and Schlegel that defines irony in his

Lectures on the History of Philosophy is here transferred to one between Solger, who has properly understood the role of irony in modern history, and Schlegel, who has not. Hegel first relates the development of a theory of irony to a new interest in Shakespeare, fostered in part by Goethe, and later attempts to imitate other foreign models (Dante, Holberg, the Nibelungenlied, Calderón). This in turn leads to a "subjectivization" of form and content, what in Shakespeare's comic scenes could be described either as "admirable nonsense," or, less kindly, a "hovering" in the void (20:141).

The unreality promulgated by what Hegel calls a "theory of irony" is appropriate for lyric. But drama requires reality, character, and action; acceptance of the theory can lead to emptiness, inconsequence, and "sprawling prosiness (aufgespreizte Nüchternheit)." Criticism, however, finds with this standpoint a "new, bold, often insolent rapture"; and it is this that so impresses the rabble, who wish to share this "aesthetic height" (141–42). Solger, in sharing Hegel's contempt for "the public," avoided the dangers of such irony, and was well situated historically to do so. He wrote after the most "bold and productive" period of such irony, the period of the Athenaeum and Schlegel's Lucinde (142); war and political circumstances prevented him from participating in the later humor of Hoffmann (142).

Hegel's review of Solger and his defense of Socrates are judgments of the relations of these men to the world and to history. Hegel's critique of Schlegel is similar, and involves the relation of Schlegel's language to the world. Schlegel's language is "empty," as Solger himself noted; it both ignores and devalues reality. It can find its referent (or explanation) only in the subjective attitude of the poet, not in the objective world. Schlegel adopts this negative stance against objectivity from Fichte's philosophy of subjectivity (160), which deals not with the world, but with "foggy imaginings, mysticism, and philosophical abstractions." It becomes known as irony, which Hegel pretends to discuss only with reluctance: "The self-conscious contempt of objectivity was named 'irony.' And since we find in our path this most distinguished ironical individuality (die ausgezeichnetste ironische Individualität), it will get short mention" (161).

Irony for Hegel, even Socratic irony, always involves relations to the world or to other persons.[5] And Hegel's critique of irony and its proponents depends not on particular analyses of irony but rather on how such analyses bear on the real world and what they imply about the social attitudes of the ironist. Hegel's ad hominem attack on Schlegel is itself a compensation for what Hegel feels is a lack of relation to worldly concerns in Schlegel's own language:

Die hier bemerkte Beziehung auf die Philosophie hat sich dieser Vater der Ironie seine ganze öffentlich Laufbahn hindurch gegeben. . . . dieß hieß aber, von der vornehmen Stellung *über der Sache* oder (um eine seiner vormaligen Erfindungen von Kategorien zu benutzen)—von der göttlichen Frechheit (und auf der Höhe der Ironie läßt sich wohl ebenso gut sagen—von der satanischen oder diabolischen Frechheit) des Urtheilens und Absprechens, auf den Boden des Philosophirens selbst und der Sache sich herablassen. Hr. Friedr. Schlegel hat auf diese Art immerfort darauf hingewiesen, daß er auf dem höchsten Gipfel der Philosophie stehe, ohne jemals zu beweisen, daß er in diese Wissenschaft eingedrungen sey, und sie auf eine nur gewöhnliche Weise inne habe. (161–62)

[Throughout his career, this father of irony kept up an appearance of relying on philosophy. . . . This means however, to descend from the noble placement "beyond things," or (to use one of his early categorical coinages) from the godly audacity (and from the summit of irony it could just as well be called the satanic or diabolic audacity) of judgment and criticism to the very ground of philosophizing and to the matter itself. Lord Fr. Schlegel always noted in this manner that he stood on the highest summit of philosophy, without ever proving that he had penetrated this knowledge and possessed it in any ordinary way.]

Schlegel's irony is mere charlatanry (162), "a notorious and pretentious phantom" (182). Solger's irony, by contrast, is a principle (*ein Princip*)—the negative principle of dialectic (182).

As in Hegel's discussion of Socrates, two forms of negativity are involved: the dialectic negativity of Solger vs. the nihilistic negativity of Schlegel. Both forms are based on Fichte's philosophy—a philosophy Hegel claims Schlegel misunderstands and abuses. Whereas Solger's irony, like Fichte's negativity, is part of a dialectical ascent, Schlegel's destroys objective reason and truth; Schlegel has turned irony against the very world it is intended to explain, and in so doing, has perverted the "guiltless" name of Socratic irony (183–84).

Solger's irony, by contrast, is not a purely abstract negativity, but arises as that negativity reflects on particular concrete concerns. Irony appears in the "transition" where the speculative category of negativity reflects on the particular, "on the field where duty, truth, and fundamental principles begin" (185). But even Solger will drop the word *Ironie*. Hegel notes that in the "speculative exposition of the highest idea," Solger does not mention irony; and that if irony is indeed "that noble secret, the great Unknown" (188), one would expect its exposition here. When what is at issue is the concrete, serious, and true, Solger's "principle" is far away, and the same criticism applies to Tieck.

According to Hegel's reading of Solger, the word *Ironie* is inadequate to deal with the highest concerns. When he explains Solger's theory of the subjective experience of the divine and divine activity (itself an objective fact), the word *Ironie* does not appear. Irony cancels itself, as it cancels itself from Hegel's discussion, when the subject matter of that discussion transcends the purely subjective.

Artistic Deception: Ironie *and* Schein
in the Lectures on Aesthetics

The artistic implications of Hegel's reading of the early romantics are set forth in his *Lectures on Aesthetics*. According to classical, eighteenth-century definitions, irony is a way of saying one thing and meaning another. Irony thus opposes appearance and reality. Although Hegel was highly critical of the equation of irony and art in early romantic theory, his language and his presuppositions concerning history in general and art history in particular show how easy that equation is to make.

Early in the introduction to these lectures, in dealing with the question of the value of art as a legitimate object of study, Hegel remarks: "Den Schein und die Täuschung dieser schlechten, vergänglichen Welt nimmt die Kunst von jenem wahrhaften Gehalt der Erscheinungen fort und gibt ihnen eine höhere, geistgeborene Wirklickheit" (28) ["Art frees the semblance and the deception of this wretched, transitory world from the genuine content of appearances and gives to them a higher, spirit-borne reality"]. Art is a way of transforming appearance into reality. According to Hegel, both the ideal and the empirical approaches are inadequate in the study of art. What is needed is a merging of both. If we speak of the history of art as a language, Hegel implies that language must not be read either according to the letter or according to pure meanings. The facts of history are read, rather, *for* their meanings, just as meanings themselves must be grounded in substance (either empirical or social). Hegel's supposed distortion of early romantic theories of irony (for which romanticists since Hettner have criticized him) is legitimate, then, insofar as the distortion of theory is based on what Hegel feels is the moral and social substance of theory. "True seriousness" can only arise through ethics, truth, things of intrinsic value, or through a "substantial interest" (101).

Hegel concludes the introduction with a short section on irony. According to Hegel, A. W. and Friedrich Schlegel were of a critical rather than a philosophical nature. And it is the critical appropriation of philosophical notions (particularly those of Fichte) that results in Friedrich Schlegel's "doctrine" and later versions of "so-called irony" (100; "Über Solgers nachgelassene Schriften," 183).

The same language of subjective mastery found elsewhere in Hegel's description of irony appears here, with what will devolve into gratuitous punning on the philosophical and social meanings of "subject" (*Lectures on Aesthetics,* 102). The relation of Fichte's philosophy to later theories of irony lies in his positing the absolute principle of knowledge as the *Ich*. This *Ich* has three forms: first, it is the absolute principle of knowledge; second, it is both negating and affirming of reality: "was ist, ist nur durch das Ich, und was durch mich ist, kann Ich ebenso sehr auch wieder vernichten" ["What exists, exists only through the I, and what is through me, I can just as easily annihilate"].[6] Over this reality (*was ist*), *Ich* rules as "Herr und Meister" (101). All else is appearance (*Schein*). But third, the *Ich* is a living, active individual—an individual who would live as an artist. For an artist, all reality is merely "ein Schein für mich" and lies entirely within the artist's might. And it is this devaluation of reality that makes a serious apprehension of it (*Ernst*) impossible.

The ironic artist thus assumes a stance that excludes all seriousness. Beneath such an artist lies the rabble: "*pauvre* borniertе Subjekte, ohne Organ und Fähigkeit, die Höhe meines Standpunktes zu erfassen und zu erreichen" (102) ["those poor foolish subjects, without the means or capacity to comprehend or to attain the heights of my standpoint"]. Schlegel's genial ironist thus lives in a continuous state of solipsism and bad faith:

Und nun erfaßt sich diese Virtuosität eines ironisch-künstlerischen Lebens als eine göttliche Genialität, für welche alles und jedes nur ein wesenloses Geschöpf ist, an das der freie Schöpfer, der vom allen sich los und ledig weiß, sich nicht bindet, indem er dasselbe vernichten wie schaffen kann. Wer auf solchem Standpunkte göttlicher Genialität steht, blickt dann vornehm auf alle übrige Menschen nieder, die für beschränkt und platt erklärt sind. (101)
[And now this virtuosity of an ironic-artistic life considers itself as a divine geniality, for which each and every thing is only a creation without being on which the free creator, who knows himself com-

pletely detached from everything, does not bind himself, in that he can annihilate the same things that he can create. He who takes up such a position of divine geniality looks down in a superior manner on all ordinary men, who are declared limited and superficial.]

Such an artist can live in the world as an individual, with relations to others (friends and lovers), but because that artist is a self-proclaimed genius such relations are worth nothing ("zugleich ein Nichtiges"). This, Hegel claims, is the meaning of "the divine genial irony" of "Lord Friedrich von Schlegel" and his imitators, an irony where the ironist lives free from all worldly bonds in the "blessedness of self-indulgence" (102).

As in the *Lectures on the History of Philosophy,* the next form taken by the negativity of irony is the contempt for all that is substantial, ethical, and valuable ("Sachlichen, Sittlichen und in sich Gehaltvollen"), the denial of all objectivity. The result is unhappiness and contradiction, for the subject desires truth and longs for objectivity, but cannot overcome its own inwardness. What results is absence of rest, absence of activity. And this, claims Hegel, we often find in Fichte's philosophy (103). This state can be resolved through art, in that the artist fashions artistic works as products of imagination:

> Das Princip dieser Produktionen, die nur in der Poesie vornehmlich hervorgehen können, ist nun wiederum die Darstellung des Göttlichen als des Ironischen. Das Ironische aber als die geniale Individualität liegt in dem Sich-Vernichten des Herrlichen, Großen, Vortrefflichen, und so werden auch die objektiven Kunstgestalten nur das Princip der sich absoluten Subjektivität darzustellen haben, indem sie, was dem Menschen Werth und Würde hat, als Nichtiges in seinem Sich-Vernichten zeigen. (104)
>
> [The principle of these productions, which can only prevail in poetry, is now again the representation of the divine as the ironic. The ironic, however, as genial individuality lies in the self-annihilation of the noble, grand, distinguished; and therefore objective art objects will only represent the principle of absolute subjectivity, since in the process of its self-annihilation, they represent what has worth and value to men as nothing.]

Irony here is nihilistic, associated with "lack of character." True character (Hegel's example is Cato)[7] depends on the ability to posit and maintain external goals on which individuals can stake their entire being (104–5).

Now if this self-annihilating irony is seen as a principle of representation ("zum Grundton der Darstellung"), then true art is impossible. For the result is an inconsistent emergence of flat figures, insubstantial forms, longings and contradictions of feeling—representations that can "awaken no true interest" (105).

This brings Hegel to Tieck and Solger, both of whom Hegel sees as representing irony as the "highest principle of art" (105). What Solger's "deep penetration into the philosophical idea" came close to discovering— was Hegel:

> Hier kam er auf das dialektische Moment der Idee, auf den Punkt, den ich "unendliche absolute Negativität" nenne, auf die Thätigkeit der Idee, sich als das Unendliche und Allgemeine zu negieren zur Endlichkeit und Besonderheit, und diese Negation ebenso sehr wieder aufzuheben, und somit das Allgemeine und Unendliche in Endlichen und Besondern wieder herzustellen. An dieser Negativität hielt Solger fest, und allerdings ist sie ein *Moment* in der spekulativen Idee, doch als diese bloße dialektische Unruhe und Auflösung des Unendlichen wie des Endlichen gefaßt, auch *nur ein Moment,* nicht aber, wie Solger es will, *die ganze Idee.* (106)

> [Here he came upon the dialectical moment of the idea, upon that point, which I call "infinite absolute negativity," upon the activity of the idea negating itself as the infinite and general in favor of the finite and particular, and to the same extent canceling this negation, and thereby again establishing the general and infinite in the finite and particular. Solger holds fast to this negativity, and to be sure it is a moment of the speculative idea, yet understood as both this mere dialectical unrest and dissolution of the infinite as well as the finite, it is only a moment, not, however, as Solger would have it, the entire idea.]

Solger died young, and because of the virtues of his character ("Festigkeit, Ernst und Tüchtigkeit"; here Hegel's invocation of Cato takes on meaning), Solger was not an "ironic artist" in the first sense, that is, not one of the so-called "apostles of irony," nor was his sense of true art itself of an ironic nature.

Hegel ends his introduction with a paragraph on Tieck (106). Tieck and other "distinguished" people were familiar with philosophical expressions without understanding them. And thus Tieck constantly demanded irony without defining it.[8] Since Tieck seldom wrote criticism, when one thinks to have the best opportunity to discover what the irony of such great works as *Romeo and Juliet* might be, "one is deceived (*betrogen*), for there is no further mention of irony." Nor do we hear more in Hegel. Here ends his introduction, as well as all discussion of irony. A discussion that began in deception ("Täuschung") ends here with deception—both by Hegel, who leaves his discussion of irony open, and by the student of Tieck, who is deceived ("betrogen") in the expectation of answers.

Modern scholars of romantic irony often have dismissed Hegel's critique. Strohschneider-Kohrs devotes only eight pages to Hegel and Kierkegaard (*Die romantische Ironie,* 215–22); Beda Allemann, following a tradition that begins with Hettner, speaks of Hegel's "willful misunderstanding" of Schlegel (*Ironie und Dichtung,* 97); Helmut Prang's judgment is similar (*Die romantische Ironie,* 79).[9] According to Strohschneider-Kohrs, Hegel's conceptions of irony have nothing to do with irony as conceived by Friedrich Schlegel; rather, his critique takes as its ground Solger's own critique of A. W. Schlegel's conception (216). Hegel misunderstands Friedrich Schlegel, who never speaks of a renunciation of objectivity, but only of a distancing from it (217).

Such criticism of Hegel is arguably correct: Hegel does misrepresent Schlegel and does not respond directly to Schlegel's supposed theory of irony. But he does not respond directly to Solger's theory either. Solger's conception of irony is less important than Solger's life and the dialectical methods Solger inadvertently discovered. The content of Solger's theories of irony is less important than is the potential of Solger's theories for incorporation into a philosophical history that will lead to Hegel's system. Schlegel's thinking is also ignored. Hegel does not deal seriously with the content of Schlegel's supposed theory because he does not accept the notion that there is a coherent theory in Schlegel; the content of Schlegel's notes on irony is secondary to its expression. Schlegel uses philosophy and art for social purposes; irony is simply a means for Schlegel to establish for himself a superior vantage—a way to become "Herr Fr. von Schlegel." To engage in a serious discussion of the content of Schlegel's work is to accept what Hegel feels are its social premises, and this Hegel refuses to do.

Hegel's text is a trap for his own detractors. To criticize Hegel requires one to accept as a basis for argumentation a system of thought that destroys the unsystematic thinking of Friedrich Schlegel. Those who criticize Hegel's polemic against Schlegel apply standards that cannot be applied to the arguments of Schlegel. Hegel's critics (Strohschneider-Kohrs, for example) require that Hegel's arguments be disinterested, logical, and consistent in order to be valid. Yet supporters of Schlegel do not insist that Schlegel's own writings be judged on such criteria.

Karl Solger: Irony and the Artist

Although never as popular as the work of Friedrich Schlegel, Solger's work was praised by Hegel and praised as well by Tieck, who claimed Hegel misrepresented it. Solger is also praised by Kierkegaard, who, like Hegel, sees Solger's work fulfilled in Hegel's own: "It is well known that Solger died prematurely, and I shall not attempt to decide whether he would have been successful in consummating the speculative thought grasped by him with so much energy, or whether his energy was not already consumed in asserting negativity. It seems most appropriate to me, however, to regard Solger as a sacrifice for Hegel's positive system" (*Concept of Irony*, 355).[10] Solger's importance to later theorists of romantic irony lies in his articulation of positive aspects of irony and his explicit characterization of irony as the sine qua non of art. Despite radical differences, Hegel, Solger, and Schlegel all contribute to the redefinition of irony as an artistic problem rather than a strictly rhetorical or philosophical one.

Solger's work has been read by enthusiasts of romantic irony (Hegel is clearly not one of them) as itself a reading of Friedrich Schlegel's theory of irony.[11] One result is an overzealous interpretation of both Solger and Schlegel; another is a deprecation of Tieck, who despite his relations with Solger and both Schlegels must be accused of failing to understand Schlegel's supposed theory.[12]

Three of Solger's works deal with theories of irony: *Erwin* (a dialogue), *Lectures on Aesthetics,* and his review of A. W. Schlegel's *Lectures on Dramatic Art and Literature.*[13] With regard to irony, the starting point for Solger is the traditional definition of irony developed by A. W. Schlegel in his lectures. Schlegel's lecture 23 is specifically addressed to the question of irony in Shakespeare.[14] In Schlegel, the distinction between the ironic and the non-ironic is equated with the distinction between tragedy and comedy. According to Schlegel, when the true tragic enters, irony ceases: "Im höchsten Tragischen höre alle Ironie auf" (quoted by Solger in his review, 566). For most theorists of romantic irony, this is in sharp contrast with the views of Friedrich Schlegel.[15]

To A. W. Schlegel, irony is what it was for earlier lexicographers: merely a form of "raillery"; its relevance for a generic system (one opposing tragedy to comedy) lies in its specific relation to the comic, or to *Scherz*. There is no place here for notions of tragic irony, however defined,[16] no room for a notion such as irony of fate, and little room for any but an extremely limited form of Socratic irony. To Solger, such irony as defined by Schlegel is false, inauthentic irony—"unechte Ironie" (567).

Solger's most important comments on irony occur earlier in this review, finding their basis in Schlegel's absolute distinction between tragedy and comedy. Solger does not accept this distinction as absolute, and argues for an inner relation between tragedy and comedy, between *Ernst* and *Scherz*. In both cases, tragedy and comedy, he argues, we transcend the nothingness of human concerns. Irony is that mood in which all contradictions are negated, a mood that makes both tragedy and comedy possible (513).

Without irony, drama is mere melodrama; we are locked into the "dismal" emotions expressed on stage. Only irony allows us to assume a detached (and by implication critical) stance as spectators. This stance "raises us over all" (514); it permits that superiority over materials characterized by Tieck, according to Köpke, as "die Herrschaft über den Stoff" (*Erinnerungen* 2:239).

To Solger, irony is central to art and to dramatic art in particular, and he treats this idea here as if it were self-evident; he feigns surprise to find that Schlegel has given so little place to irony:

> Es war dem Rec. höchst auffallend, der Ironie, in welcher er den wahren Mittelpunct der ganzen dramatischen Kunst erkennt, so daß sie auch beim philosophischen Dialog, wenn er einigermaßen dramatisch seyn soll, nicht zu entbehren ist, in dem ganzen Werke nur Einmal erwähnt zu finden, (Th. II, Abth. 2, S. 72) und noch dazu um ihr alle Einmischen in das eigentlich Tragische zu untersagen; und doch erinnert er sich an frühere Außerungen des Verfassers, welche sich an diese Idee wenigstens sehr anzunähern schienen. (514)
>
> [It was most astonishing to this reviewer to find that irony was mentioned only once in Schlegel's lectures—irony, in which I find the true center of all dramatic art, so that it is also indispensable for any philosophical dialogue that is to be at all dramatic. And moreover Schlegel prohibits any mixture of irony in the genuinely tragic. And yet, I am reminded of his earlier statements, which seemed at least very close to this idea.]

Solger then develops his own concept of irony by distinguishing true irony from Schlegel's "inauthentic" irony. True irony is not merely rhetorical, but rather has a cosmological dimension: "Die wahre Ironie geht von dem Gesichtspunct aus, daß der Mensch, so lange er in dieser gegenwärtigen Welt lebt, seine Bestimmung, auch im höchsten Sinne des Worts, nur in dieser Welt erfüllen kann" (514–15) ["True irony starts from the assumption that man, as long as he lives in this present world, can fulfill his destiny, even in the highest sense of the word, only in this very world"]. Solger will define irony as negation, but irony is not to be reduced to mere negation, nor, in terms of art, is it to be limited to the bounds of a secondary genre. It is part of man's essentially worldly condition, and as such is an essential part of the artist's being.

Solger would give two more formulations of his theories of irony, in his *Lectures on Aesthetics* and in *Erwin*. The distinctions developed in his lectures are based on a higher level of abstraction than that of *Scherz* and *Ernst*—the basis for A. W. Schlegel's own discussion in his *Lectures on Dramatic Art and Literature*. In the *Lectures on Aesthetics*, Solger defines poetry as "the inner working of the idea in the artistic spirit" (185). Art is a matter of the idea become reality, and it is in this process that irony appears, in inseparable relation with enthusiasm (*Begeisterung*). Art itself is the result of the dialectical fusion of enthusiasm and irony.[17]

The same process is defined earlier. Together with enthusiasm (*Begeisterung*), irony constitutes the center of artistic activity and all art depends on it: "Kein Kunstwerk kann ohne diese Ironie entstehen" (124). This irony must necessarily be distinguished from what Solger sees as a nihilistic form of pure subjectivity—a pure subjectivity that Hegel will later find characteristic of Friedrich Schlegel.

Solger's notion of irony owes much to earlier formulations, but he attempts to strip away some of the features most firmly associated with rhetorical irony and further to avoid the nihilistic implications of the negativity associated with irony. Solger associates irony with the artist rather than with the artwork, which is itself merely a product of artistic activity. In theory, an ironic work is ironic only metonymically, as an expression of the artist. As a consequence, Socratic irony is a privileged form of irony. Socratic irony, according to the implications of Solger's argument, is not a philosophical argument; it is a philosophical act, an expression of what Quintilian claims is Socrates' entire life of irony.

The centrality of irony in Solger's aesthetics is clear. Although it is perhaps wrong to interpret Solger here as defining irony as the highest principle of art (a formulation in *Erwin* comes closer to this), it is at least fair to say that irony here is a sine qua non of art: "Mit dieser Begeisterung aber muß nothwendig zugleich eine gewisse Aeußerung der *Ironie* verbunden sein; denn ohne Ironie gibt es überhaupt keine Kunst" (199) ["With this enthusiasm, a certain expression of irony must be bound; for without irony, there is generally no art"].

By the end of the essay, irony becomes less an artistic attitude or mood linking the artist to particular artworks than a generalized activity that links the artist to art: "Die Ironie ist keine einzelne, zufällige Stimmung des Künstlers, sondern der innerste Lebenskeim der ganzen Kunst" (245) ["Irony is no particular, occasional attitude of the artist, rather the innermost kernel of the life of all art"]. Solger abstracts the notion of irony from the particular field of artworks, but not from the particular artist, who is linked to art itself through his ironic mood.

Solger acknowledges other forms of irony, and distinguishes his new form of irony from them in language that is found in many romantic discussions of irony. True irony is to be distinguished from false irony: "Die falsche, scheinbar, gemeine Ironie entsteht aus Reflexion des gemeinen Verstandes" (245) ["False, superficial, ordinary irony arises from the reflection of the ordinary understanding"]. True irony is different: "Die echte Ironie setzt das höchste Bewußtsein voraus, vermöge dessen der menschliche Geist sich über den Gegensatz und die Einheit der Idee und der Wirklichkeit vollkommen klar ist" (247) ["Genuine irony presupposes the highest consciousness, by virtue of which the human spirit is completely clear about the opposition and the unity of the idea and reality"]. The distinction between "highest" and "common," or "vulgar" (gemein), implies the same elitism that Hegel criticizes in Schlegel's theory.

Erwin

The most extravagant claims for irony made by Solger occur in Erwin— a text that has received more attention from recent scholars than Solger's other works, although it was apparently unknown to Hegel and Kierkegaard. According to René Wellek, in Erwin "Solger drew the bold conclusion that irony is the principle of all art";[18] Hegel, not citing Erwin, makes the same claim for Solger (Vorlesungen über Ästhetik, 100). To back up Hegel's reading, Wellek must cite a text by Solger to which Hegel apparently had no access.

Erwin is a dialogue with four interlocutors: Adalbert (who seems to represent Solger himself), Anselm (Schelling), Bernhard (Fichte), and Erwin (a student). Adalbert gives an account of the dialogue to a friend. Irony is discussed at the end of the dialogue. According to Adalbert, irony is the all-embracing view of the artist: "Hier also muß der Geist des Künstlers alle Richtungen in einem, alles überschauenden Blick zusammenfassen, und diesen über allem schwebenden, alles vernichtenden Blick nennen wir die Ironie" (387) ["Here, then, must the spirit of the artist gather together all tendencies in one all-embracing glance, and this all-annihilating glance, hovering over all, we call irony"]. This claim is not made in Solger's earlier work, where the "all-embracing glance" is always a synthesis of irony and enthusiasm. Adalbert's interrogator, Anselm, is surprised by this formulation: "Ich erstaune, sprach Anselm hier, über deine Kühnheit, das ganze Wesen der Kunst in die Ironie aufzulösen, welches viele für Ruchlosigkeit halten möchten" (387) ["I am amazed, Anselm broke in, at your daring, to reduce the entire being of art to irony, which many might consider impiety"]. Adalbert then explains this irony, using familiar moves: the irony that he is discussing is different from ordinary irony, an irony he calls "Scheinironie":

> Ich sage dir, wer nicht den Mut hat, die Ideen selbst in ihrer ganzen Vergänglichkeit und Nichtigkeit aufzufassen, der ist wenigstens für die Kunst verloren. Aber es gibt freilich auch eine Scheinironie, wie Scheinwitz und Scheinbetrachtung, und daß man mir nicht diese beilege, davor muß ich mich wohl verwahren. Diese besteht aber darin, daß man dem Nichtigen ein scheinbares Dasein leiht, um es desto leichter wieder zu vernichten. . . . Dieses ist die sogenannt freundliche Lebensphilosophie, die wir beim alten Lucian und bei manchen seiner neueren Nachahmer finden. (388)
>
> [I tell you, anyone who does not have the courage to grasp the ideas themselves in their entire transitoriness and nothingness is at the very least lost for art. But there is indeed also a pseudo-irony, as there is pseudo-wit and pseudo-contemplation, and I must take care that this is not attributed to me. This consists of lending a pseudo-being to nothingness, in order to annihilate it more easily in turn. . . . This is the so-called congenial philosophy of life that we find in Lucian and in many of his more recent imitators.]

As glossed by Adalbert's interlocutor Erwin, such pseudo-irony transforms the "nothingness of the idea" into a "worldly appearance."

The distinctions between true and false irony are familiar ones. But distinctions of this type concerning irony, however analogous, are obviously not always equivalent in content. Both Solger and Friedrich Schlegel analyze irony on the basis of such distinctions between true and false, higher and lower. But these hierarchies are merely means for reevaluating a critical term. They have their artistic counterpart in the distinction between true and false poetry, their social counterpart in the distinction between true and false wit. In and of themselves, they tell us little about the content of this irony and the nature of its supporting theory.

Solger opposes irony in modern art to irony in ancient on the basis of a distinction similar to Schiller's distinction between naive and sentimental art.[19] In ancient art irony lies in things, while in modern art it lies in consciousness. Nonetheless, both ironies are legitimate; without the irony of things, modern irony would be reduced to mere subjectivity, and thus presumably subject to a critique such as Hegel's.

The dialogue nears conclusion with the radical statement that life itself is to be reduced to art, an art for which irony is central:

> So könnten wir wohl kurz sagen, unser gegenwärtiges, wirkliches Dasein, in seiner Wesentlichkeit erkannt und durchlebt, sei die Kunst; und eben darin lebe auch überall jener Mittelpunkt, worin sich Wesen und Wirklichkeit beide als Gegenwart durchdringen, die Ironie, die vollkommenste Frucht des künstlerischen Verstandes. (394)
> [For we could perhaps say, in short, that our present, actual existence, considered and lived out in its true being, is art; and that therein exists everywhere that center where being and actuality intertwine as presence—that is irony, the ripest fruit of artistic understanding.]

To speak of irony as the endpoint or as the highest principle of art (as do Hegel and Wellek) is not entirely consistent with this passage. It is not Adalbert who claims that irony is the highest principle of art; it is Anselm, who professes "amazement" at the reduction of art to irony. Adalbert never seems to consent to this oversimplification. *Erwin* thus dramatizes some of the ideas expressed somewhat more dryly in Solger's *Lectures on Aesthetics*. Irony is a sine qua non of art, and relates to the artist's point of view: the all-embracing, all-annihilating glance of the artist is what Solger (as Adalbert) says "we call" irony (387). It is a condition for the existence of art, but it is not a sufficient condition, nor a guarantee.

Furthermore, the irony that is supposed to reside in things themselves (under some interpretations, an objective irony) is for Solger a secondary concern. Solger's introduction of this concept seems to be an attempt to preempt the potential criticism that his imagined ironic artist is purely subjective. The artist's irony (a view) is related to an object: it has a correspondent in things themselves. And such an irony of things (based on the artist) is responsible for ancient art. The modern artist then realizes consciously the potential negation of ancient art. Irony is a potential when considered part of things; it is actuality in the life and point of view of the artist.

In discussions of romantic irony, readings of Solger are inextricably linked to readings of Schlegel. Hegel never discusses Solger without reference to Friedrich Schlegel, and Kierkegaard merely follows Hegel. But where modern scholars find relations in their thinking, Hegel finds only sharp contrasts. Solger's morality contrasts with Schlegel's social pretensions and his *Lucinde;*

Schlegel's nihilism must have a contrasting positive feature in Solger—a feature that is difficult to find in many of Solger's formulations. Hegel saves Solger not through an analysis of his writings but rather by placing him in a dialectical relation with history. Solger's negativity (unlike Schlegel's) is not absolute, and looks ahead to its positive counterpart in Hegel himself. Solger thus is himself a "Moment," awaiting the "ganze Idee" that will appear in Hegel.

An illegitimate reading? By some standards, yes. But is it a service to either Solger or Schlegel to assume that Hegel misreads them both?

7
Friedrich Schlegel

■

Hegel's distinction between Solger and Schlegel is not a literary judgment; it is an ethical one. Solger's seriousness, characterized as "sittlich," "sach-lich," contrasts with the social pretensions of Schlegel; Schlegel is "the distinguished Lord von Schlegel"; his irony is "divine"; he himself is an "apostle." The distinction between the two is one between *Schein* and *Ernst,* appearances and substantiality, or between the purely subjective and the objective. Hegel's implied history of modern (romantic) irony describes the transformation from one form of negation to another: from a nihilistic and self-interested negation to one that is dynamic and productive.

This history of modern irony does not rely exclusively on specific texts of Solger and Schlegel. Schlegel's public stances, personal history, and the implications of his vocabulary are as important as the direct statements in his published writings. For romanticists, the Hegelian history of irony is mere polemic, a manipulation of both Solger and Schlegel. But for a history of irony, Hegel's approach is extremely important. For it denies the myth of coherence pertaining to individual object texts in favor of a second-order coherence, critical and Hegelian. The coherence of irony lies in its own history, not in the particular theories, however original, of those who participate in that history.

The reading I have adopted for Schlegel here takes as a starting point the reading (or misreading) implied in Hegel. The key terms in Schlegel's irony are social terms—the superior standpoint Schlegel attempts to adopt and the language that supports that standpoint. The articulated theory of irony, whether philosophical, literary, or linguistic, is finally less coherent than the vantage Schlegel appears to adopt by sketching or alluding to the possibility of such a theory.

The Theory

One of the most influential nineteenth-century discussions of Schlegel is Haym's often-reprinted *Die romantische Schule* (1870). Haym assumes first that Schlegel indeed has a theory and that it is coherent. Second, in regard to irony, Haym does not consider the more conservative statements of A. W. Schlegel. Friedrich Schlegel's point of departure is Socratic irony; yet according to Haym, Socratic irony is hardly recognizable in Schlegel's *Lyceum* fragments (258–59). Rather, Schlegel develops an entirely new definition of irony:

> First, the assumption of a contradiction, of a relation of irresolvable inadequacy, and second, the triumphant sublimation into the unlimited freedom of the subject. The first definition harkens back to the philosophic manner of the Platonic Socrates, while in the second, the recoining of the concept moves into the foreground. (260)

So defined, Schlegel's irony is a "riddle" that needs solving (260), in part through the theories and vocabulary of Kant and Fichte. The solution to this riddle is Schlegel's "aesthetic doctrine" (262), which can be discovered by considering key terms such as *Ironie* and *romantische Poesie* (262).[1] The word *Ironie* for Haym becomes a locus for organizing Schlegel's fragments around a coherent thesis—a thesis that is itself a synthesis of various historical and philosophical notions. The history Schlegel fragments is resynthesized by Haym and made coherent. Schlegel, who according to Haym himself creates a riddle, is here credited with a solution—a solution that for convenience (but whose convenience?) is given the label *Ironie*.

Such an argument depends on what I have called the myth of coherence, and variants are easy to find. Strohschneider-Kohrs's influential study of romantic irony is based on the same notion of coherence, and the most recent editor of Schlegel's fragments, Hans Eichner, uses Schlegel's own statements to justify similar assumptions. The *Athenaeum* fragments are only apparently fragmentary; Schlegel is concerned both with the advantages and the dangers of system building: "Es ist gleich tödlich für den Geist, ein System zu haben und keins zu haben. Er wird sich also entschließen müssen, beides zu verbinden" (*Athenaeum* fragment 53) ["It is just as fatal for the spirit to have a system as to have none. He must resolve himself therefore to bind both together"].[2] According to Eichner, the means of effecting such a binding are the early romantic genres, the dialogue and the fragment. In a letter of 18 December 1797, Schlegel himself speaks of creating just such a system of fragments, a system of fragments which most resembles himself.[3]

Eichner's argument bears less on authorial intention than on critical reception. In proposing one reading of Schlegel, he introduces a statement from Schlegel's letters to refute another reading: the familiar argument that in his fragments, Schlegel's characteristic strategy is to mix philosophical and critical judgments. In a letter to his brother, written about 1 December 1797, Schlegel claims to have thought of a new genre for the *Athenaeum*, consisting not of individual sentences but rather of "condensed treatises and reviews"; in addition: "werde ich dabey Universalität ordentlich suchen, nicht philosophische und kritische Fragmente trennen wie im Lyceum"[4] ["I will seek universality in an orderly fashion, rather than separate philosophical and critical fragments as in the *Lyceum*"]. What Eichner and other commentators do not point out is that this letter explicitly denies that the *Lyceum* fragments are unified, and it is in the *Lyceum* fragments that Schlegel's most explicit comments on irony are found. Schlegel's readers often read as Schlegel dictates (and legitimately so); but here, in extracting a theory of irony from the *Lyceum* and *Athenaeum* fragments, they attribute to these fragments as a whole a coherence about which Schlegel himself seems to be skeptical.

Most readings of Schlegel make the same assumption: Schlegel's fragments, either initially or in terms of development, end in a coherence. To debate over the systematic nature of this coherence (for example, over the historical and theoretical relation between the *Lyceum* and *Athenaeum* fragments and the direction of Schlegel's thought) is only to shift the focus away from the initial assumption. This assumption is an important one for the consideration of romantic irony, for once made, it permits various and often elaborate aesthetic theories to be extracted from Schlegel's fragments and organized under the rubric *Ironie*. The importance of competing terms such as *Arabeske* and *Witz* has not been ignored.[5] But the critical problems posed by the existence of such terminology seem to have been dealt with by critical sleight of hand: since Schlegel is unconcerned with terminology, his terminology is fluid and particular terms are interchangeable. Therefore, in regard to romantic irony, we can legitimately patch together a theory from any number of Schlegel's own fragments. A note on *Witz* or *Paradox* may really be about irony. A new coherence thus forms, visible only to Schlegel's most enthusiastic readers.

By contrast, I have chosen as a starting point for this study a word rather than a concept. This method meets the greatest resistance when confronting romantic irony, in particular those theories of romantic irony that claim their origin in Schlegel's fragments. Both my reading of Schlegel and the way I have chosen to proceed toward that reading are based on my sense of that resistance.

Schlegel's work is conventionally divided into periods, and in the following discussion I have considered only Schlegel's early work: the published fragments, some of the notes from his notebooks (only recently made available), and some of his early essays. Although Strohschneider-Kohrs has argued for a later development of Schlegel's concept of irony, the modifications she points to, if they existed at all, had little influence on later descriptions and histories of irony.[6]

Two Early Essays: "Über Goethes Meister" and "Gespräch über die Poesie"

The main sources used to define Schlegel's conception of irony are the *Lyceum* and *Athenaeum* fragments (1797 and 1798) and the short essay from the *Athenaeum* "Über die Unverständlichkeit" (1800). Schlegel also uses the word in his early essays "Über Goethes *Meister*" (*Athenaeum* 1798) and "Gespräch über die Poesie" (*Athenaeum* 1800), and I will begin with a discussion of these two essays.[7] "Gespräch über die Poesie" appeared in two final volumes of the *Athenaeum* of 1800, two years after the *Athenaeum* fragments.[8] "Über Goethes *Meister*" appeared in the second volume of 1798 (1/2), which contained the fragments as well. These early works suggest Schlegel's tentative setting forth of a new and extravagant understanding of irony, along with its almost immediate withdrawal.

Taken alone, "Gespräch über die Poesie" gives little warrant for a new theory of irony and is perfectly consistent with classical statements on irony. The essay is a dialogue that includes several self-contained essays. The word irony appears only occasionally, and always in a subordinate position. Ludoviko's "Rede über die Mythologie" deals with the possibility of establishing a "new mythology"—a synthesizing force that will make one poem of ancient poetry and will itself be "an artwork of Nature" (312, 318). The great wit of romantic poetry, according to Ludoviko, appears only in the construction of the whole, as in Cervantes and Shakespeare. He continues:

> Ja diese künstlich geordnete Verwirrung, diese reizende Symmetrie von Widersprüchen, dieser wunderbare ewige Wechsel von Enthusiasmus und Ironie, der selbst in den kleinsten Gliedern des Ganzen lebt, scheinen mir schon selbst eine indirekte Mythologie zu sein. (318–19) [Indeed this artificially ordered disorder, this appealing symmetry of

> contradictions, this marvelous eternal fluctuation of enthusiasm and
> irony—a fluctuation that lives even in the tiniest parts of the whole—
> seems to me to be already an indirect mythology.]

The phrase "ewige Wechsel von Enthusiasmus und Ironie" is similar to
phrases from the *Athenaeum*.[9] But the word *Ironie* here is only a negative
element, one of the opposed poles of a *Wechsel* (alternation, or fluctuation)—the opposite of *Enthusiasmus* (compare Solger's dialectic of *Ironie* and
Begeisterung).

In the discussion that follows this section, the word appears again.
Antonio here has denied the notion that the romantic or the didactic can
constitute a genre, since any work should be both didactic and romantic.

> Auch machen wir diese Foderung überall, ohne eben den Namen zu
> gebrauchen. Selbst in ganz populären Arten wie z.B. im Schauspiele,
> fodern wir Ironie; wir fodern, daß die Begebenheiten, die Menschen,
> kurz das ganz Spiel des Lebens wirklich auch als Spiel genommen und
> dargestellt sei. (323)
> [So we make this demand everywhere, without actually using the
> terms. Even in popular genres, for example, in the theater, we demand
> irony. We demand that the events, characters, and in short the entire
> play of life be truly conceived and represented as a play.]

Irony here seems to mean an artwork's consciousness of itself, a description
that would apply to Tieck's drama (Lussky's secondary form of irony, or
what Immerwahr calls merely subjective irony). But the emphasis is not on
irony per se; it is rather on the notion of nature as self-created art, which
the artist in turn imitates. To say (ironically) that life is merely a play is to
recognize that nature is itself play.[10]

But Schlegel does not follow up any of the implications of this notion.
In another essay contained in the dialogue, "Brief über den Roman," the
novel is defined as "the romantic book," but the word irony does not appear
at all. It appears later in a list: "Metrum, Sprache, Form . . . der ruhige
weiche Ton, der antike Styl, die Ironie der Reflexion" (345) ["meter, diction, form . . . a quiet soft tone, antique style, irony of reflection"]; irony
is simply one of many techniques whereby old genres reform themselves.[11]
By 1800, then, Schlegel no longer considers irony central to a theory of
romantic poetry, or to a theory of the novel.

In his earlier essay, "Über Goethes *Meister*," Schlegel uses the word in a
far stronger sense. Here, Schlegel is speaking of book 2 of the novel:

Nur dem, der vorlesen kann, und sie vollkommen versteht, muß es überlassen bleiben, die Ironie, die über dem ganzen Werke schwebt, hier aber vorzüglich laut wird, denen die den Sinn dafür haben, ganz fühlbar zu machen. Dieser sich selbst belächelnde Schein von Würde und Bedeutsamkeit in dem periodischen Styl, diese scheinbaren Nachlässigkeiten und Tautologien, welche die Bedingungen so vollenden, daß sie mit dem Bedingten wieder eins werden, und wie es die Gelegenheit gibt, alles oder nichts zu sagen oder sagen zu wollen scheinen, dieses höchst Prosaische mitten in der poetischen Stimmung des dargestellten oder komödierten Subjekts, der absichtliche Anhauch von poetischer Pedanterie bei sehr prosaischen Veranlassungen; sie beruhen oft auf einem einzigen Wort, ja auf einen Akzent. (137–38; emphasis added)

[Only one who reads aloud and understands it perfectly can make the irony entirely felt to those who have a sense for it—an irony that hovers over the entire work but comes forth very prominently here. This self-deriding appearance of value and meaning in the periodic style, this apparent carelessness, the tautologies, which provide such perfect definitions that they become one with the things defined and seem to say or wish to say all or nothing as the opportunity arises, this highest prosaic in the middle of the poetic mood of the represented or comically staged subject, the intentional breath of poetic pedantry at very prosaic occasions—these rest often on a particular word, indeed on a single accent.]

Irony here is not a local matter but a characteristic of the entire work.[12] Furthermore, it is a quality of the work that is perceptible only to select readers. Yet even this extravagant definition has clear roots in earlier definitions of irony. Irony is first and foremost a matter of a presentational situation: there is irony in the text, but it can only emerge in a particular situation. It requires a knowing speaker and a sympathetic listener, and will often appear in a single "accent"—or, as earlier rhetoricians noted, in the pronunciation alone. This irony has a source in the work itself, but is described in largely rhetorical terms. Irony establishes a community of speaker and listener—a community here that seems to exist apart from the text itself, and apart from ordinary readers as well. The "hovering over," a characteristic of irony, is transferred to those who express or receive irony—those ideal literary receivers and critics with perfect understanding who will hover over the mass of ordinary hearers.

Fragments

Schlegel's theory of irony depends finally on his fragments, in particular the *Lyceum* fragments (1797) and the *Athenaeum* fragments (1798). These are supported by fragments in *Ideen* (in the 1800 *Athenaeum*)[13] and by the fragments in his notebooks, many only recently published. The description of this theory varies widely: most scholars agree, however, that Schlegel defines irony in deliberate opposition to older forms and that this new irony involves at least the self-conscious relation of the artist to his work and the destroying of artistic illusion—the two forms described by Immerwahr as objective and subjective irony. To these basic notions, others can be added— for example, Strohschneider-Kohrs's description of romantic irony as an activity (*Tätigkeit*) of the creative process, a description certainly applicable to Solger's theories.

Schlegel's use of the word *Ironie,* as many scholars have noted, is implicated in his general poetic (and philosophic) theory. The opposition between various forms of irony is itself a variant of the opposition between ancient and modern literature, objectivity and subjectivity, Schiller's theory of naive and sentimental literature. Irony blurs into such terms as romantic, wit, humor, and parody, and even such coinages found in Schlegel's notebooks as "Parekbasis" (from the "parabasis" of Old Comedy). But each of these terms had a history as well, and those histories themselves were trapped in the polarities used by Schlegel to organize history.

The word *Ironie* appears in some dozen fragments of the *Lyceum* and the *Athenaeum,* often with important restrictions implied by the contexts. Although Schlegel's theories of art depended on various unsettled terms such as *romantisch,* it will be the thesis here that little of Schlegel's original thought develops in conjunction with the word *Ironie.* I will examine the fragments on the basis of two questions: Are the uses and associations of the word *Ironie* consistent? Are they intelligible within earlier forms and definitions of irony?

Uses and Non-Uses

What has been regarded as the most important fragment written by Schlegel is *Athenaeum* fragment 116 ("Die romantische Poesie ist eine progressive Universalpoesie . . ."). It is one of Schlegel's longest fragments and appears in all discussions of romantic irony I know of. This fragment describes romantic poetry as a mixing of poetry and prose, of geniality and criticism;

it "hovers" between the poet and subject matter, and is the poet's self-representation as well as the mirror of the world; it is infinite, free. . . . In modern descriptions of romantic irony, we often find such language, calqued from this fragment. But the word *Ironie* does not appear here, nor does it appear in another often cited fragment, *Lyceum* fragment 37. In fact, the word *Ironie* is surprisingly rare in these published fragments, appearing only four times in the *Lyceum* (fragments 7, 42, 48, 108), seven times in the *Athenaeum* (fragments 51, 121, 253, 305, 344, 362, 431), once in *Ideen* (fragment 69). In *Ideen,* art is most consistently described in religious and political terms (fragments 11, 46, 114, 131, 149); art forms part of (or serves as a substitute for) religion and politics. But the word *Ironie* is absent from these discussions as well. If Schlegel originally associated his poetic theories with the word *Ironie,* it seems that he later withdrew that association. Hegel notes that when Solger speaks of the highest matters, the word *Ironie* is absent; the same seems to be true of Schlegel.

The most suggestive uses of the word come from Schlegel's notebooks, unpublished in his lifetime. There are many references to irony in these notebooks, many more than appear in the published fragments. The most often cited is from a philosophical notebook: "Ironie ist eine permanente Parekbase"[14] ["Irony is a permanent parabasis"]. The reference is apparently to the parabasis of Old Comedy, during which the chorus could drop its disguise and step forward to speak to the audience in the persona of the poet. This fragment has been emphasized by many romanticists; Strohschneider-Kohrs claims that all of Schlegel's fragments dealing with romantic irony can be reduced to it.[15] Other fragments are less striking, but nonetheless support many of the various theories of romantic irony, for example, from his literary notebooks, fragment V, 700 (LN 696): "Die vollendete absolute Ironie hört auf Ironie zu seyn und wird ernsthaft.—" (p. 144) ["Perfected, absolute irony ceases to be irony and becomes serious"] and fragment 809 (LN 802): "*Ironie* ist Analyse der These und d.[er] Antithese.—" (p. 154) ["Irony is the analysis of thesis and antithesis"]. Irony is often involved in various (and inconsistent) schemata involving parody, urbanity, and the comic, for example, fragment VIII, 534: "*Urbanität* = moralischer Witz. *Ironie* = [philosophischer]. *Parodie* = [poetischer]. — *Caricatur* [mimischer] Witz = Humor musikal[ischer] Witz, Groteske pitt[oresker] Witz. [physischer] Witz = Combinat[orisches] Genie" (p. 298).[16]

But irony is also defined in a purely negative sense, for example in fragment V, 1056 (LN 1047): "Nichts ist platter als die leere Form d[er] Ironie ohne Enthus[iasmus] und ohne Id[eal-]Re[alismus]" (p. 172) ["Nothing is more superficial than the empty form of irony without enthusiasm and without ideal-realism"]; or in the phrase "annihilirend oder ironirend" in fragment 902 (p. 162; compare LN 826).

These unpublished fragments can be considered a search for the definitions and limitations of the word irony, as Strohschneider-Kohrs views them (34); they could also be taken as rejected formulations, although I know of no scholar on romantic irony who has so taken them. Is Schlegel working in his notebooks to reject the negative associations of the word *Ironie* found in fragment 902? Or does he reject the more extravagant, positive interpretation of *Ironie* implied in fragment 809 (LN 802) that later romanticists give particular emphasis? With few exceptions (most notably Strohschneider-Kohrs), scholars agree that with his later conversion to Catholicism, Schlegel does drop his earlier theories on irony; but perhaps those theories (if they ever existed) were dropped as soon as they began to be formulated.

Schlegel's notebooks undeniably offer possible interpretations or readings of the later published fragments, even if some of the more elaborate schemata cannot be taken too seriously. The question of how Schlegel realizes the often contradictory potential of the notebook formulations is one that must be answered on the basis of his published fragments. Do such notions as "perfected absolute irony" (fragment 700) or irony as synthesis (fragment 809) find support in the *Lyceum* and *Athenaeum* fragments? Or do they retain the older senses of the word irony, and the largely negative senses for which Hegel criticizes Schlegel?

The Athenaeum *Fragments (1798) and* the Lyceum *Fragments (1797)*

The word *Ironie* appears often in the *Athenaeum* fragments, but these uses are less striking than those in the *Lyceum* fragments and in the unpublished fragments. The typical phrase in which it is used in the *Athenaeum* fragments is "bis zur Ironie," a phrase that occurs frequently in the notebooks (for example, LN 505, 1141, 1144). What this seems to mean is a resolution in negation: "Naiv ist, was bis zur Ironie, oder bis zum steten Wechsel von Selbstschöpfung und Selbstvernichtung natürlich, individuell oder klassisch ist, oder scheint" (*Athenaeum* fragment 51) ["The naive is what is or seems individual or classical to the point of irony or to the continual fluctuation of self-creation and self-annihilation"]. If this fragment defines irony as the "eternal fluctuation of self-creation and self-annihilation," irony has taken on a new meaning. But the word "oder" ("bis zur Ironie, *oder* bis zum steten Wechsel") may signal an either/or variation, not necessarily a gloss. *Athe-*

naeum fragment 121 is similar: "Eine Idee ist ein bis zur Ironie vollendeter Begriff, eine absolute synthesis absoluter Antithesen, der stete sich selbst erzeugende Wechsel zwei streitender Gedanken. Ein Ideal ist zugleich Idee und Faktum" ["An idea is a concept perfected to the point of irony, an absolute synthesis of absolute antitheses, a constantly self-producing fluctuation of two conflicting thoughts. An idea is at the same time an idea and a fact"]. The vocabulary of these fragments is similar. But in the second formulation, it is clear that the higher synthesis is the *Idee*, not *Ironie* itself; and beyond that remains a higher synthesis represented as the *Ideal* (compare the notebook fragment 809, quoted above). *Athenaeum* fragment 51 refers to a limited type of art (the naive) and seems to define irony as one limit of that art; the naive limits itself either in irony or (more strongly) in the "continuous fluctuation of self-creation and self-annihilation." The "continuous fluctuation," even if construed as a gloss on the word *Ironie,* is a step beyond irony, which here and elsewhere in the published fragments seems to mark a negative limit to be transcended by a new (terminological) entity.[17]

The association often found in the notebooks between parody and irony is made in *Athenaeum* fragment 253, but again only in a subordinate phrase, "durch Parodie . . . und durch Ironie."[18] And finally, *Athenaeum* fragment 431 is simply a clever combination of the ordinary rhetorical language about irony found as early as Cicero: "Opfer den Grazien, heißt, wenn es einem Philosophen gesagt wird, so viel als: Schaffe dir Ironie und bilde dich zur Urbanität" ["If said to a philosopher, 'sacrifice to the Graces' essentially means 'create irony and cultivate urbanity' "]. Anyone familiar with the rhetorical tradition will recognize in the association of irony and urbanity the standard Latin vocabulary attached to Socrates. There simply is no theory of irony propounded in the *Athenaeum* fragments, and nothing comparable to the most radical experimental uses of the word found in the notebooks.

Let us turn then to the *Lyceum* fragments, published a year earlier, in 1797. The word *Ironie* only appears four times.[19] Fragment 48 reads: "Ironie ist die Form des Paradoxen. Paradox ist alles, was zugleich gut und groß ist" ["Anything that is good and great is a paradox. And irony is the form of paradox"]. Irony, therefore, is the form in which disparate qualities (of ethics and of power?) are combined. The logic of this fragment is less clear than its social implications. Irony is a mark of moral and individual superiority. I, inasmuch as I appear paradoxical, am thus good and great. And the sign of such a situation is the word *Ironie*. I overread this fragment deliberately, and clearly through Hegel's eyes.

Lyceum fragments 42 and 108 should be quoted in full. They are the only two fragments in which Schlegel discusses irony in any detail. Both fragments take their starting point in Socrates, and the familiar language associated with Socrates in the rhetorical tradition appears (*Urbanität, Verstellung*).

Die Philosophie ist die eigentliche Heimat der Ironie, welche man logische Schönheit definieren möchte: denn überall wo in mündlichen oder geschriebenen Gesprächen, und nur nicht ganz systematisch philosophiert wird, soll man Ironie leisten und fordern; und sogar die Stoiker hielten die Urbanität für eine Tugend. Frielich gibts auch eine rhetorische Ironie, welche sparsam gebraucht vortreffliche Wirkung tut, besonders im Polemischen; doch ist sie gegen die erhabne Urbanität der sokratischen Muse, was die Pracht der glänzendsten Kunstrede gegen eine alte Tragödie in hohem Style. Die Poesie allein kann sich auch von dieser Seite bis zur Höhe der Philosophie erheben, und ist nicht auf ironische Stellen gegründet, wie die Rhetorik. Es gibt alte und moderne Gedichte, die durchgängig im Ganzen und überall den göttlichen Hauch der Ironie atmen. Es lebt in ihnen eine wirklich transzendentale Buffonerie. Im Innern, die Stimmung, welche alles übersieht, und sich über alles Bedingte unendlich erhebt, auch über eigne Kunst, Tugend, oder Genialität: im Äußern, in der Ausführung die mimische Maniere eines gewöhnlichen guten italiänischen Buffo.
[Philosophy is the proper home of irony, which can be defined as logical beauty: for wherever philosophy is found in oral or written dialogues (and not only in strictly systematic philosophy), there irony should be demanded and provided. And even the stoics considered urbanity a virtue. Of course there is also rhetorical irony, which is extremely effective when used sparingly, particularly in polemic; still, compared to the noble urbanity of the Socratic muse, it is no more than the charm of flashy oratory compared to a tragedy in the high style. Poetry alone can in this way raise itself to the realm of philosophy, and it is not based on ironic passages, as is rhetoric. There are ancient and modern poems that throughout and everywhere breathe the divine breath of irony. There is in them a truly transcendental buffoonery. Internally, the mood that oversees all, and raises itself infinitely over all limits, even over its own art, virtue, or geniality; externally, in the production, the mimic manner of an ordinarily skilled Italian buffo.]

And fragment 108:

Die Sokratische Ironie ist die einzige durchaus unwillkürliche, und doch durchaus besonnene Verstellung. Es ist gleich unmöglich sie zu erkünsteln, und sie zu verraten. Wer sie nicht hat, dem bleibt sie auch nach dem offensten Geständnis ein Rätsel. Sie soll niemanden täuschen, als die, welche sie für Täuschung halten, und entweder ihre Freude haben an der herrlichen Schalkheit, alle Welt zum besten zu haben, oder böse werden, wenn sie ahnden, sie wären wohl auch mit gemeint. In ihr soll alles Scherz und alles Ernst sein, alles treuherzig offen, und alles tief verstellt. Sie entspringt aus der Vereinigung von Lebenskunstsinn und wissenschaftlichem Geist, aus dem Zusammentreffen vollendeter Naturphilosophie und vollendeter Kunstphilosophie. Sie enthält und erregt ein Gefühl von dem unauflöslichen Widerstreit des Unbedingten und des Bedingten, der Unmöglichkeit und Notwendigkeit einer vollständigen Mitteilung. Sie ist die freieste aller Lizenzen, denn durch sie setzt man sich über sich sebst weg; und doch auch die gesetzlichste, denn sie ist unbedingt notwendig. Es ist ein sehr gutes Zeichen, wenn die harmonisch Platten gar nicht wissen, wie sie diese stete Selbstparodie zu nehmen haben, immer wieder von neuem glauben und mißglauben, bis sie schwindlicht werden, den Scherz grade für Ernst, und den Ernst für Scherz halten. Lessings Ironie ist Instinkt; bei Hemsterhuys ist's klassisches Studium; Hülsens Ironie entspringt aus Philosophie der Philosophie, und kann die jener noch weit übertreffen.

[Socratic irony is the only thoroughly unwilled and still thoroughly intentional dissimulation. It is as impossible to assume it artificially as to reveal it. Even in its most open avowal, it remains a riddle to anyone who does not have it. It aims at deceiving no one except those who consider it deception, and either take pleasure in the wonderful knavishness of tricking the whole world or become upset when they suspect that they too are intended as its targets. In it, all is both joking and serious, all is sincerely open and deeply dissembled. It arises from the unity of the artistic sense of life and a scientific spirit, from the convergence of perfected philosophy of nature and perfected philosophy of art. It contains and excites a feeling of the unresolvable conflict of the indefinite and the definite, of the impossibility and necessity of a complete communication. It is the most free of all licenses, for through it, one overcomes oneself; and still it is the most rule-bound, for it is absolutely necessary. It is a very good sign, if the unsophisticated rabble (*die harmonisch Platten*) hardly know how they are to take this continuous self-parody, and again and again believe and disbelieve, until they become dizzy and take a joke for something serious and something serious for a joke. Lessing's irony is instinct; with Hemster- huis it is classical study; Hülsen's irony arises from the philosophy of philosophy, and widely surpasses these.]

In fragment 42, Schlegel distinguishes two forms of irony: one rhetorical, the other Socratic—the same strategy to be used by Solger in distinguish- ing true from false irony. Neither of these conceptions of irony is essentially new. Poetry, according to Schlegel, should simply move from one clearly identified irony to another; it should remove itself from rhetorical hand- books and follow Socrates. The "divine breath" of irony, the "transcendental buffoonery"—these are suggestive phrases and have caused considerable theorizing. But they seem, in this context, to be restricted through their association with Socrates. The notion of a moderately skilled Italian buffo does not go beyond the notion of Socrates as the Silenus.[20]

Fragment 108 clarifies some of these implications. Again, Schlegel takes Socratic irony as his starting point. But here, rather than opposing it to a rhetorical irony, he describes it in terms of its reception. Irony is a form of deception and self-deception. Its victims are those who imagine they understand it. The relation to Socrates is unmistakable: Socrates' claim of ignorance is most deceptive to those who imagine it is untrue (or ironic). But Schlegel revels in this deception: irony is a manner of mixing the serious and the trivial; it is also a matter of distinguishing ordinary hearers from initiates. It is a paradox—the freest of all licenses but the most rule- bound—and anyone who does not understand this or accept it is superficial and unsophisticated (one of the "harmonisch Platten")—someone who at- tends to the logic of language rather than to the extralinguistic possibilities of virtue and knowledge once associated with Socrates but now associated with the modern poet.

What Schlegel contributes to a theory of irony here is his focus on the relation between the producer of a text (however chaotic) and its receptor. The relation is absolutely clear: the producer (the ironist) defines through irony a standpoint of superiority over those who receive it. Those who enjoy the superiority afforded by irony are not the elect hearers who understand it; in fact, those who understand irony for what Schlegel says it is (de- ception) are those who are most thoroughly deceived by it. Rather, those who can attain the superior vantage of the ironist are those who have and produce irony, that is, other ironists.

Those scholars who have pointed out that romantic irony, or its formulation by Schlegel, involves the establishment of a community are I think absolutely correct. But Schlegel's community is a restricted one. According to Schlegel's formulation, it is not even a community of hearers and initiates that is established but rather a community of creators, in which the function of the listener is only to define the superiority of the creator.

If this reading of the published fragments is valid, then a second reading of the unpublished fragments is possible. The most extravagant (and most interesting) claims become less statements about irony than expressions of its function. They are symptoms in their obscurity of the situation Schlegel defines through invocation of the word irony. They are the mechanical products of the producer who has already defined a superior vantage. But their content, however intriguing, no longer constitutes a theory of irony.

"Über die Unverständlichkeit"

This mysterious essay by Schlegel appeared in part 2 of the third volume of the *Athenaeum* (1800), the final issue to appear. Wellek has described the *Athenaeum* as "the crucial document" for romanticism;[21] "Über die Unverständlichkeit," at least materially, functions as its conclusion.

Although seldom the basis for readings of Schlegel, the essay has served to support many. Strohschneider-Kohrs considers it against the background of Schlegel's fragments, in particular *Lyceum* fragment 42, and claims that while Schlegel speaks about (romantic) irony in this essay ("die hohe Ironie"), the essay itself does not embody it (278–80). Anne Mellor clearly takes the essay as a serious statement concerning irony, as do Helmut Prang and Marshall Brown. Lilian Furst takes the essay in the context of an audience: the "elaborate hierarchies" of irony relate to lower and higher audiences. Schlegel himself characterized it only as an "ironic fugue composed of bits and pieces of an earlier essay."[22]

The essay opens with the claim that the *Athenaeum* is a series of "tests of the possibilities of communication" (363) and that such tests necessarily lead to confusion. Midway through the essay, Schlegel begins what appears to be part 2: "Ein großer Teil von der Unverständlichkeit des *Athenaeums* liegt unstreitig in der *Ironie,* die sich mehr oder mindern überall darin äußert" (368) ["A great part of the incomprehensibility of the *Athenaeum* lies unquestionably in the irony that more or less emerges everywhere"]. He then quotes *Lyceum* fragment 108 nearly in full (omitting only the final sentence concerning Lessing, Hemsterhuys, etc.) and *Lyceum* fragment 48 ("Ironie ist die Form des Paradoxen. Paradox ist alles was zugleich gut und groß ist"). He follows with a (mock?) catalog of ironies:

Um die Übersicht vom ganzen System der Ironie zu erleichtern, wollen wir einige der vorzüglichsten Arten anführen. Die erste und vornehmste von allen ist die grobe Ironie; findet sich am meisten in der wirklichen Natur der Dinge und ist einer ihrer allgemein verbreitetsten Stoffe; in der Geschichte der Menschheit ist sie recht eigentlich zu Hause. Dann kommt die feine oder die delikate Ironie; dann die extrafeine. (369)

[In order to throw some light on our survey of the entire system of irony, we will describe the most preeminent kinds. The first and foremost of all is coarse irony; we find this most often in the actual nature of things and it is one of their most common elements; it is most properly at home in the history of man. Then comes fine or delicate irony, then extra-fine.]

This type of fine or extra-fine irony is a form of deception, found "in old gardens" that lure the "sentimental friend of nature" and then splash him with water. He continues:

Ferner die dramatische Ironie, wenn der Dichter drei Akte geschrieben hat, dann wider Vermuten ein andrer Mensch wird, und nun die beiden letzten Akte schreiben muß. Die doppelte Ironie, wenn zwei Linien von Ironie parallel nebeneinander laufen ohne sich zu stören, eine fürs Parterre, die andre für die Logen, wobei noch kleine Funken in die Coulissen fahren können. Endlich die Ironie der Ironie. Im allgemeinen ist das wohl die gründlichste Ironie der Ironie, daß man sie doch eben auch überdrüssig wird, wenn sie uns überall und immer wider geboten wird. Was wir aber hier zunächst unter Ironie der Ironie verstanden wissen wollen, das entsteht auf mehr als einem Wege. Wenn man ohne Ironie von der Ironie redet, wie es soeben der Fall war; wenn man mit Ironie von einer Ironie redet, ohne zu merken, daß man sich zu eben der Zeit in einer andren viel auffallenderen Ironie befindet; wenn man nicht wieder aus der Ironie herauskommen kann, wie es in diesem Versuch über die Unverständlichkeit zu sein scheint; wenn die Ironie Manier wird, und so den Dichter gleichsam wieder ironiert; wenn man Ironie zu einem überflüssigen Taschenbuch versprochen hat, ohne seinen Vorrat vorher zu überschlagen und nun wider Willen Ironie machen muß, wie ein Schauspielkünstler der Leibschmerzen hat; wenn die Ironie wild wird, und sich gar nich mehr regieren läßt.

Welche Götter werden uns von allen diesen Ironien erretten können? (369)

[Then there is dramatic irony, when the writer has written three acts, then against all probability becomes someone else and now has to write the last two acts. Doubled irony, when two lines of irony run parallel without disturbing each other, one for the groundlings, the other for those in the boxes, while some tiny sparks also manage to get into the wings. Finally irony of irony. In general, perhaps the most fundamental irony of irony is that one soon gets tired of being presented with it all the time. However, what we wish to understand here by irony of irony is something that is created in a variety of ways. When one speaks of irony without using irony, as I just now did; when one speaks of irony with irony, without noticing that at the same time one falls into an even more obvious irony; when one cannot escape from irony, as appears to be happening in this essay on incomprehensibility; when irony becomes a manner, and thus ironizes the writer in turn; when one has promised irony for some superfluous paperback, without looking over his supply and now has to produce irony against his will, like an actor who has a stomachache; when irony grows wild, and can no longer be ruled.

What gods will rescue us from all these ironies?]

This is a whimsical catalog of the uses to which the word may be put, and not all of those uses are those of Schlegel himself. The phrase "dramatic irony" was not current, although, as we have seen, irony in relation to drama was a common topic, generally relating to discussions of Greek drama and the distinctions between tragedy and comedy. Here, Schlegel transfers that distinction of genre into a distinction of audience, giving us, I think, the coordinates with which his own irony is to be understood. And it is this notion of dramatic irony that leads Schlegel into the apparent self-reflection of the irony of ironies. He is trapped in his (discussion of) irony; he is producing a discussion of irony for what will be only another superfluous paperback; his irony has turned on him; his (catalog of) irony has grown wild and can no longer be controlled.

Clearly Schlegel felt that this discussion was related to *Lyceum* fragment 42 ("Die Philosophie ist die eigentliche Heimat der Ironie . . ."). It is, however, not a culmination of the earlier discussion, but its antithesis and negation—its ironic counterpart, if we allow the word ironic to refer here to a temporal negation. The philosophical pretenses of *Lyceum* fragment 42 form one-half of a paradox (the paradoxical nature of irony is defined in *Lyceum* fragment 48, quoted by Schlegel immediately after he quotes *Lyceum* fragment 108). This irony of thought is negated by the purely verbal irony—

the mechanical sorting and cataloging of various phrases that can be formed about irony. To ironize his own discussion of irony (in whatever sense we wish to take "ironize"), Schlegel reduces it to verbiage.

Finally, this essay seems to identify one of the paradoxes of irony for Schlegel, that involving a hierarchical relation between the ironist and unsophisticated hearers. The paradoxical danger of such irony lies in the threats it poses to the ironist; any hierarchy (particularly one with a historical lineage involving Socratic and Erasmian Sileni) can easily be reversed.

Schlegel's repeated references to drama do not merely allude to the destruction of illusion characteristic of *commedia dell' arte,* nor do they simply provide a variant on the topic of dramatic illusion and verisimilitude that was a staple of traditional dramatic criticism (Johnson's "Preface to Shakespeare" is a late example). Drama is an appropriate metaphor because of the separation of levels: the absolute distinction between stage and audience (a distinction that is threatened, but in a physical theater never destroyed); and the equally material distinction between levels of audience (a distinction concretized in the physical structure of theaters). The ironist, as dramatist, has two audiences—a higher audience and a lower one. And it is that higher status to which the romantic ironist metaphorically lays claim; the ironist takes a seat in the boxes, "hovering" over the groundlings below. Even such a metaphor is nostalgic; theaters with large and more distant balconies had already transformed and blurred the relation between seating level and social rank. But Schlegel's simplified representation of the theater is a product of the social distinctions that seem inseparable from his conception of irony.

The origins of the *Athenaeum* leave little doubt as to Schlegel's conception of this relation between audiences and between the writer and his audience. In an often quoted letter to his brother, of 31 October 1979, he states:

Nähmlich ein Journal von uns beyden nicht bloß ediert, sondern *ganz allein* geschrieben, ohne alle ⟨regelm. [äßigen]⟩ Mitarbeiter, wo *weder Form noch Stoff näher bestimmt* wäre, außer daß alles was ganz *unpopulär* wäre, oder ein *großes Werk* oder Theil eines solchen wäre, ausgeschlossen bliebe. . . . Ich sagte zwar, *keine REGELMÄßIGE Mitarbeiter,* weil man doch nur für sich allein stehen kann. Doch mit der Ausnahme, daß wir *Meisterstücke der höhern Kritik und Polemik* aufspürten wo sie zufinden wären.—Ja überhaupt alles, was sich durch *erhabne Frechheit* auszeichnete, und für alle andren Journale *zu gut* wäre.[23]
[Namely, for us both not only to edit a journal, but to write it all by ourselves, without any regular contributors, where neither form

nor content would be determined, except that all that is thoroughly unpopular or a great work or part of one would be excluded. . . . I did say no regular contributors, because one can only stand for oneself alone. But still with the exception that we track down masterworks of high criticism and polemic where they are to be found. Indeed all that is distinguished by sublime audacity and is too good for all other journals.]

This journal will have a particular advantage:

Ein andrer großer Vortheil dieses Unternehmens würde wohl seyn, daß wir uns eine große Autorität in der Kritik machen, hinreichend, um nach 5–10 Jahren kritischen Diktatoren Deutschl.[ands] zu seyn, die A.[llgemeine] L.[iteratur-] Z.[eitung] zu Grunde zu richten und eine kritische Zeitschrift zu geben, die keinen andren Zweck hätte als Kritik. ([*Letters*], ed. Immerwahr, 31–32)

[Another great advantage of this undertaking will probably be that we establish for ourselves a great authority in criticism, wide ranging, such that in five to ten years we will be critical dictators of Germany, smash the *Allgemeine Literatur-Zeitung* to the ground and produce a critical journal that has no other purpose except criticism.]

This letter is surely not without its own irony—in whatever sense the word may be taken. It is not a critical manifesto. And if the *Athenaeum* did not fulfill the plan in its details, it may have done so in its tone.

To quote such a letter again is perhaps to make the same methodological assumption that I have criticized in other discussions of romantic irony. It is dangerous to assume that a writer is discussing a certain topic when that topic is not mentioned. But the letter does seem to indicate Schlegel's thinking—as indeed do all his comments on wit, paradox, humor, dialectic, and romanticism—and the word irony and its related definitions are products of that thinking. Schlegel's aesthetics privilege the artist-critic. When Schlegel's thinking is realized as a theory of irony, that position of superiority is conflated with the essential features of rhetorical irony, defined by schoolmasters centuries earlier. Irony is a matter of hierarchies—hierarchies of meanings, hierarchies of understanding, and indeed the quasi-religious hierarchies of the type outlined in *Ideen,* whereby the artist becomes an educator-priest.[24] The difference between romantic and rhetorical irony lies not in the presence or absence of hierarchical structure, which characterizes both, but rather in the contents of that hierarchical structure. In rhetorical irony, both verbal and higher nonverbal levels are expressible as statements.

In romantic irony (or in what would come to be known as romantic irony), the higher extraverbal level is either a subjective social or spiritual state of the ironist, or an objective meaning no longer expressible in language. Schlegel repersonalized irony by insisting on the figure of Socrates, not as an exemplum of a virtue, but rather as an exemplum of a philosophical process of thinking—one that finds its locus in the philosopher-poet.

What is known as the self-reflexivity of romantic irony is less intelligible as a direct product of Socrates' own self-awareness and its romantic reception than as a shift in the language pertaining to irony and in the focus of irony. What is at issue in discussions of romantic irony is the romantic poet and philosopher—the writing subject. Self-reflexivity is an incidental product of this reorientation, reinforced by Schlegel's reliance on the vocabulary of Fichte. It would fall to twentieth-century critics of the romantics to shift this focus even further.

Although I have drawn a skeptical history of romantic irony, I do not imply by my skepticism that romantic irony does not exist. It is, rather, one of many literary myths, with its own scripture and its own evolving dogma. Surely romantic irony exists for romanticists, and it may well exist for a modern novelist such as Thomas Mann. But romantic irony cannot be reduced legitimately to a definition, nor can the claims made for it be taken at face value. Romantic irony, like irony itself, exists within the history that both produces and describes it; and only by ignoring that history can romanticists speak intelligibly of its practice or indeed of its historical origins.

PART FOUR

POSTROMANTIC

IRONIES

8

Dramatic Irony

■

I have chosen two focal points in the modern history of the word irony: romantic irony and what I call New Critical irony—the use of irony as a tool for analyzing literary works of art. The notions of irony that developed in the nineteenth century can be considered a bridge: the ironist changes in character from a philosopher-poet to a critic.

Two noteworthy developments in the history of the word occur during the nineteenth century. The first is the development of notions of tragic irony and dramatic irony from various suggestions in German romanticism. The phrase "dramatic irony," generally associated with Connop Thirlwall's 1833 essay on the irony of Sophocles (Thirlwall himself does not use the phrase), was to become a staple of dramatic criticism. A second development is what I will call the general critical domestication of irony as an evaluative term. The word irony becomes routinely used to describe good, or interesting, literature.

These developments involve a reconception of the history of irony, in part through the casual acceptance of the metaphoric uses of the words drama and dramatic. Dramatic irony can mean not only "an irony pertaining to drama" but also "a dramatic form of irony." Tragic irony can mean not only "an irony pertaining to dramatic tragedy" but also "an irony that has tragic overtones." In *Lectures on the History of Philosophy,* Hegel uses the term to describe an ethical form of Socrates' irony.[1] New generic relations are implied through such simple metaphors. Even when the phrases are applied specifically to drama in recent criticism, more than the history of drama and its critical terminology appears to be involved, for example:

> Tragedy is the art form, above all, that makes the most of what is called discrepant awareness—what one character knows and the other doesn't or what none of the characters know but the audi-

ence does. Thus it is that irony is tragedy's characteristic trope, that several levels of meaning operate at the same time. Characters speak without knowing what they say, and misreading is the typical and predictable response to the various cues that others give. . . . Other factors make for dramatic irony, particularly in connection with the deceptive powers of the feminine and the special verbal skills that accompany these.[2]

Here dramatic irony seems to refer not only to deception and self-deception but to general conflicts of meaning as well. It thus can serve as a convenient transition to any form of criticism that assumes that literature involves such conflicts.

The development of these phrases parallels the development of what is called romantic irony. Many of the disputes over romantic irony and its definition are more properly linguistic ones: is romantic irony a type of irony? a theory of irony? or simply the word irony as used by the romantics? Literary scholars necessarily blur such distinctions: perhaps to enlarge an otherwise specialized topic, or perhaps simply to enable them to engage in critical discussions of irony in the first place.

Most American literary students are familiar with the special sense of dramatic irony. It is defined in the leading definition in the *Princeton Encyclopedia of Poetry and Poetics* as follows: "*Dramatic i[rony]* is a plot device according to which . . . the spectators know more than the protagonist."[3] This simple formulation is clearly applicable to a play such as Sophocles' *Oedipus*. But what is not at all obvious from the *Encyclopedia* is the modernity of this simple formulation—a modernity that is suppressed through the citation of ancient drama and relatively early essays, in particular Thirlwall's essay of 1833, cited even by the *Oxford English Dictionary*.[4] The definition of dramatic irony given above is not prominent until the twentieth century. It is in one sense a reduction of various romantic notions of irony in drama, but in another sense a wide extension of them. Here I will consider two early nineteenth-century essays that focus specifically on the problem of irony in drama: Adam Müller's "Ironie, Lustspiel, Aristophanes" (1808) and Connop Thirlwall's often cited "Of Irony in Sophocles" (1833).

Adam Müller

Adam Müller (1779–1829) was associated with many of the major romantics (for example, Schlegel, Brentano, and Kleist) and is called by Curtius "one of the great unrecognized men of the German intellectual heritage."[5]

Müller's importance in the history of irony is due largely to a single essay, "Ironie, Lustspiel, Aristophanes," from his Dresden lectures on dramatic art (1806).[6]

A. W. Schlegel, in his nearly contemporary *Lectures on Dramatic Art and Literature* (1808), discussed irony as a form of comedy—certainly the easiest and clearest way to situate irony within the dramatic opposition of comedy and tragedy. In his formulation, comedy is opposed to tragedy as *Scherz* is to *Ernst;* irony, a form of *Scherz,* is thus limited to comedy, and so it appears both in Greek comedy and in Shakespeare. As we have seen, Solger would express dissatisfaction with this formulation, and many modern scholars argue that Hegel and Kierkegaard incorrectly read Friedrich Schlegel's theories of irony as nothing more than a striking variant. The claims Müller made for irony in 1806 are far more radical, and they are presented by Müller himself as a reading of Friedrich Schlegel—a reading that could not have been influenced by association with the views of irony presented by A. W. Schlegel in 1808. Modern scholars, in defending Friedrich Schlegel against Hegel's polemic, may well be reading Friedrich Schlegel not through his brother and not through Hegel, but rather through an enthusiastic Adam Müller.[7]

Müller does not attempt to define a particular type of irony that is specifically dramatic; rather he attempts to expand the meaning of the word *Ironie* with reference to drama and with particular reference to the limitations placed on irony through its association with comedy. Müller recognizes a type of irony that A. W. Schlegel would deny in 1808—tragic irony. Just as there are two possible types of irony, so are there two types of tragedy: a tragedy without irony, something we might describe as merely pathos or melodrama, and tragedy with irony. The word tragedy had long had evaluative connotations; in this equation, the word irony partakes of that evaluative force.

Midway through the essay on Aristophanes, Müller identifies Schlegel as his source, and complains (perhaps prophetically) that Schlegel has been seriously misinterpreted:

> Nachdem der Begriff der Ironie durch Friedrich Schlegel wieder aufgestellt worden, fiel ein Heer von poetisierenden Modephilosophen über das Wort her, und von der Schlegelschen, selbst noch unvollständigen Erklärung wieder nur den halben Sinn aufgreifend, ward *entweder* eine gewisse träumerische Gleichgültigkeit gegen die ernsteren Verhältnisse des Lebens, gegen bürgerliche Geschäfte; ein gewisses satirisierendes Scherztreiben mit heiligen Dingen und uralten Sitten;

ein gewisses Streben, den Schein von Unverständlichkeit und Unbe-
greiflichkeit vor schlichten, gutgesinnten Leuten durchzusetzen, *oder*
wohl gar das noch elendere Streben, den ungemeinen, den ganz beson-
dern, den Verächter der Zeit und der Umgebungen zu spielen, mit
jenem ehrwürdigen Namen bezeichnet. (242)
[After the concept of irony was reestablished by Friedrich Schlegel, an
army of poetic mode-philosophers fell upon the word, and taking only
the partial sense of Schlegel's still incomplete explanation, used that
honorable name to designate *either* a certain dreamy indifference to
serious relations of life, to bourgeois affairs; a certain satiric spoofing of
holy things and ancient customs; a certain striving to set before simple
and well-meaning folk the appearance of incomprehensibility and un-
intelligibility; *or* perhaps that even more miserable attempt to play the
uncommon, entirely unique despiser of time and circumstance.]

Müller's strategy is the same adopted by many other romantics: there are
two levels of irony, or of interpretation of Friedrich Schlegel—Müller's
own and various vulgar degradations:

Um dieses Wort zu bewähren, lassen Sie mich zuvörderst einen
griechischen Begriff entwickeln, der vor einigen Jahren von geistrei-
chen Freunden der Kunst wieder hergestellt, nachher aber von kindi-
schen Nachahmern derselben durch ekelhaften Mißbrauch zertreten
worden, nichts destoweniger aber das ganze Geheimnis des künstlerischen Lebens in seiner wahren ursprünglichen Gestalt ausdrückt, den
Begriff der *Ironie.* Verlangen Sie eine deutsche Übersetzung des Worts,
so weiß ich Ihnen keine beßre zu geben als: *Offenbarung der Freiheit des
Künstlers oder des Menschen.* (234)
[In order to validate this word, allow me first to develop a Greek concept that a few years ago was reestablished by certain magnanimous
friends of art, and that since, however, has been trampled in disgust-
ing misuse by their childish imitators—a concept that nonetheless
expresses the entire secret of artistic life in its true original form, the
concept of irony. If you desire a translation of the word, I can offer
you none better than the following: the revelation of the freedom of
the artist or of man.]

A few lines later irony is glossed as "die göttliche Freiheit des Geistes" ["the
divine freedom of the spirit"], without which there can be no idea of the
holy nor of love (235).
Müller then distinguishes the two corresponding genres of irony: comic

and tragic. The common limitation of the ironic to the comic is part of what Müller feels is a vulgar degradation of the word. True seriousness reveals itself as ironic. When the serious is expressed without irony, we have mere pathos ("das Weinerliche"), whereas if the serious is combined with irony, and thus with God and freedom, we have the tragic. In parallel fashion, "der Scherz" without irony yields merely the ridiculous ("das Lächerliche"), whereas satire, in combination with irony, yields the comic (240–41).

As long as these elements are mixed, the serious will not be bigoted and "monologic," nor will "der Scherz" be frivolous and "dialogic." Rather, monologue and dialogue will be entwined in the dramatic, that is, in one spirit. Tragic irony occurs when belief and doubt are represented together, and the dramatic example given by Müller is the King and the Fool in *King Lear* (243).[8] But this mixture of belief and doubt also leads Müller to a more radical statement; irony is apotheosized:[9]

> Nennen Sie diesen nun den Geist der Liebe oder den Geist der Frei-heit, nennen Sie ihn Herz oder Gott—mir schien in der Beziehung auf den individuellen Gegenstand dieser Vorlesungen am geratensten, ihn mit dem bewegtesten, zartesten, geflügelsten Geist der alten Welt, mit dem Zeitgenossen des Aristophanes, mit *Platon: Ironie* zu nennen. (241) [You can call this the spirit of love or the spirit of freedom, you can call it heart or God—but to me, given the particular object of these lectures, it seems most appropriate to name it in accordance with that most dynamic, delicate, winged spirit of the ancient world, with the contemporary of Aristophanes, with Plato—"irony."]

In "Prolegomena einer Kunst-Philosophie" (1808), Müller has additional notes on irony, which is defined with specific reference to the artist rather than to the artistic work. Irony is a response to fundamental philosophical dichotomies: life and death, Fichte's *Ich* and *Gegenich*.[10] These are resolved in irony; Nature herself "moves from life to death and from death to life with infinite ease and irony" (157). The philosopher is expected to do the same: the philosopher who lives in consciousness of this movement, that is, "in genuine Platonic irony," who knows how to transform this conscious-ness into belief, assumes an identity similar to the artist-priest sketched in Schlegel's *Ideen*: "der ist Künstler und Gelehrter zugleich, und so und nicht anders soll sein heiliges Amt gedacht werden" (158) ["he is artist and scholar at the same time, and thus and in no other way should his holy office be imagined"]. Müller's philosopher evolves toward the artist-scholar. Artist and scholar are not defined in terms of an opposition that is resolved in philosophy; rather, philosophical knowledge is itself posited as a conflict to be resolved in a unitary being of artist-scholar.

Connop Thirlwall's "On the Irony of Sophocles" (1833)

Connop Thirlwall, in his 1833 essay, is more modest in his specific claims for irony than Müller; but the essay was to prove far more influential than Müller's, even if much of that influence was and still is indirect.[11] The notions for which Thirlwall is cited as an early authority are peripheral to his main concerns. Thirlwall's contribution to the history of irony is twofold. First, he was familiar with German criticism and instrumental in transferring much of its terminology to English. Second and more important was his tentative and almost casual formulation of that special, limited sense of dramatic irony referring to the privileged position and knowledge of the spectator—the limited sense that has become the leading definition in English literary handbooks.

By the turn of the century, the essay was commonly referred to in English discussions of Sophocles, and although now relatively inaccessible, it was reprinted in Thirlwall's collected papers (1878) and later summarized (reasonably accurately) in Alan Thompson's The Dry Mock (1948).[12] Although Thirlwall is often credited with developing the concept of dramatic irony, he does not use the term. This much is generally noted in discussions of Thirlwall.[13] What is mentioned less often is that he does not expound in any detail the modern concept of dramatic irony itself.

Thirlwall begins as do Schlegel, Solger, and Müller. There are two types of irony—irony as commonly understood and a more complex form of irony that it is his business to expound:

> Some readers may be a little surprised to see *irony* attributed to a tragic poet. . . . We must begin with a remark or two on the more ordinary use of the word, on that which to distinguish it from the subject of our present enquiry, we will call *verbal irony*. This most familiar species of irony may be described as a figure which enables the speaker to convey his meaning with greater force by means of a contrast between his thought and his expression, or to speak more accurately, between the thought which he evidently designs to express, and that which his words properly signify. (483)

Although much of Thirlwall's discussion of particular plays concentrates almost exclusively on verbal irony—the analysis of *Ajax* focuses on various possible interpretations of Ajax's speeches (514–20)—Thirlwall distinguishes this form of irony from what he calls "practical irony": "Without departing from the analogy that pervades the various kinds of verbal irony, we may speak of a *practical irony*, which is independent of all forms of speech, and needs not the aid of words. Life affords as many illustrations of this, as conversation and books of the other" (485). There are various kinds of practical irony, but essentially Thirlwall has done no more than extend the notion of verbal irony into the nonverbal realm. Reality is a language that has conflicting meanings: what is expected is not the same as what actually happens.

Between these two types of irony, Thirlwall defines a third, but this third type of irony has nothing to do with his discussion of drama. This irony, which Thirlwall calls "dialectic irony," is associated with Plato. Thirlwall's language, however, seems indebted to the romantics, and some of the concepts will correspond to those pertaining to practical irony: "There is however an irony which deserves to be distinguished from the ordinary species by a different name, and which may be properly called *dialectic irony*. This, instead of being concentrated in insulated passages, and rendered prominent by its contrast with the prevailing tone of the composition, pervades every part, and is spread over the whole like a transparent vesture closely fitted to every limb of the body" (484). The metaphor suggests that Thirlwall could be talking about the kind of irony Schlegel and others found in *Wilhelm Meister*—an all-pervasive irony. But he means something quite different:

> The writer effects his purpose by placing the opinion of his adversary in the foreground, and saluting it with every demonstration of respect, while he is busied in withdrawing one by one all the supports on which it rests: and he never ceases to approach it with an air of deference until he has completely undermined it, when he leaves it to sink by the weight of its own absurdity. Examples of this species are as rare as those of the other are common. The most perfect ever produced are those which occur in Plato's dialogues. (484)

Many classicists would distinguish Socratic irony from this limited sense of it; for example, in the *Meno,* Socrates does not demolish arguments but rather produces them in another. Thirlwall, however, is not seeking to incorporate his understanding of Socratic irony into his notion of irony in drama. And he does not mention this form of irony again.[14]

Thirlwall then turns to various forms of "practical irony." The most striking is not given a particular name by Thirlwall, but could be called judicial irony—the irony of the judge:

> There is always a slight cast of irony in the grave, calm, respectful attention impartially bestowed by an intelligent judge on two contending parties, who are pleading their causes before him with all the earnestness of deep conviction, and of excited feeling. What makes the contrast interesting is, that the right and the truth lie on neither side exclusively: that there is no fraudulent purpose, no gross imbecility of intellect, on either: but both have plausible claims and specious reasons to alledge, though each is too much blinded by prejudice or passion to do justice to the views of his adversary. For here the irony lies not in the demeanor of the judge, but is deeply seated in the case itself, which seems to favour each of the litigants, but really eludes them both. (489–90)

This seems to me the most innovative part of the essay. But in his discussion of particular plays, Thirlwall applies this theoretical conception only to the *Antigone* (525). Thirlwall's notion of judicial irony may well have been developed with unique reference to that play and may represent no more than his own interpretation of it.

How does Thirlwall come to consider such a play and such an aspect of the play ironic? What makes a judicial stance ironic? The answer seems to lie in the notion of irony as detachment: "Yet it is not so: the poet himself preserves an ironical composure, and while he excites our esteem and pity for the suffering hero, guards us against sharing the detestation Philoctetes feels for the authors of his calamity" (532). This meaning of detachment (a motif that will recur in modern discussions of irony) seems to result from the combination of two ideas: first, the notion that irony involves a conflict that must be judged (verbal irony entails a conflict of word and thought; "practical" irony entails a contrast between events and their interpretation); and second, the notion of a poet as a god: "The dramatic poet is the creator of a little world, in which he rules with absolute sway, and may shape the destinies of the imaginary beings to whom he gives life and breath according to any plan that he may choose" (490).[15] On the following page, Thirlwall relates this invisible power directly to religion: "The essential character therefore of all dramatic poetry must depend on the poet's religious or philosophical sentiments, on the light in which he contemplates history and life, on the belief he entertains as to the unseen hand that regulates their events" (491). To Thirlwall, irony always involves a level of "superior understanding": "A man of superior understanding may often find himself compelled to assent to propositions which he knows, though true in themselves, will lead to very erroneous inferences in the mind of the speaker. . . . Such is the conduct of the affectionate father in the parable" (486). What Thirlwall calls "tragic irony"—an irony that must be glossed as "irony in tragedy" since it includes both verbal and practical irony (537)—seems to combine the notions of irony of fate and the poet as god.

Thirlwall's direct relation to modern theories of dramatic irony is tenuous. But his indirect relation lies in his notion of the man of superior understanding—a theoretical being comparable to Müller's *Künstler-Gelehrter*. This man of superior understanding is either the poet, a judge, or a critic: when Thirlwall refers to "intelligent judges of such matters" he is referring to "the most eminent German critics, a Winkelmann, a Lessing, a Herder" (531). Dramatic irony involves an audience, but Thirlwall, although he mentions the spectator, refers generally to readers of plays—for example, "the most superficial reader" (491). And it is only with his first mention of the spectator that a concept similar to the modern notion of dramatic irony is set forth. Here, Thirlwall is discussing *Oedipus Rex:*

> During this pause the spectator has leisure to reflect, how different all is from what it seems. The wrath of heaven has been pointed against the afflicted city, only that it might fall with concentrated force on the head of a single man; and he who is its object stands alone calm and secure: unconscious of his own misery he can afford pity for the unfortunate: to him all look up for succour: and, as in the plenitude of wisdom and power, he undertakes to trace the evil, of which he is himself the sole author, to its secret source. (496)

But this paragraph is isolated: it occurs during his analysis of the play, and in itself constitutes the very pause it describes. It is only here that Thirlwall mentions the contrast between the understanding of the spectator and that of the character—a contrast on which modern theories of dramatic irony are based. Elsewhere, what makes up irony in Sophocles are "contrasts"— contrasts that are noticed by the "attentive reader": "Here, . . . the main theme of the poet's irony is the contrast between the appearance of good and the reality of evil" (500); Thirlwall's contrast between "the spectator" and "the attentive reader" is directly analogous (498).[16]

Thirlwall's main contribution to the history of irony is in the introduction into English of various concepts of irony found in German writers. Occasionally (as in the notion of irony as a calm detachment), these incidental and partially illustrative or even figurative statements assume more importance than his main discussion and the clear expostulation of the three types of irony: verbal, dialectic, and practical. The modern notion of dramatic irony that develops from Thirlwall, however, arises in the same manner as does the notion of tragic irony.[17] A phrase that means "irony in drama" or "irony in tragedy" is interpreted as meaning a particular type of irony. This type of irony is then itself subject to reinterpretations that depend largely on the contemporaneous critical reception of particular plays. Thus dramatic irony comes to be defined by our literary-critical interpretation of Sophocles' Oedipus plays. Dramatic irony is only as dramatic or even ironic as are our own literary-critical objects and interpretations.

Thirlwall's Reception

The notion of dramatic irony is clearly established by the early twentieth century, although often, in deference to Thirlwall's essay, such a notion is described as "Sophoclean irony." G. G. Sedgewick (1935) provides a classic formulation: "Dramatic irony . . . is the sense of contradiction felt by spectators of a drama who see a character acting in ignorance of his condition."[18] Sedgewick discusses Thirlwall's essay in precisely these terms: "The spectator knows the facts, the people in the play do not" (26). A decade earlier, J. A. K. Thomson described the same notion as "Sophoclean Irony." After arguing for the essential unity of tragic and comic irony, Thomson states: "There is a thing traditionally called 'Sophoclean Irony.' It is the device, often strikingly effective, which puts in the mouth of a character language whose full significance is not perceived by himself but only by his hearers, who know, as he does not, the doom that awaits him. There are scholars who write as if, in mentioning this verbal form of Irony, they had exhausted the subject" (*Irony: An Historical Introduction*, 35). According to Thomson, such notions are old hat. And perhaps so. A similar view of irony had clearly been accepted by A. C. Bradley in 1904. Here Bradley is referring to the production of a "dread of the presence of evil":

> It is enhanced . . . by the use of a literary expedient. Not even in
> *Richard III*, which in this, as in other respects, has resemblances to
> *Macbeth*, is there so much of Irony. I do not refer to irony in the ordinary sense; to speeches, for example where the speaker is intentionally
> ironical, like that of Lennox in III.vi. I refer to irony on the part of
> the author himself, to ironical juxtapositions of persons and events,
> and especially to the "Sophoclean irony" by which a speaker is made to

use words bearing to the audience, in addition to his own meaning, a further and ominous sense, hidden from himself and, usually, from the other persons on the stage. The very first words uttered by Macbeth:

So foul and fair a day I have not seen,

are an example to which attention has often been drawn; for they startle the reader by recalling the words of the Witches in the first scene,

Fair is foul, and foul is fair.

When Macbeth, emerging from his murderous reverie, turns to the nobles saying "Let us toward the King," his words are innocent, but to the reader have a double meaning.[19]

Like Thirlwall, Bradley considers the audience of *Macbeth* a reading audience, which only enhances the superior vantage enjoyed by the spectator-critic.[20]

Most interesting is the reception of the notion of irony by Lewis Campbell in two works: first, in an essay in his 1871 edition of Sophocles, and second, in a book-length study of Aeschylus, Sophocles, and Shakespeare published in 1904. Campbell is not in sympathy with any notion of irony applied to Greek drama, but by 1904, he admits he is fighting a losing battle.[21]

Campbell's 1871 essay is entitled "On the So-called Irony of Sophocles." This short essay focuses on Thirlwall, and if not the best critique of Thirlwall, it is at least one of the best articles for showing what seems to be at stake in the invocation of various types of ironies. The article is frankly polemical. Under the phrase "The Irony of Sophocles" Campbell finds at least five different things:

The truth which this phrase, "The Irony of Sophocles," is intended to comprehend in one, is better expressed by speaking separately—(1) of the power of God as an element in Greek tragedy; (2) of the effect of contrast in exciting wonder, and intensifying pity and fear; (3) of the subtle use of language in pointing contrasts through *litotes,* double meanings, and suggestions of the truth; (4) of the ethical genius of Sophocles, unobtrusively making felt the full meaning of every situation; (5) of the pathetic force with which by a few simple touches he stirs the deepest springs of feeling. (132)

But the word irony will not do; for "it confuses the feeling of the spectator with a supposed intention in the mind of the author . . . [and] detracts from the simplicity and tenderness which are amongst the chief merits of the Sophoclean drama. It injures the profound pathos of Greek tragedy by suggesting the suspicion of an *arrière pensée,* of the poet's face behind the mask, surveying his own creations with a sardonic smile" (133).

In this summary, the notion of dramatic irony as we know it does not appear. Campbell introduces such a notion, apparently from Thirlwall, only as a rhetorical straw man. Campbell ridicules the notion that the artist's intention is to assume a position of power over his materials and over his audience (128–29). Sophoclean irony, according to Campbell, can be viewed in different ways: "Is the Irony of Sophocles, then, an irony of the poet, or of an imaginary Fate or Providence, or, thirdly, of the spectator?" (129). And no one type of irony, no one type of ironist (whether a creator or viewer), should be privileged. Greek drama was communal: "The intention of the poet is one with the feeling of the spectator. If irony was what the spectator enjoyed, then irony was what the poet meant, but not otherwise" (129). Campbell rejects irony because of the implied hierarchy of poet, characters, and spectators:

> The Greeks, like other people, delighted in contrast. . . . But is every contrast between appearance and reality to have the name of irony? . . . And what was the frame of mind with which the spectator saw the culmination and overthrow of the power of Agamemnon or Oedipus? Did he mentally assume the position of a superior being, watching with tranquil interest the ignorance and vainglory of an ephemeral creature, or, like the refined critic of a later age, 'hold the balance even' between conflicting interests? (130)

Campbell rejects this: the spectator is "swayed by the emotions of pity, awe, and fear"; because of this, "it is mere confusion to speak of such feelings as the enjoyment of irony" (130).

Some thirty years later, Campbell returns to this point in *Tragic Drama in Aeschylus, Sophocles, and Shakespeare: An Essay* (1904). Again, he notes the prevalence of the term irony: "For the contrast of situations—present and future, apparent and real—'tragic irony' is a term which in our language seems to be firmly established in common use" (169–70). But Campbell seems to have given up his attempt to suppress this term; rather, it must be modified: "It is essential to plead that the term 'irony' in this connection should be stripped of some associations which ordinarily cleave to it; such as the smile of conscious superiority, the dissembled laugh, the secret mockery of the unfortunate—everything in short which impairs the fulness of emotional sympathy" (171). He had rejected the term in the 1871 edition precisely because these associations conflicted with his view of Sophocles:

"For the word 'irony' in ordinary use . . . implies the absence or suppression of sympathy" (126); "For irony is not the natural language of absolute power, but of power which for the moment is withheld" (128). A disparaging quotation of Thirlwall's essay follows: "the look which a superior intelligence, exempt from our passions . . . would cast upon the tumultuous workings of our blind ambition . . . (128; he refers to "On the Irony of Sophocles," 487).

In his 1871 edition, Campbell claims that irony is an inappropriate description of Sophoclean drama because it implies hierarchical relations of power between author, character, and audience. In 1904, Campbell can no longer argue for a suppression of the term itself; he hopes merely that these ordinary meanings of irony can be stripped away. What I have been arguing here is something quite different: such meanings cannot be stripped away; they are to be viewed, rather, as part of the critical strategy involved in invoking irony.[22]

The critical concept of dramatic irony as defined by Sedgewick and repeated in many handbooks since is essentially a twentieth-century one. It results from a reading of certain classical dramas and also from a reading of their reception. When Thirlwall's essay is discussed by Campbell or by Sedgewick, it is at least subject to critique. When it is cited as an authoritative source (for "irony of fate") in the *Oxford English Dictionary,* it assumes a canonical status, providing an apparent historical source for meanings of irony Thirlwall seems not to have formulated.[23]

I turn again to the handbook definition from the *Princeton Encyclopedia of Poetics:* "*Dramatic i[rony]* is a plot device according to which (a) the spectators know more than the protagonist." Although it may well be impossible to date the origin of this conception precisely, it is easy enough to see the immense advantage the simple formulation has over earlier formulations. Müller's conception of irony is too extravagant and eccentric to be useful to any critic other than one who shares his romantic assumptions. Schlegel's enigmatic pronouncements on irony, if assumed to be coherent, present similar difficulties. And according to some scholars, the very notion of romantic irony must be split in order to be intelligible. Lussky's distinction between two tendencies in romantic irony can be seen as the opting of literary history for intelligible formulas—ones that are simple and teachable. The "breaking of dramatic illusion" is one thing; "artistic self-reflection" is another. And romanticists may privilege whichever they prefer.

Dramatic irony has been subject to a similar reception. The modern notion of dramatic irony originates in early discussions of the relation of irony to the generic distinction between tragedy and comedy. To understand irony within this context requires an understanding (or interpretation) of the artistic and cultural context of Greek drama; and irony will be affected by the ordinary polemic, both literary and political, associated with such matters. Most early discussions of tragic irony involve, in addition, the dialectical relation of the artist to artistic materials, at best a difficult and abstruse matter to resolve. Any potential clarity of the term is further obscured by evaluative considerations: tragic irony must be a virtue; the phrase "bad tragic irony" is oxymoronic.

Sedgewick's lectures are not addressed to students of philosophy. They are addressed to students of literature. And what occurs is the transformation of a philosophical concept into a literary-critical one (Hegel criticizes an analogous usurpation of philosophical language by Schlegel). This in itself involves, first, the elimination of the more abstruse philosophical baggage. But second, it involves a redefinition of some key elements: the artist-philosopher is transformed into the critic, and the whole notion of irony is conceived as a literary-critical one, not as an artistic-philosophical one. Müller's *Künstler-Gelehrter* becomes a *Gelehrter* pure and simple—one who identifies neither with the artist nor the text, but rather with the (critical) audience. The double-edged statement, the expression of an artistic point of view—these yield to the authority of a superior audience. The learned reader transcends all other participants in the artistic process. We seem well on the way to Rorty's nightmarish utopian vision of "liberal ironists."

9

The Myth of
Chaucerian Irony:
Medieval
Misprisions 3

■

The following section could be considered a practical study in the history of irony. Thus far, I have been looking at the word itself and its transformation. Here, I will look at the transformations that word effects in the reception of a specific author. How did the word irony come to be used of Chaucer? What changes does that word indicate (and effect) in the critical characterization of Chaucer? And finally—a question that has been present throughout this study—what is the function of the invocation of the word?[1]

The Chaucer I will be looking at here is one developed from the eighteenth through the twentieth centuries; there is nothing particularly medieval about him. I have placed the chapter here—preceding a fuller discussion of New Criticism and later views of irony—because the ironic Chaucer of twentieth-century criticism is based as much on late nineteenth-century conceptions of irony as on modern ones. When Chaucerians invoke Chaucerian irony, they are invoking a nineteenth-century critical notion modified inconsistently and sporadically to suit various developments in modern critical theory. This practical study of Chaucerian irony can thus be considered an introduction to the theoretical work (New Criticism) on which much of that irony seems to be based.

The word irony is seldom used of Chaucer's work before the nineteenth century. It is not used in Warton's *History of English Poetry* (1774) nor in his earlier *Observations on the Faerie Queene of Spenser* (1754, 1762); the one occurrence I have found in Tyrwhitt's 1775 edition of Chaucer clearly refers to rhetorical irony: one thing is said; something else is meant.[2]

When modern Chaucerians speak of Chaucerian irony, they mean something different from this. Their understanding of irony is shaped principally by George Lyman Kittredge, by critical proponents of romantic irony, by American New Critics. We hear of Chaucer's "complex irony, which can be understood as a way of saying opposite things simultaneously, without either being undermined by the other."[3] Chaucerian irony, according to such a formulation, is egalitarian. It is also an aspect of Chaucerian narration; E. Talbot Donaldson speaks of the narrator as "the victim of the poet's pervasive—not merely sporadic—irony. And as such he is also the chief agent by which the poet achieves his wonderfully complex, ironic, comic, serious vision of the world."[4] Donald R. Howard also assumes irony is at the heart of Chaucer's work, associating that irony with "realism" (50), "high seriousness" (51), "role-playing" (5, 184), Chaucer's "impartial or distanced stance" toward his world (55); the words "irony" and "ironic" appear a total of twenty times on page 118, and Howard concludes that "the ironies hover over the whole conception of the work" (119).[5] No single definition of irony could account for Donaldson's and Howard's uses of the word; nor could it account for what I believe is the intelligibility of such uses of the word to most twentieth-century readers and particularly to Chaucerians.

But how did the word come to have such a range of meanings? And what does the history of the word suggest we are importing into Chaucer's text when we describe it as ironic in these various ways?

Whereas most discussions of Chaucerian irony (or other privileged forms of irony) begin by discrediting rhetorical irony, my argument here is that the popularity of the word irony in literary criticism is firmly rooted in the implications of rhetorical irony. Rhetorical irony involves an appeal to an absent authority—a meaning opposed to the superficial statement. Under later theoretical forms of irony, such an authority is not canceled; it is rather displaced, either onto the poet (romantic irony) or onto the critic. Chaucerian irony, through its lack of definition, has exploited the critical advantages (or advantages to the critic) of both these forms.

In rhetorical irony, an authoritative meaning dominates an unauthoritative statement: X is said, but Y is meant. Although various forms of rhetorical irony are possible, such as irony of words and irony of thoughts, all such ironies imply the dominance of a literal statement by an implied, articulable meaning. Romantic irony, by contrast, and forms of irony based on it, lack such an authoritative meaning. According to its theorists, romantic irony involves other matters—the self-conscious relation of artists to their work; the subversion of authority through parody; the eternal poetic fluctuation between self-creation and self-annihilation. Irony, accordingly, is something undefined that "hovers" over an entire work. Chaucerian irony (as understood by twentieth-century Chaucerians) shares many of the characteristics of romantic irony, without its acerbic polemic: Chaucer is a self-conscious artist, of "genial and tolerant realism"; his irony "embraces, displays, enjoys, makes capital" of the "contradictions and disparities of late-medieval life."[6] Chaucer (as understood today) is a precursor of romanticism (also as understood today).

The above paragraph constitutes an intelligible history of Chaucerian irony. But this modern history of irony is itself part of the history it describes; it assigns positive values to literary and literary-critical strategies similar to its own, for example, the concealing of authority and the transformation of the poet into a critic. We can understand this history better by refusing to accept its myths at face value. Rather than a subversion of authority, what this history reveals is a displacement of authority. The authority of the poet's meaning has yielded to the authority of the poet's sensibility, and to the authority of the critic who analyzes these matters.

Chaucerians and Modern Irony

During the nineteenth century, the word irony takes on a variety of meanings. It is associated with wit, humor, comedy. It develops dramatic associations, leading to the modern notions of tragic or dramatic irony. The metaphorical notions of situational irony and irony of fate are extended, and the implications of the ancient association of irony with Socrates are extended.

Medievalists in general, and Chaucerians in particular, have been faced with a choice: either to accept the historical development of the word or to adopt a conservative attitude toward irony. D. W. Robertson, Jr., retains the rhetorical sense of the word. According to Robertson, we can recognize irony only when we find a statement that contradicts what we assume to be the meaning of the text.[7] But even the most traditional rhetorical definitions of irony can be subject to romantic or New Critical misreadings, as we have seen earlier in the interpretation of the comments on irony by Donatus and Pompeius. Medievalists have been trained in modern theories of irony. What we think of as a Chaucerian is a nineteenth- and twentieth-century entity, and the views of such a critic and scholar on irony are formed accordingly.

The critical language used by Chaucerians is in part a borrowing of the critical language associated with Shakespeare; by the late nineteenth century, this language had been affected by A. W. Schlegel's widely disseminated *Lectures on Dramatic Art and Literature*. The borrowing of such terminology by Chaucerians privileged Chaucer (placing him in a category with Shakespeare) and also entailed a new understanding of Chaucer's irony, one that changed the relations between the poet, his now dramatic text, and his audience.

In the late eighteenth century, the word irony is rarely used of Chaucer. The few occurrences refer unambiguously to what I call rhetorical irony: something is said, something else is meant. When Thomas Tyrwhitt uses the word of Chaucer in his influential edition of 1775 (often considered the first modern edition of Chaucer), this is what he means. Tyrwhitt is commenting on line 1932 of the Summoner's Tale, "Hir praier is of ful gret reverence": "The Editt. have changed this to 'ful litel'; but the reading of the Mss. may stand, if it be understood ironically." According to Tyrwhitt, Chaucer says "gret," but means the contrary, "litel." [8]

To mid-nineteenth-century critics such as Leigh Hunt, irony continued to mean what it meant to seventeenth- and eighteenth-century critics and to Tyrwhitt. In an anthology entitled Wit and Humor (1846), Hunt does not use the word in a fifty-page section on Chaucer including selections and comment. In his introduction, irony is listed as the fourth of twelve varieties of Wit and Humour (the first three are simile, metaphor, and "the Poetical Process"). It is defined as "Dissimulation" and "Saying one thing and Meaning another." The association with Socrates, dissimulation, and hierarchies of meaning and statement are all familiar themes from the preromantic history of the word. [9]

In the later nineteenth century, we begin to see the effect of romantic terminology. Adolphus William Ward's Chaucer appeared in the English Men of Letters series in 1879. Ward introduces the term "self-irony" in a passage that shows clearly his association of such a term with a poet. He is speaking of the Host's description of Chaucer:

> From this passage we may gather, not only that Chaucer was, as the Host of the Tabard's transparent self-irony implies, small of stature and slender. . . . Modesty of this stamp is perfectly compatible with a certain self-consciousness which is hardly ever absent from greatness, and which at all events supplies a stimulus not easily dispensed with except by sustained effort on the part of a poet. The two qualities seem naturally to combine into that self-containedness (very different from self-contentedness) which distinguishes Chaucer. [10]

The phrase "the Host's . . . self-irony" has to do with Chaucer, despite its grammatical construction; it has to do with poetic "self-consciousness" and "self-containedness," qualities which are denied to the mere Host. Irony is still a variety of "Humour," but Ward's use of the word implies that he means more than raillery or dissimulation:

Closely allied to Chaucer's liveliness and gaiety of disposition, and in part springing from them, are his keen sense of the ridiculous and the power of satire which he has at his command. His humour has many varieties, ranging from the refined and half-melancholy irony of the *House of Fame* to the ready wit of the sagacious uncle of Cressid, the burlesque fun of the inimitable Nun's Priest's Tale, and the very gross salt of the Reeve, the Miller, and one or two others. (179–80)

John W. Hales's "Chaucer and Shakespeare" appeared in 1873 and was reprinted in his *Notes and Essays on Shakespeare* (1884).[11] Hales draws on two sources for his notion of irony, A. W. Schlegel and Connop Thirlwall. Hales defines Chaucer as a "lesser Shakespeare" (58) and interprets him through Shakespeare:

Another respect in which Chaucer is not unworthy of some comparison with his greater successor is his irony. We use the word in the sense in which Dr. Thirlwall uses it of Sophocles in his excellent paper printed in the *Philological Museum* some forty years ago, and in which Schlegel, in his *Lectures on Dramatic Literature,* uses it of Shakespeare, to denote that dissembling, so to speak, that self-retention and reticence, or, at least, indirect presentment, that is a frequent characteristic of the consummate dramatist, or the consummate writer of any kind who aims at portraying life in all its breadth. We are told often enough of the universal sympathy that inspires the greatest souls, and it is well; but let us consider that universal sympathy does not mean blind, undiscriminating, wholesale sympathy, but precisely the opposite. Only that sympathy can be all-inclusive that is profoundly intelligent as well as intense; and this profound intelligence is incompatible with any complete and unmitigated adoration. . . . [Shakespeare's] irony consists in the earnest, heartfelt, profound representation of [his characters], while yet he is fully alive to their failings and failures. It is observable only in the supremest geniuses. Men of inferior knowledge and dimmer light are more easily satisfied. . . . Chaucer, too, in a similar way abounds in secondary meanings. . . . He hates without bigotry; he loves without folly; he worships without idolatry. . . . It is because his spirit enjoyed and retained this lofty freedom that it was so tolerant and capacious. (78–79)[12]

Hales's view of irony here is subject to the same criticism leveled against Friedrich Schlegel by Hegel. It is essentially negative, grounded in "the precise opposite of universal sympathy." The opposite of universal sympathy is logically universal contempt, but Hales denies this. Extending Thirl-wall's notion of the "man of superior understanding," he characterizes irony as "profound intelligence," "superiority," a quality possessed only by the "greatest souls." If we are unable to accept Hales's argument, we must be one of those "men of inferior knowledge and dimmer light" who are unable to attain such heights. Again, despite the romantic terminology, the basic structure of rhetorical irony underlies this description. If we are "men of inferior knowledge and dimmer light," we are victims of an ironic meaning that transcends mere statements. The hierarchy of statement and meaning has been transferred to a hierarchy of audience and poet.

Skeat's edition of Chaucer, published in the 1890s, has been used to some extent by every Chaucerian since. And when Skeat uses the word irony, which he does very rarely, he, like Tyrwhitt, means rhetorical irony. His comment on line 1251 of the Merchant's Tale is exemplary. Chaucer says the worthy knight follows his bodily delight after women "As doon thise fooles that been seculeer." Skeat comments, "seculeer, secular: as distinguished from the monks and friars. Chaucer probably speaks ironically, meaning that these holy orders were as bad as the rest. See 1. 1322 [I speke of folk in seculer estaat]." [13] According to Skeat, Chaucer ostensibly makes a moral distinction between regular and secular (this is what he says); in fact, the distinction is invalid (this is what he means). Chaucer's meaning is thus contrary to his statement. But that was Skeat, who defined his own role as a Chaucerian in a one-page section in his introduction, entitled "Criticism":

> The conspicuous avoidance, in this edition, of any approach to what has been called aesthetic criticism, has been intentional. Let it not be hence inferred that I fail to appreciate the easy charm of Chaucer's narrative, the delicious flow of his melodious verse, the saneness of his opinions, the artistic skill with which his characters are drawn, his gentle humour, and his broad sympathy. It is left to the professed critic to enlarge upon this theme; he can be trusted to do it thoroughly. (6:xxiii)

Among these "professed critics" were George Saintsbury, Thomas Louns-bury, Frederick Tupper, John Livingston Lowes, and most importantly, Kittredge.[14] Saintsbury, in his article on Chaucer in the Cambridge History of English Literature, discusses the end of the Knight's Tale and notes Chaucer's "famous touches of ironic comment on life and thought, which, though they have been unduly developed upon as indicating a Voltairian tone in Chaucer, certainly are ironical in their treatment of the riddles of the painful earth" (218). Tupper and Lowes, in a dispute over Chaucer's use of the Seven Deadly Sins, also extend the meaning of the word irony. Lowes disagrees with Tupper's reductive application of the Seven Deadly Sins to Chaucer. Accordingly, he accuses Tupper of an equally reductive use of the word irony:

> Furthermore, Chaucer's unsurpassed and unsurpassable *Irony* is independent of any formal schematizing of a group of Tales. This mastery of irony on Chaucer's part is no discovery of Mr. Tupper's, nor would he for a moment claim it as his own. *Vixere fortes ante Agamemnona multi.* What he has seemingly overlooked is the fact that ironical inconsistency between precept and practice has been the fruitful theme of comedy and satire from Aristophanes to Meredith, with no thought of the Seven Deadly Sins. (369)

Chaucer's irony now has precedents and successors, even though neither ancient nor modern writers can surpass it.

The most influential of Skeat's professed critics is Kittredge. The various senses of the word irony in modern Chaucer criticism are all indebted to him. Tupper and Lowes view irony as a conflict between precept and practice. In *Chaucer and His Poetry,* Kittredge presents Chaucer's relation to his work as ironical, and this view significantly widens the implications of poetic irony. One meaning of irony in Kittredge is irony of events: "It is a very pregnant manifestation of Chaucer's feeling for the irony of life and circumstance when he makes Pandarus the exponent of chivalric love" (136). An irony of events is an extension of the structure of rhetorical irony: what man expects (or states) is unauthoritative; what happens is authoritative. Kittredge also calls Chaucer ironic in a Socratic sense: "Almost all Chaucer's references to himself are ironical. He is an outsider—so he tells us—in the courts of love, the *servus servorum* of the god. He invents nothing: all his work is that of a faithful copyist" (31). This statement could be analyzed as "Chaucer says that he is unknowledgeable; he means that he is knowledgeable." But what Kittredge has in mind here is probably something different: "With his usual irony, of the Socratic sort, he ascribes this breach of decorum to his feeble intellect" (14). Whenever Kittredge uses the word irony with reference to Chaucer himself, he seems to be equating Chaucer with Socrates. The poet feigns ignorance, and in so doing evinces an even higher intelligence: "The great sympathetic ironist drops his mask, and we find that he has once more been studying human life from the point of view of a ruling passion" (143). The various senses of the word irony are blurred:

the rhetorical meaning shifts to metaphysical and philosophical meanings, as classical precedent (Socrates is an *eirōn*) and romantic poetics (poets are philosophical) are combined.[15]

Since Kittredge, irony has become an increasingly privileged term in Chaucer criticism, although its meanings have continued to expand. Germaine Dempster sanctioned the use of the term dramatic irony with respect to Chaucer in a monograph of 1932—a term not even used of drama (let alone narrative) until the nineteenth century.[16] Two articles by Earle Birney, originally published in 1939 and 1942 and recently reprinted, are symptomatic of the slippage in the term.[17] In 1939, Birney notes various types of irony in Chaucer, including dramatic irony. Birney's 1942 article is entitled "Is Chaucer's Irony a Modern Discovery?" and attempts to show that irony (the phenomenon) was recognized by Chaucerians before irony (the name) was used of it. What Birney calls irony in his titles is something he names variously in his texts: "humour," "broad mirth," "slyest innuendo" (303); "incongruities," "hidden satire," "irony of circumstance," "comic drama" (304); "subtleties of comic characterization" (305); "satiric allegories," "wit" (307); "structural ironies" (311); "delicacies of Chaucer's humor" (313); "ambiguities" (315, 317). Birney argues (against Spurgeon) that these qualities had been recognized in Chaucer before Warton; the proof consists of phrases from Dart's "Life of Chaucer" included in Urry's 1721 edition—"pleasant Wit," "gay humour," "gallantry" (314). Birney thus universalizes a modern concept of irony in two ways: not only did the thing itself exist (irony as understood by modern critics), a concept of the (unnamed) thing existed as well; eighteenth-century criticism is to be regarded as twentieth-century criticism in a different language.

The definition of the word irony in contemporary Chaucer criticism must be understood as a conflation of all these factors: the influence of Kittredge's use of the term, its convenient and simple rhetorical definition, the understanding of the term by romanticists, its supplanting of competing terms such as wit and humor in the nineteenth century.

The evaluative force of the word owes even more to American New Criticism and particularly to the work of Cleanth Brooks. Though few Chaucerians today acknowledge their debt to American New Critics, that influence is pervasive. Charles Muscatine's justly influential *Chaucer and the French Tradition* (1957) cites Brooks directly, and Donaldson's "Chaucer the Pilgrim" (1954) has its theoretical counterpart in the nearly contemporary refutation of historical fallacies by Wimsatt and Beardsley in *The Verbal Icon*.[18] Robertson's reaction against New Criticism involved both an attack on its romantic origins and a revision in the use of the word irony—a word that

Robertson tried to confine to its rhetorical meaning. And the more recent attempts by some Chaucerians to distance themselves from their New
Critical roots often take the form of an attack on irony.[19]

I will discuss the New Critical conception of irony in a separate chapter.
In brief, it is responsible for the association of irony with ambiguity or tension and the consequent implication that the relation between competing
meanings in irony is horizontal rather than vertical. The notion of such
egalitarian relations between meanings produces the definition of "complex irony" quoted at the beginning of this chapter and the misreadings of
Pompeius I discussed in chapter 4.

Donaldson the Critic

When romantic poets or New Critics assert such a multiplicity of competing meanings and call that multiplicity irony, they adopt for themselves the
role of authority attributed in rhetorical irony to an articulable meaning.
Nowhere is this clearer than in the work of E. Talbot Donaldson, and in
what may be the single most influential article on Chaucer. Donaldson's
analysis of the *Canterbury Tales* in terms of a poet and a naive narrator are
according to Donaldson a variation of the problem of Chaucerian irony:

> Now a Chaucer with tongue-in-cheek is a vast improvement over a
> simple-minded Chaucer when one is trying to define the whole man,
> but it must lead to a loss of critical perception and in particular to a
> confused notion of Chaucerian irony, to see in the Prologue a reporter
> who is acutely aware of the significance of what he sees but who
> sometimes, for ironic emphasis, interprets the evidence presented by
> his observation in a fashion directly contrary to what we expect. The
> proposition ought to be expressed in reverse: the reporter is, usually,
> acutely unaware of the significance of what he sees, no matter how
> sharply he sees it. He is, to be sure, permitted his lucid intervals,
> but in general he is the victim of the poet's pervasive—not merely
> sporadic—irony. And as such he is also the chief agent by which the
> poet achieves his wonderfully complex, ironic, comic, serious vision
> of the world which is but a devious and confused, infinitely various
> pilgrimage to a certain shrine.[20]

The Poet is the ironist; the Pilgrim is his victim, as are the imperceptive
critics who do not recognize this difference.

Donaldson's notion of Chaucer the Pilgrim and its own confused reception give some idea of what is at stake here. Donaldson had much precedent

for the notion of an identifiable Chaucerian narrator; and the notion of a master teller is an extension of the association of individual tale with teller, characteristic of the work of Kittredge and of Donaldson's contemporary, Lumiansky. It was Donaldson's article, however, that canonized the word persona as descriptive of this narrative and critical strategy and associated with that the word irony.

Although Donaldson is generally given credit for the notion of two Chaucers (Chaucer the Man and Chaucer the Pilgrim), Donaldson actually describes three Chaucers: Chaucer the Man (the biographical Chaucer rejected by Donaldson, following Kittredge), Chaucer the Pilgrim (the naive narrator, or what Donaldson implies is Chaucer the persona—Donaldson himself never explicitly identifies them), and a third Chaucer, Chaucer the Poet who transcends both Chaucers: "I think it time that [Chaucer the Pilgrim] was rescued from the comparatively dull record of history and put back into his poem. He is not really Chaucer the poet—nor, for that matter, is either the poet, or the poem's protagonist, that Geoffrey Chaucer frequently mentioned in contemporary historical records as a distinguished civil servant, but never as a poet" (1). Although Donaldson's article bears a strong relation to the comments of Wimsatt and Beardsley, it has earlier roots in Kittredge, one of only four critics cited by Donaldson. According to Kittredge, Chaucer is more sophisticated than the narrator of the *Tales* suggests: "A naif Collector of Customs would be a paradoxical monster" (quoted by Donaldson, "Chaucer the Pilgrim," 2). Donaldson agrees, but he revives the naive Chaucer ridiculed by Kittredge. This naive Chaucer is no longer a historical being (a Collector of Customs) but a fictional one—Chaucer the Pilgrim.

Grammatically and logically, Donaldson's three Chaucers ought to exist in a hierarchy: Chaucer the Man writes in the guise (or persona) of Chaucer the Poet who writes in the guise (or persona) of Chaucer the Pilgrim.[21] Donaldson denies this particular hierarchy, however. His understanding of "poet" is a romantic one. Chaucer the Poet is a synthesis of the two unauthoritative Chaucers (the Man and the Pilgrim) who transcends what is mortal and human within them: "The third entity, Chaucer the poet, operates in a realm which is above and subsumes those in which Chaucer the man and Chaucer the pilgrim have their being" (11).

Donaldson opposes the biographical fallacy, which implies that Chaucer the Man is an authority for the work of Chaucer the Poet. He introduces a poetic-biographical fallacy, however, by attributing to each of his three Chaucers a personality and a psychology. Each has a set of opinions, and each has a biography: "The several Chaucers must have inhabited one body, and in that sense the fictional first person is no fiction at all" (10); "Chaucer the pilgrim may not be said merely to have liked the Prioress very much, he thought she was utterly charming. In the first twenty-odd lines of her portrait (A 118ff.) he employs, among other superlatives, the adverb *ful* seven times" (3). Here, Chaucer the Pilgrim is given credit for speaking and for having an emotional relationship with the Prioress. He is responsible for all the words of the text and for the opinions they imply. Chaucer the Poet, however, is somehow responsible for the fact that those words are Poetry. He is the author of the personality who speaks, and he has authority over this fictional being. Proponents of the intentional fallacy or the biographical fallacy, which Donaldson opposes, assume that Chaucer the Man has authority over the meaning of his own poetic language. Here, that authoritative relation of the man over his work is transformed into an identical relation of authority between Chaucer the Poet and Chaucer the Pilgrim.[22]

The concept of Chaucerian irony is a response to textual statements whose authority is suspect: is the Knight "worthy" as the General Prologue states? is the Prioress "charitable"? is no "bettre felawe" to be found than the Summoner? The critical language of irony acts to recover this authority on a deeper, or higher, level—a level which becomes more remote from the text as critical discourse becomes more elaborate. A Chaucerian poet who transcends his narrator; a Chaucerian critic who transcends both poet and narrator; Chaucerian metacritics who transcend their own tradition.

The word irony has a rich critical history, and we should be careful to distinguish what aspect of that history our use of the word invokes. For example, one critic writes: "Medieval irony . . . involves a recognition of mutability as a dominant feature of earthly life, and failure as the necessary outcome of all man's attempts in and concerning this world"; "we may thus say that at the heart of Chaucer's poetry lies an ironic self-awareness, a sense that his poetry . . . is fulfilled only when it is superseded or gone beyond."[23] When we hear Chaucer described this way, we are confronting a Chaucer in the guise of a romantic poet. Similarly, when we hear an aesthetically dissatisfying tale saved through a virtuosic ironic reading, we are dealing to some extent with a New Critical sense of irony; a Great Poet must write Great Poems—great poems the critic has been sensitive enough to appreciate by invoking irony.[24]

We may want such Chaucers: ambiguous, self-reflective, urbane, transcendent; and a purely medieval Chaucer with his concomitant medieval irony is neither possible nor even desirable. But we can at least confront the impossibility of that medieval Chaucer by understanding some of the more outlandish Chaucers beneath whom we have buried him.

PART FIVE

MODERN

AND POSTMODERN

MYSTIQUE

Cleanth Brooks
and New
Critical Irony

■

By the end of the nineteenth century, the word irony and its cognates had lost both the specificity of the earlier rhetorical definitions and the philosophical potential of early romantic uses of the word. Irony had become associated with wit and humor and the word itself had taken on an evaluative function. Ironic literature was more clever, more complex, and better than non-ironic literature.

During the twentieth century, the meanings of the word continued to be modified in accordance with developing literary genres, critical theory, and the institutions controlling that critical theory. In relation to the lyric, irony has become closely associated with an American New Criticism. And in part as a reaction against New Criticism, there have been attempts to rehistoricize irony by literary critics such as Northrop Frye and cultural critics such as Hayden White. This modern transformation of the relation between irony and history is the subject of the chapters below.

Cleanth Brooks

The contribution of Brooks and New Criticism to the history of irony is substantial. By the thirties, the word irony had become a weakly defined commonplace in literary criticism, and its primary application was to narrative and drama.[1] Brooks applied the word to lyric poetry, strengthened the evaluative force of the word, and attempted to redefine irony not as a vertical hierarchy of statement and meaning but rather as a horizontal tension. Ironic literature was better than other literature (and so had it been for earlier critics such as Kittredge); but it was better in terms of form and structure, not in terms of an implied "Socratic" philosophical stance.

Brooks's program was related both directly and indirectly to pedagogic concerns, and before discussing Brooks's views, it is well to consider the often noted relation of those views to the institutional setting in which they developed.[2] By deemphasizing past historical contexts, Brooks unquestionably emphasized his own. His apparent limitation of what he calls "context" to verbal or thematic context rather than to particular historical contexts dehistoricized lyric poetry and, in so doing, obscured the social basis of those lyrics, for example, the elite society for which a poet such as Donne wrote. Having declared that past society of listeners irrelevant, Brooks then rebuilt it as a society of modern readers. Donne's elect audience became the seemingly more democratic audience of Brooks's own readers and students.[3]

The literary community associated with New Criticism is a familiar one, and variants on it and on its history are easily found. Schlegel explicitly speaks of the establishment of an elite audience, a religion of literature complete with a hierarchy of priest-critics. Much of Schlegel's work was designed for and addressed to elite audiences—the readers of the *Athenaeum* and the much more exclusive audience for his Cologne lectures.[4] An even closer parallel to the institutional history of New Criticism can be seen in Antoine Compagnon's recent study on the influence of Gustav Lanson on French literary studies. The same themes of attempted democratization, emphasis on explication, and the formation of elites through professionalization appear. Lanson's program of literary history and explication of texts was linked to his political program advocating the democratization of education.[5] The result, however, was Lansonism, characterized first by a critical elite, and finally by an academic elite (157); because explication takes place in an institutional setting, such explications themselves must be taught and the ability to produce them evaluated.

As we have seen, the meaning of the word irony has more to do with the literary community it implies than with its lexical definition. The democratic rhetoric associated with American criticism often comes into conflict with its own institutional background. For example, we find irony recently defined as follows: "the power to entertain widely divergent possible interpretations—to provoke the reader into seeing that there is a radical uncertainty surrounding the processes by which meanings get determined in texts and interpreted by readers."[6] This poststructuralist representation of irony is quite similar to the New Critical statement quoted at the beginning of the previous chapter, equating irony with unresolved oppositions.[7] Yet the nature of an academic environment belies such rhetoric. The meanings selected by students and those selected by the professors who grade those students are not equal. Nor are the scholarly works of those professors considered equal when subjected to the peer review process adopted by most presses, journals, and departments. The history of such literary communities parallels that of the critical language associated with them. And irony can never be fully democratized, even in New Critical hands.

Let us return to Brooks's *Well-Wrought Urn* and finally to a passage with which I began this study. The opening strategy is familiar; Brooks distinguishes ordinary, inauthentic irony from a newly defined genuine irony. According to Brooks, there are two types of wit—the wit of the soul (true wit) and the wit of the intellect (a lower form). There are also two types of readers—genuine readers, and those (earlier critics?) who are trapped in illegitimate neoclassical assumptions. There are also, by implication, readers such as Brooks, who transcend these categories. True readers of poetry long for the language of the soul, but do not realize that the true language of the soul is expressed in precisely those categories associated with mere intellect: "Few of us are prepared to accept the statement that the language of poetry is the language of paradox. Paradox is the language of sophistry, hard, bright, witty; it is hardly the language of the soul" (3). Brooks forces us here to assume a romantic posture: because we have a romantic view of the relation of poetry to expression, we are disinclined to believe that paradox is essential to poetry. Brooks then reintroduces the "hard, bright, witty" assumptions we might associate with a neoclassical theory of poetry; since we have assumed a romantic posture, we reinterpret these paradoxes in a romantic fashion.

The key word for Brooks is irony—a word that he uses in full consciousness of its expanded nineteenth-century meanings, even when he attempts to dismiss that history as irrelevant. Brooks thus lends theoretical legitimacy to what could be otherwise described as the normal (and in certain cases opportunistic) slippage in the meaning of a critical concept. Donne shows "ironical tenderness" (17); the "character of paradox" has "twin concomitants of irony and wonder" (17); "ironical devices" are "rich" and "intricate" (111). And most important, our recognition of irony distinguishes us from our critical predecessors:

> If the structure of poetry is a structure of the order described, that fact may explain (if not justify) the frequency with which I have had to have recourse, in the foregoing chapters, to terms like "irony" and "paradox." By using the term irony, one risks, of course, making the poem seem arch and self-conscious, since irony, for most readers of poetry, is associated with satire, *vers de société,* and other "intellectual" poetries. Yet, the necessity for some such term ought to be apparent; and irony is the most general term that we have for the kind of qualification which the various elements in a context receive from the

context. This kind of qualification, as we have seen, is of tremendous importance in any poem. Moreover, irony is our most general term for indicating that recognition of incongruities—which, again, pervades all poetry to a degree far beyond what our conventional criticism has been heretofore willing to allow. (209–10)

Brooks's treatment of terms such as "self-conscious" is of particular note: this quality (a positive one for romantics) is viewed as potentially negative. So too is the notion of an elite audience and its taste for mere *vers de société*. So too is a certain kind of intellectualism so suspect that it must be given inverted commas. Brooks then rejects (or seems to reject) all the notions associated with these hierarchies. This gesture, if carried through, would indeed lead to what I have called the egalitarian theory of irony, which occasionally finds expression in late New Criticism of the sixties and seventies and more recently in the notion of the smorgasbord of meanings a text offers to the critic.

But such an expansion of Brooks's theory is also its falsification. Brooks will not dispense with the terms he seems to reject: ". . . the necessity for some such term ought to be apparent." In other words, the situation in which Brooks discusses literature requires the very terms he seems to reject. Brooks appeals to his readers to purify their conceptions of irony and of literary society but insists that they retain the suspect terms. History cannot be purged of its traditional associations. The notion of an elite audience evoked here by Brooks is present throughout New Critical discussions of literature.[8]

If irony were simply Brooks's word for what is interesting in poetry, there could be no objection—no objection, as long as we accept the premise that the rhetorical meanings of the word (which Brooks dismisses as characteristic of "intellectual" poetries) can be excluded from later, more general meanings of the word, and as long as what interests Brooks interests us. But in reading poems, Brooks rewrites them. A poem in Brooks's hands acquires a new content, one presumably freed of (past) historical associations and interpretive constraints. This new content, based on Brooks's own sensitivity, is called irony. It has its origins in the sensitivity of the critic, a sensitivity that is projected onto the text of the poem. The New Critics' emphasis on the text is equally an emphasis on their own reading of that text. Irony, in the passage from *The Well-Wrought Urn* quoted above, is defined not as the textual incongruities of a poem; such a definition would center the value (irony) of a poem in the text. Rather "irony is . . . that recognition of incongruities"—in other words, the irony of a poem and consequently its value is in the critic, not, as New Critical theory claims, in the text itself.

A similar strategy is used by Brooks in an article cited in nearly all histories of irony, "Irony as a Principle of Structure" (1951), which was expanded from an article published in *College English* in 1948.[9] Here, his ambivalence toward the term irony is stated directly. Brooks establishes a hierarchy of poetic concerns: the first, mentioned in the opening sentence, is metaphor—"One can sum up modern poetic technique by calling it the rediscovery of metaphor and the full commitment to metaphor" (729). This leads to a concern with what Brooks calls "particulars"—a poem is comparable to the "tail wagging the dog," or the "tail flying the kite"—and to the assertion of the necessity of an organic relation between the particulars in a poem. Only then does Brooks introduce the term irony. "The memorable verses in poetry . . . show on inspection that they derive their poetic quality from their relation to a particular context. . . . Now the *obvious* warping of a statement by the context we characterize as 'ironical'" (730). And the most obvious form of such irony is called "sarcasm." We should note that Brooks's use of the word ironical here shows again that he is not simply concerned with the text. The context by which we recognize irony or sarcasm is extratextual—it is the speaker's "tone of voice" (730).

This is close to Brooks's statement in *The Well-Wrought Urn:* irony involves incongruities of meaning and the recognition of those incongruities. But Brooks continues to qualify the notion of irony:

> As one who has certainly tended to overuse the term *irony* and perhaps, on occasion, has abused the term, I am closely concerned here. But I want to make quite clear what that concern is: it is not to justify the term *irony* as such, but rather to indicate why modern critics are so often tempted to use it. We have doubtless stretched the term too much, but it has been almost the only term available by which to point to a general and important aspect of poetry. (732)

Brooks handles the term in a manner that some might describe as ironic in itself: the term appears in inverted commas, or it is underlined and treated with an apparently critical self-consciousness.

Brooks lists various types of irony (what he calls "modes"), "tragic irony, self-irony, playful, arch, mocking, or gentle irony, etc." (731); but the key distinction is a binary one and an evaluative one, similar to that often seen in romantic criticism. Brooks gives an example from "Dover Beach" and then applies what he calls "Eliot's test": "We are forced to raise the question as to whether the statement grows properly out of a context; whether it acknowledges the pressures of the context; whether it is 'ironical'—or merely callow, glib, and sentimental" (732). Irony, thus, is an evaluative term. But Brooks retracts this almost immediately. There is a poetry that transcends irony, I. A. Richards's poetry of synthesis, "which does not leave out what is apparently hostile to its dominant tone, and which, because it is able to fuse the irrelevant and discordant, has come to terms with itself and is *invulnerable to irony*. Irony, then, in this further sense, is not only an acknowledgment of the pressures of a context. Invulnerability to irony is the stability of a context in which the internal pressures balance and support each other" (732–33; emphasis added).[10]

What are we to make of this? Irony is on the one hand that which takes poetry beyond the "merely callow, glib, or sentimental," but on the other hand it is a danger to which certain great poetry makes itself invulnerable. Such stability is similar to that which characterizes the only statements that Brooks says have no ironical potential—mathematical ones ("two plus two equals four").[11]

Brooks's attitude remains ambivalent throughout his readings. Following an analysis of "A Slumber did my Spirit Seal," in which he points out various "ironical contrasts," Brooks asks: "Ought we, then, to apply the term *ironical* to Wordsworth's poem? Not necessarily. I am trying to account for my temptation to call such a poem ironical—not to justify my yielding to the temptation—least of all to insist that others so transgress" (737).[12] Irony, therefore, is a temptation; and the entire question of irony is recentered. Irony is no longer a poetic technique; it is rather a critical problem.

Despite his ahistorical approach, Brooks incorporates certain historicized views of irony, for example that irony is a late form. On the one hand, irony is a universal: "Irony, taken as the acknowledgment of the pressures of context, is to be found in poetry of every period and even in simple lyrical poetry" (738). On the other hand, modern poetry is especially ironic. And why? Because of a "breakdown of a common symbolism," "the general skepticism as to universals," "the depletion and corruption of the very language itself" (738). Irony is the symptom of some evil. And the critics who invoke irony may be part of this: "Those critics who attribute the use of ironic techniques to the poet's own bloodless sophistication and tired skepticism would be better advised to refer these vices to his potential readers, a public corrupted by Hollywood and the Book of the Month Club. For the modern poet is not addressing simple primitives but a public sophisticated by commercial art" (738). Irony is thus both a symptom of the disease of modernity and belatedness and the means of curing that disease. Readers can transcend a godless age by reinventing their readings as prayers, their texts as scripture. This new religion is one of self-reflection and introspection:

> At his best, Jarrell manages to bring us, by an act of imagination, to the most penetrating insight. Participating in that insight, we doubtless become better citizens. (One of the "uses" of poetry, I should agree, is to make us better citizens.) But poetry is not the eloquent rendition of the citizen's creed. It is not even the accurate rendition of his creed. Poetry must carry us beyond the abstract creed into the very matrix out of which, and from which, our creeds are abstracted. That is what "The Eighth Air Force" does. That is what, I am convinced, all good poetry does. (740)

What good poetry must do is to transform the reader-critic into a self-conscious reader. It must define that reader in a manner reminiscent of Friedrich Schlegel's characterization of the poet. We become better citizens through the self-conscious contemplation of our creeds. And this is where both the irony of the poem and the irony of the critic (Brooks's own discussion of irony) lead us.[13]

Irony as Impurity

The theory of New Criticism is in part an institutional attempt to free literature from dependence on other disciplines. The theory of the autonomy of literature is from an academic standpoint an appeal for the autonomy of literature departments in the face of competition from other departments—sociology, psychology, history. But Brooks's arguments never rule these disciplines out of court, any more than the academy could do away with the corresponding departments, and the truism concerning the New Critical emphasis on the autonomy of the text has often been exposed as inaccurate.[14] The very definition of the word irony as "pressures of context" precludes an absolute autonomy of text (or poem) as object; one of the first examples of context given by Brooks in "Irony as a Principle of Structure" is "tone of voice" (730)—the same extratextual matter that in classical rhetoric distinguishes two materially identical written texts.[15] The New Critical strategy whereby such extratextual matters are kept in play can be seen in a nearly contemporary article by Robert Penn Warren entitled "Pure and Impure Poetry."[16] Warren makes a distinction between poetry and the poem, a distinction the Chicago critic R. S. Crane, in a harsh review, claims is missing in Brooks.[17] But Warren, unlike Crane, privileges the poem and its irony over poetry. Explication, by implication, is a higher art than poetics. To Warren, a poem is essentially its own referential impurities. Irony is one of the impurities characteristic of all poems; but irony is excluded from such abstract notions as poetry: "Poetry wants to be pure, but poems do not. . . . [Poems] mar themselves with cacophonies, jagged rhythms, ugly words and ugly thoughts, colloquialisms, clichés, sterile technical terms, head work and argument, self-contradictions, clevernesses, irony, realism— all things which call us back to the world of prose and imperfection" (367). What I am forced to call Warren's own irony is apparent. On the one hand, Warren opposes the notion that poetry is essentially ironic, or that irony is the essence of literariness. On the other hand, he reintroduces the implications of such a claim by discrediting abstract theoretical views of poetry. Warren, like Brooks, situates his theoretical argument in practical readings—readings that are the basis for a theory rather than an applica- tion of it. Warren then usurps for this practical notion of the poem all the (evaluative) claims that could be applied to poetry, drawing (figura- tively?) on the association already seen in Schlegel's *Ideen* between poetry and religion: "The saint proves his vision by stepping cheerfully into the fires. The poet, somewhat less spectacularly, proves his vision by submitting it to the fires of irony—to the drama of his structure—in the hope that the fires will refine it. In other words, the poet wishes to indicate that his vision has been earned, that it can survive reference to the complexities and contradictions of experience. And irony is one such device of reference" (377–78).[18] Warren never makes a theoretical claim for irony—there is no need to do so. For theory itself has been reduced to a shadowy abstraction, a poetics without poems. Irony becomes a defining quality of (good) poems through its presumably antipoetic referential qualities.

Any literary work involves a context, part of which is its own reading; and the proper reading of poetry leads us back to our roles as critics. What New Criticism in the hands of a Brooks or a Warren does is to transform the romantic poet into a modern critic—and here, given Crane's attack on New Criticism, it is useful to distinguish the critic from the theorist. It is the good citizenship of the readers about which Brooks is concerned—not that of the poet, nor that of the text.

Old meanings of irony continue to be revived and deployed by Brooks and other New Critics. On the one hand, irony enjoys a privileged status— it is the general word for what is important in poetry. On the other hand, its status is arbitrary—other words would do as well; irony is a word chosen to refer to a phenomenon that is beyond words (to Brooks) or that is essentially a referential problem (Warren).

The word irony, in its history as a critical term, expresses the critic's

relation to literary material. The critic stands above literature as an inter-
preter and enjoys a certain detachment—but a knowing detachment, in
much the same way a spectator enjoys a superiority over a drama in terms
of dramatic irony. Because of the mere literariness of the materials, this
relation is ironic in both a positive sense (referring solely to the viewer) and
a negative sense (what is the intrinsic value of the merely literary?). Irony
is a term that can express all these conflicting relations of the critic to a
literary text.

In Brooks, even the oldest meanings of the word find their place: *eirōn* in
Aristophanes was clearly a term of reproach, and even in the texts of Plato
it is by no means complimentary. To Brooks, such ironies are sophistical,
and his own catalog of the merely ironic is essentially a description of the
sophists and their tastes for what is clever and paradoxical. The ordinary
spectator, according to Brooks, is inclined to interpret irony in this way,
that is, as a form of sophistry. This spectator (or reader) misses the referential value of irony, which concerns the expert reader (the critic) and the
relation of that reader to other readers. A history of irony could also be
written in accordance with this theme: this history of irony reveals more
than merely the diminution of reproach. The Aristophanic *eirōn* finds a
counterpart in those "poor subjects" Hegel says cannot share the heights
of the romantic ironist, and finally in those ordinary readers or insensitive
critics who still believe irony is deception and neither recognize nor share
the higher egalitarianism proclaimed above them.

The Rehistoricization of New Criticism and Irony

Everywhere in Brooks's writing is revealed the attempt to purge criticism of
dogmatism. Universals are subordinated to particulars; definitions of guid-
ing principles are qualified; terminology is transformed and in certain cases
ignored. Brooks's key article on irony places the word itself in a tertiary
role. It is a statement of the twentieth-century purposes of explication, the
democratization that Compagnon has shown was sought by French critics
such as Lanson.

But democratization is impossible in an academic environment that is in
its very structure undemocratic and authoritarian.[19] And in that context, it is
impossible to remove the authoritarian connotations of the word irony and
the authoritarian interpretative hierarchies the corresponding phenomenon
(however defined) implies. In criticism, we can see this redogmatization of
irony occurring within a few years of Brooks's statements, made in the late
forties. Irony for Brooks was a historical phenomenon only insofar as its

readers were living in history; the history involved in irony is seen as the ethical history of readers. After Brooks, irony is rehistoricized, for example by Northrop Frye, whose history seems both a reaction to New Criticism and a product of many of its assumptions. Familiar clichés are retained: irony is a late phenomenon in history, a modern phenomenon, a decadent phenomenon. But irony itself is placed on a higher level of abstraction—the level of literature rather than the level of particular literary works, precisely the level disparaged by Warren.

To Frye, irony is a historical phase, but a phase itself useful only as a heuristic or educational device; irony is a phase of history not because of historical events but rather because we need a context through which to make literary works intelligible to our students. History thus seems to creep back into literary criticism; but history was never completely absent. For New Criticism was locked in its own institutional history—a history it could not escape, and a history it continued to exploit.

Brooks's work and his strategies represent the final movement I am describing in this study—the transferring of the authority characteristic of irony from the text to the poet to the critic reading that poet. The history of irony, in this reading, runs parallel to the history of the critical institution in which it is defined. In what I have called rhetorical irony, the authority lies in the text and in its presentation: the text has two meanings, one a literal meaning, the other a higher meaning. In what I have called romantic irony, that authority is transferred to the author: the final meaning of the text is not articulable; it "hovers" over the text in the form of the sensitivity of the poet and it is the task of the reader to join the poet on this elevated plane. In New Critical irony, the notion of romantic irony is extended: poets are reduced to their texts and become metonymies for their texts, and it is the sensitive critic who becomes the authority for poetic meaning.[20]

The presumed opponents to New Criticism I study in the following chapter do not alter this history. Frye and, following his lead, Hayden White simply broaden the implications of Brooks's argument by associating late historical phases (whether in literature, history, or historiography) with the word irony. For both critics and metacritics, this is a convenient myth of origins, disguising as historical inevitability the stance of superiority they have attempted to seize. The assumption that history has an end-phase in such ironic stances is a congenial one for those whose accidental position in history and in academic institutions permits them to write of such things.

Viconian Ironies

∎

In *Scienza Nuova,* Vico characterizes *ironia* as one of the primary tropes, "tutti i primi tropi" (sec. 404), to which all others can be reduced (sec. 409). The other three are metonymy, synecdoche, and metaphor, which is "la più luminosa e, perché più luminosa, più necessaria e più spessa" (sec. 404) ["the most luminous and, because most luminous, most necessary and most frequent"]. The same four primary tropes are named in his *Institutiones oratoriae:*

> Tropi sunt qui vocem a propria ac nativa significatione ad impropriam et alienam deflectunt. . . . Invertitur autem significatio quadrupliciter, vel a toto ad partem, et contra, vel a causis ad effecta, et vicissim, vel a similibus, vel ab oppositis. Hinc quatuor primarii tropi, synecdoche, metonymia, metaphora, et ironia, ad quos caeteri omnes revocantur. (101)[1]
> [Tropes are defined as turning an expression from its proper and native signification to an improper and alien signification. . . . Signification is changed in four ways: either from the whole to the part and vice versa, or from the causes to effects, and vice versa, or from like things, or from opposites. Hence we have the four primary tropes: synecdoche, metonymy, metaphor, and irony, to which all the others are reduced.]

The full discussion of irony, in a later section of *Scienza Nuova,* is as follows:

> L'ironia certamente non poté cominciare che da' tempi della riflessione, perch'ella è formata dal falso in forza d'una reflessione che prende maschera di verità. E qui esce un gran principio di cose umane, che conferma l'origine della poesia qui scoverta: che i primi uomini della gentilità essendo stati semplicissimi quanto i fanciulli, i quali per natura son veritieri, le prime favole non poterono fingere nulla di

falso; per lo dovettero necessariamente essere, quali sopra ci vennero diffinite, vere narrazioni. (Sec. 408)
[Irony certainly could not begin except in a time of reflection, since it is formed of a falsehood by means of a reflection which takes the mask of truth. And here arises a great principle of human affairs, which confirms the origin of poetry revealed here: since the first men of the pagan world were simple like children (who are by nature truthful), the first fables could fabricate nothing false; so they must necessarily have been true narrations, as they were defined for us above.]

I quote these passages in full because I wish to present all that Vico has to say about irony in his published writings. The questions I will consider in the following pages are several. To what extent can statements such as Vico's be used to legitimize postromantic theories of irony? And what are the implications of universalizing the developments in the literary uses of the word irony (in particular, those I have outlined in the preceding chapter)?

In *Scienza Nuova,* Vico organizes knowledge and history under three movements, phases, or ages: the age of gods, the age of heroes, and the age of men (sec. 31). To these three ages correspond three languages: a language of mute signs and gestures; a language of heroic emblems, images, and metaphors; and, lastly, conventional human language. These Vico further explains as hieroglyphic, symbolic, and epistolary or vulgar (secs. 31 and 173). Further triads, not specifically related to these, are introduced later, for example the three customs common to all cultures: religion, marriages, burial (sec. 333). The triadic form in this particular case is arbitrary, and Vico does not suggest that such a triad can be mapped onto the historical movements.

Recent readers of Vico, in particular Hayden White, have attempted to correlate the fourfold division of tropes discussed in sections 404 through 409 with the threefold division of ages and its variants. Whereas Vico himself privileges metaphor as the master trope in section 404, these twentieth-century readers of Vico privilege irony. Irony is the endpoint of culture and the reflective mode in which modern science and history must be written.

White's explication of *Scienza Nuova,* section 408, makes some significant additions:

It was only after the recognition of disparities between these figurative representations of reality and the objects they were meant literally to characterize that the fourth major trope, irony, became possible.

Irony, Vico says, "is fashioned of falsehood by dint of a reflection which wears the mask of truth." Irony represents a stage in the evolution of consciousness in which language itself has become an object of reflection, *and the sensed inadequacy of language to the full representation of its object has become perceived as a problem.* Ironic speech presupposed an awareness of the possibility of feigning or of lying or dissimulating. Thus, Vico says, "Irony certainly could not have begun until the period of reflection," for "since the first men of the gentile world had the simplicity of children, who were truthful by nature, the first fables could not feign anything false" (sec. 408). That is to say, the fables of primitive man were taken to represent the true report of reality. (*Tropics of Discourse,* 207; emphasis added)[2]

Vico's point is only that poetry, in particular early poetry, is true. The truth of early poetry is contrasted by Vico with the lies and dissembling characteristic of a later period, the age of reflection. White's expansion, emphasized above, is an interpretation of irony, not of Vico, in late twentieth-century terms. And it is one that owes its formulation to White's own introductory chapter in *Metahistory:*

> It can be seen immediately that Irony is in one sense metatropological, for it is deployed in the self-conscious awareness of the possible misuse of figurative language. Irony presupposes the occupation of a "realistic" perspective on reality, from which a nonfigurative representation of the world of experience might be provided. Irony thus represents a stage of consciousness in which the problematical nature of language itself has become recognized. . . . In Irony, figurative language folds back upon itself and brings its own potentialities for distorting perception under question. . . . The trope of Irony, then, provides a linguistic paradigm of a mode of thought which is radically self-critical. (*Metahistory,* 37)[3]

Vico's scheme is also provided with a classical lineage: "Vico argues that all figures of speech may be reduced to four modes or tropes: metaphor, synecdoche, metonymy, and irony (secs. 404–9). This contention follows Aristotle but with this difference: Vico restricts the meaning of the mental operation indicated by each trope" (*Tropics of Discourse,* 204). Vico scholars, including White himself, have traced the fourfold division of tropes back to Ramus.[4] But Aristotle, as far as I know, has no comparable fourfold division of tropes. White is clearly inspired here by Kenneth Burke's brief essay "Four Master Tropes," and may well be thinking of Aristotle's fourfold explanation of metaphor in *Poetics* (1475b).[5]

In *Metahistory,* White pushes this scheme further: it is first of all a means of categorizing nineteenth-century historians. Secondly, it is the historical movement in which those historians themselves wrote. In other words, White's literary-critical categories are assumed to correspond to actual as well as written history.

On the face of it, this is a bold and aggressively ahistorical means of considering both history and historians—one that reflects its own origins in mid-twentieth-century American literary theory. But White depends on Vico for methodological support, particularly on Vico's notion, from *Scienza Nuova,* that poetic truth and metaphysical truth are the same, and that when physical truth is opposed to these, it must be regarded as false (sec. 205; *Tropics of Discourse,* 198). Applied to White's own work, or to its literary-critical background, this means that when critical statements conflict with the statements of an object text, the critical statements are true; for a historian, it means that when the facts of history oppose the historian's representation of them, the historian is correct. Such assumptions are common in recent literary criticism (the work of Harold Bloom is only one example). And White's application of them is not invalidated only because they so strongly oppose the assumptions of the nineteenth-century historians he studies.

It is reasonable to claim that when we read Ranke, Michelet, and Burckhardt, the history they wrote about is less important than the historiographical and literary context in which they lived, although there seems to me to be a logical problem in assuming that the dominant mode for Michelet, who lived through much of the history he describes, is metaphoric rather than reflective (White's "ironic" mode).[6] What seems to be less reasonable is the apparent corollary: that as a discipline, history should be transformed into a stylistics. The privileging of the term irony is a product of its Viconian definition as reflection—history-writing transforms itself into its proper subject matter.

To literary historians, White's tactics are familiar; they are perhaps less so to historians. He attempts to find an organizing scheme for a body of texts. Once these texts are defined as literary, a number of traditional formulas present themselves: "ancient vs. modern," "modern vs. postmodern," "classical vs. romantic," and many structuralist variants. Literary historians who utilize such categories generally do not confuse their schemata with the (literary) reality they describe—the schemata are heuristic or simply convenient. White differs from traditional literary historians (although less so from some contemporary ones) in claiming that there is no difference.[7]

White's attempt to map the four master tropes onto Vico's threefold history leads to some peculiar results. A most telling case is the chart that appears on page 209 of *Tropics of Discourse*. Here, White correlates the four master tropes with three stages (religious, heroic, and human), three types of human nature (poetic, and again heroic, and human), three "sub-phases" (birth and growth, maturity, decadence and dissolution). To the three historical stages that serve as headings, White adds a fourth stage: re-prise. There are thus four matching columns headed: "Religious," "Heroic," "Human," "Reprise." But beneath those four headings there is a blurring between columns three and four. Under the third column ("Human") and the fourth column ("Reprise"), listed as single entries, are "synecdoche to irony" and "decadence and dissolution" (although these items each contain two nouns, they are defined as a single movement). Below that, the two columns "Human" and "Reprise" are again distinguished pictorially. But the apparent pictorial reality of the fourth column is the result of typographical sleight of hand. The only items listed under the fourth column are the sec-tion numbers for the preceding triads; reading across for the heading "Type of human society" we have the four entries "poetic," "heroic," "human," and "secs. 916–18." White's fourth column is purely visual, and contains only the references for the first three.

This final phase, which is in part fictitious, is highly privileged. Irony is a self-reflective mode, the only critical mode, and thus the mode in which White himself, and other writers in Vico's fourth phase, must write. By writing within this trope, they write outside all tropes, since irony is defined by White (although not to my knowledge in Vico) as "metatropological" (*Metahistory*, xii, 37).

This is not, according to White, an arbitrary critical stance, since self-privileging positions of critical stances are themselves legitimate. History has a spiritual deep structure identical to the deep structure that gives rise to the tropes and, presumably, to the belated (but valid) discourse of fourth-phase historians (*Tropics of Discourse*, 197ff.). In White's introduction to *Tropics of Discourse*, focused largely on Piaget, he comments on his earlier work as follows:

> I have shown in *Metahistory*, and in a number of the essays contained in this book, how specific analysts of processes of consciousness seem to project the fourfold pattern of tropes onto them, in order to emplot them, and to chart the growth from what might be called naive (or metaphorical) apprehensions of reality to self-reflective (ironic) com-prehensions of it. This pattern of emplotment is analyzed, I think, as the "logic" of *poiesis* by Vico and Nietzsche and as the logic of *noesis* by Hegel and Marx. (*Tropics of Discourse*, 12)[8]

The romantic origins of this handling of Vico are obvious and acknowl-
edged frequently, if somewhat indirectly, by White himself. But a more
important inspiration for White is American literary-critical theory of the
fifties. White notes in *Metahistory* (3 n. 4) that he has "depended heavily on
two literary theorists whose works represent virtual philosophical systems,"
Frye and Burke. White also refers to Frye in a nearly contemporary essay
reprinted in *Tropics of Discourse:* "By an extension of Frye's ideas, it can be
argued that interpretation in history consists of the provisions of a plot
structure for a sequence of events so that their nature as a comprehensible
process is revealed by their figuration as a *story of a particular kind*" (58).[9]
White revises history as literature, that is to say, literature as understood
by American literary critics of the 1950s.

For his notion of a fourth mode, White owes much to New Criticism,
although I find no citation to particular New Critics such as Brooks. Here
he is discussing Burke's four master tropes: "Burke has suggested that irony
is inherently *dialectical*. . . . I am not sure this is the case. To be sure, irony
sanctions the ambiguous, and possibly even the ambivalent, statement. It
is a kind of metaphor, but one that surreptitiously signals a denial of the
assertion of similitude or difference contained in the literal sense of the
proposition, or at least sets a crucial qualification on it" (*Tropics of Discourse,*
73). White follows this with a citation to Vico. Yet nowhere in the passages
of Vico or Burke referred to will one find irony described as a "kind" of
metaphor: Vico's symmetry places it in opposition to metaphor (it makes
comparisons through opposites rather than similarities). White's statement,
with the words "ambiguity," "ambivalence," is, however, very much in the
tradition of American New Criticism, as is his final assertion that irony is
a means of setting a "crucial qualification." Despite the slight Derridean
interference, this is precisely what Brooks stated some twenty years earlier.

It is not my purpose here to critique in detail White's analysis of the
particular historians in *Metahistory.* A single example of his technique will
suffice:

> For example, in Michelet the idiographic form of explanation is
> coupled with the plot structure of the Romance; in Ranke the organi-
> cist explanation is coupled with the Comic plot structure; in Tocque-
> ville the mechanistic mode of explanation is used to complement and
> illuminate an essentially Tragic conception of the historical process;
> and in Burckhardt a contextualist explanatory mode appears in con-
> junction with a narrative form that is essentially satirical. (*Tropics of
> Discourse,* 66)

No one would deny the virtuosity of such a reading. Yet neither here nor in *Metahistory* are such readings held up for scrutiny against extensive citation of the texts they are supposed to explain. White's methods and the abstract readings that result may well appeal to literary specialists, who will have seen many similar statements in the past applied to any number of literary texts. Here, a historian legitimizes as history the explicative skills in which American literary scholars have been institutionally trained. If we accept White, those skills that could be criticized as mere cleverness and verbal sophistry are redefined, first as "historical" and second, through the romantic and New Critical associations of the word irony, as "critical." History-makers, historians, and historiographers are simply poets awaiting their belated reviews. White reduces history to literature. And literature understood by his American readers of the seventies was a literature already thoroughly "read" by New Criticism.

Northrop Frye

White's theories come directly from Frye's *Anatomy of Criticism* (1957), as White acknowledges.[10] Frye's stated aim is to suggest "the possibility of a synoptic view of the scope, theory, principles, and techniques of literary criticism" (3), a "comprehensive view of what [literary criticism] is actually doing" (12). Contemporary criticism has not distinguished "criticism as a body of knowledge" (Frye's subject) from "the direct experience of literature, where every act is unique, and classification has no place" (29). By defining criticism as a science (a "body of knowledge"), Frye will have provided a tool with which readers and students can collectively organize their diverse and unique literary experiences. The tone, if not the result, appears anti-romantic; and Frye is critical of the tradition in criticism from Schlegel to the New Critics that sees literary study as a religion: "What critics now have is a mystery-religion without a gospel, and they are initiates who can communicate, or quarrel, only with one another" (14).[11] A "genuine poetics" is to Frye a "theory of criticism whose principles apply to the whole of literature and account for every valid type of critical procedure" (14):

> I suggest that it is time for criticism to leap to a new ground from which it can discover what the organizing or containing forms of its conceptual framework are. Criticism seems to be badly in need of a coordinating principle, a central hypothesis which, like the theory of evolution in biology, will see the phenomena it deals with as parts of a whole.

> The first postulate of this inductive leap is the same as that of any
> science: the assumption of total coherence. (16)

I have already discussed the general problems of a similar assumption of
total coherence in relation to romantic irony, and I will be returning to it
again. But what warrant do Frye's theories provide for notions that irony
can be regarded as a historical phase?

The notion that irony itself is a phase of history has its roots in the notion
of world-irony. Metaphoric uses of similar phrases can be traced as far as
Pascal and are also found in Nietzsche and in Hegel, although Hegel himself
does not, as far as I can determine, ever articulate the notion that irony
can be a historical principle or an outlook governing a historical period.[12]
Frye's use of the word irony as a historical (or literary) phase is a strict
temporalization of what in Hegel is a casual phrase.

Irony is a component of Frye's principal "organizing or containing forms,"
and this irony cannot be strictly characterized as a principle, a concept,
or a word. Frye's apparently simple and clear terminology is quite fluid.
And the total coherence he offers, albeit based on a few simple and readily
intelligible forms, becomes extremely complex. Frye has many definitions
of irony. It is the last of the five modes and, with satire, constitutes the
last of four (seasonal) mythoi.[13] In addition, it is one of six phases through
which each of the four archetypal narratives must move (comic, romantic, tragic, and ironic).[14] The ironic phase is the first phase of the seasonal
myth of comedy (177) and the first phase of the seasonal myth of irony
and satire (226); in tragedy and romance (the other two seasonal mythoi),
it is, I believe, the fifth.[15] In addition, the opposition between *eirōn* and *alazōn* figures prominently in Frye, providing an additional complexity to the
understanding of the ironic (172–74).

Irony can be related to hierarchies of authors, subjects, and readers. The
five modes are based on the relation of the hero to ordinary men (33–34):
(1) myth (if hero is superior in kind to other men), (2) romance (if superior
in degree to other men), (3) high mimetic (if superior in degree to other
men but not to environment), (4) low mimetic (if superior to neither),
(5) ironic (if inferior in power or intelligence to ourselves). The ironic mode
is thus one in which we, as spectators, are superior to the hero; Frye seems
to be drawing on those twentieth-century notions of dramatic irony I have
discussed in chapter 8.

And as irony defines the relation of the critic-spectator to the hero, so
does it locate that relation in time. Modern viewers are privileged over
ancient viewers, insofar as we are now in an ironic phase of literature; Frye

refers to this as a "fact" (46). As a type of literature, irony can be understood as partaking of a movement in the cycle of literature through three
"organizations of myths and archetypal symbols in literature." These are
defined as (1) undisplaced myth (metaphorical—apocalyptic and demonic),
(2) romantic, (3) "the tendency toward 'realism'" (139–40): "Ironic literature begins with realism and tends toward myth, its mythical patterns being
as a rule more suggestive of the demonic than of the apocalyptic, though
sometimes it simply continues the romantic tradition of stylization" (140).
Even as a type of literature, irony is set within time, and the examples listed
in the same paragraph are, from the standpoint of world literature, quite
modern: Hawthorne, Poe, Conrad, Hardy, Virginia Woolf.

Frye's assumption of total coherence in his subject matter does not lead
to a similar coherence in his own discussion. Irony is a phase, a mode, a
mythos. The word permits easy shifting between these; even a seemingly
specific phrase such as "ironic phase" has multiple definitions. It would be
extremely difficult to apply Frye's total system directly. Nonetheless, parts
of it are easily cannibalized, as White's use of Frye's notion of irony shows.
As a temporal mode, Frye's irony is an endpoint—one that will lead to the
renewal of a cycle. The relation of this to Vico's scheme of history is now
easily seen: irony leads to its opposite myth. But such equations seem to me
to involve serious reductions of both Frye and Vico.

What lends Frye's discussion its power is the ability of his often conflicting schemata to organize an extremely wide range of material, and to leave
implicit the value judgments he characterizes as those "odious comparisons of greatness" (27). Frye selects a canonical body of texts and creates
a language to describe them. This language provides a number of linguistic
bridges—a mode can become a phase can become a myth. As literary history, Frye's schemata are a way of transforming the diachronies of earlier
literary history into flexible structural synchronies.

The most important point for our purposes is Frye's privileging of irony.
Whether a mode or a phase, irony is no longer a rhetorical term, nor even
a philosophical one connected to Socrates. As a mode, it is situated tem-
porally as the endpoint out of which renewal springs. As a phase (at least
in one of the senses of "phase") it is our phase (46)—the time in which
we receive literature, the phase (or period) in which both Frye and his
successors define themselves. Irony is refashioned in the image of the critic-
historian as critical self-reflection. And with this image, the romantic and
New Critical assumptions suppressed elsewhere in Frye reemerge.

Frye constructs a history and a generic system in part as a reaction
against the New Critical notion of literary history as a series of disconnected

texts and their associated readings. Instead of virtuosic readings of individual texts, Frye provides an equally virtuosic reading of literary history. What emerges from Frye is an idealized history rather than a traditional history—a history first read by the critic as a text, then redefined as the historical (archetypal) basis for all texts; a history two steps removed from a traditional history of literary, political, or cultural events.

To transfer Frye's theories to fields other than literary study is to universalize their particular historical foundations. Within Frye's theory can be found the diverse elements of its contemporary literary history: Aristotelianism, neo-Aristotelianism, New Criticism, romanticism, mythological criticism. As literary theory, it contains an implied history of literary history; as historical theory, it does not contain a similar history of historiography. Frye's assumption of total coherence addresses the special needs of literary scholars within educational institutions, and I assume those needs are different from the needs of historians.

Both Frye and White rely on the rhetorical tradition. Frye metaphorizes rhetorical terms as historical genres. White remetaphorizes these terms and these historical genres as history, thus returning to history a critical language stripped of its own history. White's version of history is historical only insofar as it exists within the history it purports to describe, although it does not exist in that history in the way it claims. White accepts the self-images of cultural criticism, and such self-definitions have their own history, in this case one extending from Friedrich Schlegel to American New Criticism. But these New Critical sources are concealed in White's own recourse to pre–New Critical and post–New Critical texts.[16]

Coda: On the Ironic Mode in Contemporary Criticism with Specific Reference to Roland Barthes

But what if the Viconians are right?

The following pages are intended to suggest why I do not believe that question is worth pursuing, and to explain the skepticism I have toward any claim that there exists a specifically ironic mode in recent criticism or that recent criticism can be usefully described in this way. Such a statement might come as a surprise; isn't that the direction in which this very study tends? And what of Barthes? What of Derrida? Is their criticism not an ironic criticism, with clear and demonstrable links to Socratic irony, rhetorical irony, the romantic irony of Schlegel, the genial irony of nineteenth-century critics? To such questions, I could easily answer yes. But the particular value of this study results from holding to an original assumption: that statements about irony will be statements in which the word irony appears. Once we conceptualize irony as a trope, a technique, a literary attitude, the literary itself, a world-historical phase, or any related abstraction, we begin to construct a philosophy of irony and not a critique of one. Notwithstanding my admiration for Roland Barthes and the appeal the various figures in the history of irony have for me, to combine these under the rubric "Irony" would involve the very critical strategies I have rejected.

Barthes is far removed from American New Criticism, much farther removed than is Paul de Man, whose "Rhetoric of Temporality" I will discuss in the following chapter. This is due to matters of institutional affiliation, nationality, and finally, to Barthes's own long association with structuralism. Barthes does not "read" as a New Critic; he "explicates" as a Lansonian. And the very crediting to Barthes of a theory of irony may well be one of the disguised fruits of American New Criticism.

To begin with, Barthes uses the word irony very infrequently. Despite the proliferation of headings in Barthes's work, the word irony is almost never so used (I will discuss an exceptional case below). When Barthes does use the word, he usually applies it to the classical pole of his various binary oppositions: irony is generally associated with, say, a "readable" rather than a "writable" text. When Candace Lang describes Barthes's work through the dichotomy irony/humor, she identifies as irony the classical, bourgeois pole of the opposition.[17]

Lang's description of Barthes is just and I certainly do not quarrel with its critical utility, but it leads to the same type of result I studied earlier in my chapter on romantic irony. To assume a good and a bad form of irony is useful primarily as a weapon for promulgating new theories of irony and denouncing old ones, as Barthes himself realized full well. And to use such a polemical technique in relation to Barthes's own work leaves us with what is less a critical description than an evaluation. Furthermore, Barthes's own use of the word irony seems to me inconsistent and, even in those passages that clearly do support Lang's categories, rather casual.[18]

In *Le Plaisir du texte,* Barthes lists *ironie* under the subheading "Plaisir du texte": "Culture. . . . Intelligence. Ironie. Délicatesse. Euphorie. Maîtrise. Sécurité." Under "Textes du jouissance," we have "Le plaisir en pièces; la langue en pièces; la culture en pièces" (82). This is analogous to the distinction in *Critique et vérité* between two types of irony: "la pauvre ironie voltairienne" is opposed to "une autre ironie, que, faute de mieux, l'on appellera *baroque.*" But in *Critique et vérité,* either pole can be characterized as ironic; Barthes's tactic is exactly the same as the romantic tactic of distinguishing an ordinary irony from a newer one. Barthes's "baroque irony" responds to the introductory definition of irony given earlier in the paragraph: "Irony is nothing other than the question posed of language by language. . . . There is an irony of symbols, a way of placing language in question by apparent declared excesses of language" (74–75).[19] Barthes's "baroque irony" is what Lang characterizes as "humor." All this can be defended, but the restriction of the word irony to the negative pole of this opposition certainly contradicts the spirit of this passage, since the fundamental definition of irony that introduces the distinction of ironies involves precisely this "baroque irony"; Barthes introduces the notion of a "poor Voltairian irony" only as a matter of clarification.[20] Lang's effort to pin the analysis on the word irony seems especially vulnerable to the very critical techniques that are at issue. Lang seems to me to be superimposing with these dichotomies a metaphysics of irony, one that disregards the levels of language and signifiers that were of primary concern to Barthes.[21]

Barthes is simply not consistent in his use of the word. One of the few times it is even used as a heading is in *Sade, Fourier, Loyola.* What Barthes here claims constitutes the irony of Sade is quite different from the classical ironic codes cited in *S/Z;* it is closer to the definition of baroque irony given in *Critique et vérité,* "the placing of language into question." Irony is a method of "ruining" a culture that cannot be verbally effaced; it accomplishes this by the "suppression of the aesthetic division of languages," by the active cultivation of a language "mutilated" of its past grace, by the planting of a language in new language fields (where it might function as a weed, I assume), by "metonymic explosions" of maxims (152–53). Barthes's description of Sade's technique is close to his description of his own method in the preface, where he claims to "deplace the social responsibility of the text." In the face of the totality of bourgeois ideology, "the only possible riposte is neither confrontation nor destruction, but only theft: to fragment the old text of culture, of science, of literature, and to disseminate its traits according to unrecognizable formulates, in the same way that one disguises (*maquiller*) stolen goods" (15).[22]

The word irony simply never develops into a key word nor into an object of meditation for Barthes. Those who have seen it as such have read sometimes alien traditions and alien ironies into Barthes, whether German romantic, Socratic, or American New Critical. I am equally skeptical of the supposed relation to irony of such Derridean terms as *jeu.* If there is such a relation, it does not occur prominently in the works of Derrida with which I am familiar. I would be grateful, however, for the specific references that challenge this conclusion.[23]

I do not claim to have done any more here than register an objection. The assertion that an overriding concept (or technique) exists in the writing of Barthes or Derrida that is indifferently named, say, *ironie, écriture,* or *jeu,* is the type of argument their critical endeavors seem most especially directed against.

12

Paul de Man

■

The following chapter and my conclusion originate in Paul de Man's 1969 essay, "The Rhetoric of Temporality."[1] They attempt to sketch some of the implications of this study in relation to contemporary critical issues that so far I have touched on only indirectly. De Man's essay has achieved near classic status and deservedly so; no essay of the past thirty years of comparable importance to literary criticism deals with irony in such a serious and focused way.

The critique I have been developing here is certainly one that could be applied to the branch of contemporary criticism known as deconstruction. The two histories, of criticism and of irony, run parallel: each reveals the dual struggle first of the romantic to wrest authority from the text and to privilege the romantic poet as the object of literary concern, and second of the critic to wrest authority away from the poet and to reorient literary studies on criticism. Deconstruction is an endpoint of that critical history and thus partakes of it; the same is true of other forms of contemporary criticism that acknowledge a significant relation, whether positive or negative, to a past criticism. Deconstruction would be charged with continuing the program already implicit in New Criticism, with reintroducing authority into a literary universe through critical authoritarianism—all in the guise of a subversion or a revision of traditional canons, ideas, and ideologies.

But that version of deconstruction is properly the subject of a critique of criticism. And what I am writing here is neither that critique nor a history of literary consciousness or literary techniques. As characterized here, a representative text of deconstruction is only one example of how the critical and literary forces studied in the preceding chapters emerge in contemporary literary thought.

The word irony occurs with some frequency in de Man's work and, unlike Barthes or Derrida, de Man does not use the word casually. De Man's stated interests as well as his institutional affiliations placed him in direct relation to many of the important traditions in the history of irony: philosophical, rhetorical, German romantic, and perhaps most important New Critical.[2] De Man's essay, which can be read as an attempt to renounce this last association, both contains and reenacts the history of irony I have outlined here. Historically, it is a locus where various literary, critical, and lexical histories converge with the occurrence of the word irony; as criticism, it not only describes this history but draws on the particular critical tactics associated with it. In de Man's essay, irony evolves from a word into a concept (undefined) and finally into a mode of consciousness, while a parallel attempt is being made to supplant irony with allegory—a term that will serve as the basis for much of de Man's later work.[3] Despite this denigration of the word irony, what might be called its attendant critical metaphysics remains.

De Man's essay is in two parts entitled "Allegory and Symbol" and "Irony." His apparent intention is to revive the romantic distinction between allegory and symbol and to reverse the poles of that distinction, privileging allegory over symbol. Having discredited the term symbol, de Man then substitutes for it the term irony, through reference to a different set of romantic texts. Irony never wins back the position lost by symbol, but neither is it completely overshadowed by the key term allegory.

De Man's conclusions concerning allegory and irony seem reasonably straightforward. Allegory and irony can be distinguished through the categories of time and space: "Irony is a synchronic structure, while allegory appears as a successive mode capable of engendering duration as the illusion of a continuity that it knows to be illusionary" (226). The result of this argument is the rehabilitation of allegory as an exegetical mode (a different allegory from the one discredited in the romantic opposition between allegory and symbol). Irony by contrast is *merely* realistic and mimetic: "In this respect, irony comes closer to the pattern of factual experience and recaptures some of the factitiousness of human existence as a succession of isolated moments lived by a divided self" (226)—a statement de Man almost immediately modifies. Irony thus is defined indirectly as a poetic trope, allegory as a critical one.

But the reasons for de Man's project are never given. Certainly, the argument in part one is a valid one and the reasons for such an argument are obvious enough. But why does de Man move from the opposition allegory/symbol to allegory/irony? Even more troubling to my reading is the shifting meaning of irony:

The fundamental structure of allegory reappears here in the tendency of the language toward narrative, the spreading out along the axis of an imaginary time in order to give duration to what is, in fact, simultaneous within the subject.

The structure of irony, however, is the reversed mirror-image of this form. In practically all the quotations from Baudelaire and Schlegel, irony appears as an instantaneous process that takes place rapidly, suddenly, in one single moment. . . . Baudelaire speaks of "*la force de se dédoubler* rapidement," "*la puissance d'être* à la fois *soi-même et un autre*"; irony is instantaneous like an "explosion" and the fall is sudden. (225)

But what is this irony that "appears"? Certainly not a word, because the word does not appear in the quotations de Man refers to. What concept or mode of consciousness it could be is also undefined. To read this essay as itself the response to de Man's appeal for such clarification would be extremely difficult, nor do I find satisfying the possible solution of labeling as ironic de Man's very calls for definition (as if they are meant only to expose the necessary failure of any attempt at definition): "The terms [irony and allegory] are rarely used as a means to reach a sharper definition, which, especially in the case of irony, is greatly needed" (209); "We cannot escape, therefore, the need for a definition toward which this essay is oriented" (211). The type of master definition de Man claims to be seeking here would, I suppose, declare incorrect the historical uses of the word de Man studies; but the logic of the essay implies that such a master definition would not restrict de Man's own use of these words. Irony evolves in this essay from a word in romantic texts to a specific rhetorical trope; but before being analyzed in detail, it becomes an undefined concept or consciousness that (in the language of romantic irony) hovers over the rest of the essay.

I return to my primary question: if de Man's goal is to establish the "priority of allegory" (204)—*Allegories of Reading* would then be a logical next step—why does irony need to be involved at all? The essay is strewn with difficulties, despite the apparent elegance of its argument. By reading through these difficulties, I hope to get at why such apparently unproblematic conclusions are so unsettling.

De Man begins his essay with an objection to the "subjectivist critical vocabulary" through which traditional rhetorical terms such as mimesis, metaphor, allegory, and irony have fallen into "disrepute." This disrepute was, however, only "a temporary matter," which various twentieth-century critics have worked to correct. In his note, de Man identifies these as

Barthes, Foucault, Genette, and Benjamin, and the note ends with the statement: "The evolution from the New Criticism to the criticism of Northrop Frye in North America tends in the same direction" (187 n. 1). This is the first of many direct and indirect allusions to New Criticism. They are highlighted by de Man's implied insistence that his readers bracket the obvious connection between New Criticism and the word irony.

The problem for de Man is "the association of rhetorical terms with value judgments that blur distinctions and hide the real structures" (188). The particular system of judgments de Man wishes to undo is connected with the romantic distinction between allegory and symbol. De Man will undo this distinction by lending priority to allegory.

The word allegory has many meanings—meanings de Man pretends to ignore, but which he manipulates to advantage. For de Man's essay, the two most important to distinguish are personification allegory and what could be called allegoresis, that is, allegory as a mode of interpretation. De Man's description of the romantic distinction between symbol and allegory does not identify what to Goethe and to Coleridge was at issue; the allegory they disparage is personification allegory, one they claim is limited and bound by a predetermined conceptual content (the idea virtue, for example, limits the artistic personification Virtue). De Man objects to "a certain degree of ambiguity" in Coleridge's distinction between symbol and allegory from *The Statesman's Manual;* and while such ambiguity exists, much of it would disappear if more of Coleridge's often quoted statement were given by de Man. What precedes the somewhat dense definition of symbol is Coleridge's definition of allegory: "An allegory is but a translation of abstract notions into a picture-language, which is itself nothing but an abstraction from the objects of the senses; the principal being more worthless than its phantom proxy, both alike unsubstantial, and the former shapeless to boot. On the other hand a symbol . . ."[4] With such a background, it is somewhat clearer what Coleridge may mean when he describes the symbol as "the translucence of the special in the individual, or the general in the special, or of the universal in the general; above all by the translucence of the eternal through and in the temporal." The particular kind of allegory against which he is defining symbol is personification.[5]

I am uncertain why de Man needs to ignore this, since the romantics he cites speak of higher and lower types of allegory in the same way they speak of higher and lower types of irony. In a polemical aside, de Man takes Hans Eichner to task for saying that a passage from Schlegel's "Gespräch über die Poesie" suggests that Schlegel uses the word allegory where we would use symbol.[6] Eichner, in the brief note cited by de Man, says only that when Schlegel says things like "all beauty is allegory," he is speaking of a higher form of allegory than that commonly designated by the term. In the same note, Eichner provides references to several lucid statements by Schlegel concerning this hierarchy of allegories—statements that clearly identify the type of common allegories disparaged by the romantics as personification allegory and simple didactic allegory.[7] My only explanation for de Man's ignoring such passages is that the particular distinctions made are not useful to him. Even Schlegel's "higher allegories" remain artistic modes. The allegories de Man has in mind are exegetical and critical.

The allegory attacked by Goethe, Coleridge, and Schlegel is specific and limited. But de Man's argument relies for its coherence on the multivalence of the word allegory. De Man retains the association with personification through reference to the *Roman de la rose* but blurs the technique allegory (itself limited) with the potential referents and functions of that technique: "Thus Defoe's gardens, far from being realistic natural settings, are stylized emblems, quite similar in structure and detail to the gardens of the *Roman de la rose*. But they serve primarily a redemptive, ethical function" (204).[8] Allegory is redefined: "The prevalence of allegory always corresponds to the unveiling of an authentically temporal destiny" (206); and related explicitly to the medieval doctrine of four allegorical levels: "the failure of the attempt to conceive of a language that would be symbolical as well as allegorical, the suppression, in the allegory, of the analogical and anagogical levels . . ." (207). At this point, no definable (or conceivable) sense of allegory is possible. This last allegory is clearly enough an exegetical one, and the shift from the artistic to the critical sense of the word takes place with its emergence. Yet de Man's sentence, however suggestive, does not describe the medieval levels of allegory in any stable way. What is the (rejected) "analogical" level? If it is the second, historical level (the level that equates Noah with Christ), then I assume what de Man has done is to secularize allegory, leaving only the third, moral level of medieval exegesis—recalling the "redemptive, ethical function" of Defoe's gardens (204). A secular version of that level would be a close exegetical variant of the "allegories offering simple moral instruction" so disparaged by Schlegel.

Rousseau's *La Nouvelle Héloise* concludes as will de Man: "This conflict is ultimately resolved in the triumph of a controlled and lucid renunciation of the values associated with a cult of the moment, and this renunciation establishes the priority of an allegorical over a symbolic diction" (204). Since de Man will not allow the word allegory to settle into place as a poetic technique, what his statement implies is the priority of an exegetical over a poetic diction, the priority of the reader over the text, the critic over the poet (the position to be taken in *Allegories of Reading*).

The second part of the essay introduces into the dialectic of symbol/ allegory the term irony. A shift occurs in the meaning of the word irony that is parallel to the earlier shift in the word allegory.

In the first part of the essay, de Man initially pretended to define allegory by accepting as legitimate the romantic distinction between allegory and symbol. He then ignored that definition, effecting most of the more important transitions verbally, relying on the multiple meanings the word has developed historically. In the second part of the essay, the more striking transitions are effected in a different manner, by assuming the existence of a unitary abstraction (irony) that has many names in history (one of which is irony). Such logic enables de Man to proceed from a precise rhetorical definition of a trope, to the history of the novel, to a Baudelaire essay that nowhere mentions irony, and finally to Schlegel's essay "Über die Unverständlichkeit." I will discuss a few of these transitions here, and look finally at de Man's own concluding parody of the Three Temptations.

De Man begins with a doubling, describing the trope in the language of the trope: "Around the same time that the tension between symbol and allegory finds expression in the works and the theoretical speculations of the early romantics, the problem of irony also receives more and more self-conscious attention" (208). Symbol and allegory "find expression"; irony receives "self-conscious attention." But what irony? De Man does not define it before stating flatly that irony is "conspicuously absent" in Rousseau, Wordsworth, and Hölderlin. Even more startling to me is the assertion of the "implicit and rather enigmatic link between allegory and irony which runs through the history of rhetoric" (208). Anyone who knows enough to make heads or tails of de Man's argument knows this is false; such a link is explicit in most traditional rhetorics and not in the least bit enigmatic, since both tropes involve "saying one thing and meaning another," as de Man states (209).[9] Despite the continuous and coherent history the words enjoy in the very rhetorical tradition de Man cites both here and in his opening sentence, he claims: "The relationship between allegory and irony appears in history as a casual and apparently contingent fact, in the form of a common concern of some writers with both modes" (209). Irony is both derhetoricized and delexicalized, becoming here not a word but a "common concern" of a select group of writers.[10]

The irony to be excluded from time is first excluded from history. De Man's conclusions are completely contained in the assumptions (all unstated) in the introductory paragraphs on irony:

> In the case of irony one cannot so easily take refuge in the need for a historical de-mystification of the term, as when we tried to show that the term "symbol" had in fact been substituted for that of "allegory" in an act of ontological bad faith. The tension between allegory and symbol justified this procedure: the mystification is a fact of history and must therefore be dealt with in a historical manner before actual theorization can start. But in the case of irony one has to start out from the structure of the trope itself, taking one's cue from texts that are de-mystified and, to a large extent, themselves ironical. (211)

Irony is assumed in this formulation to be a trope that exists prior to the (historical) rhetoric manuals that describe it. De Man states: "It is a historical fact that irony becomes increasingly conscious of itself in the course of demonstrating the impossibility of our being historical. In speaking of irony we are dealing not with the history of an error but with a problem that exists within the self" (211). Irony here is given a consciousness; our speaking of irony leads in turn to our own consciousness. What at first glance seems a striking set of false alternatives in de Man's prose (*not* the history of an error *but rather* a problem within the self) represents the shift in the meaning of irony. One can associate irony with language that reveals the error of all language about the world (nihilism), but there is a consciousness that is superior to both nihilistic irony and its objects. The nihilistic function of irony is here negated, as de Man's discussion of irony builds a language model where statements are dominated by consciousness, that is, a model analogous to "the structure of the trope of irony" whereby authoritative meanings dominate literal statements (the precise opposite of the critical enterprise undertaken by Barthes).

From here, de Man makes a transition to Baudelaire: "Thus freed from the necessity of respecting historical chronology, we can take Baudelaire's text, 'De l'essence du rire,' as a starting point" (211). I assume I am only one of many who, with LaCapra, have noted the absence of the word irony from Baudelaire's essay: "It is, moreover, the height of irony that a reader of de Man's essay would never realize that Baudelaire's *De l'essence du rire* is not about irony. In fact the word is never mentioned."[11] LaCapra's reading of de Man proceeds undisturbed, and perhaps that is the function of his own critical invocation of irony here. But his statement does not flatter de Man's readers, who surely ought to suspect much of what LaCapra claims they will never realize. They do not have to read Baudelaire's essay; all they must do is note the absence of the word in de Man's quotations.

Further transitions are similar. De Man parenthetically glosses Baudelaire's "le comique absolu" with "by which he designates that which, at other moments in his work, he calls irony" (212). But where these passages are, de Man does not say.[12] The final passage of Baudelaire cited by de Man allows for a bridge between Baudelaire's "le comique absolu" and earlier statements by Schlegel about irony; Baudelaire speaks of the experience of vertigo while watching pantomime, and de Man summarizes: "Irony is unrelieved *vertige,* dizziness to the point of madness" (215). De Man's word "madness" I assume is suggested by Baudelaire's "ce delire," a phrase that appears in the sentence of Baudelaire's essay that immediately follows the point where de Man's quotation ends. The word irony, however, is de Man's alone. Or de Man's and Schlegel's, whose *Lyceum* fragment 42 is the *locus classicus* for the relation of irony to the Italian buffo. De Man is back to the classic texts of romantic irony, and his critique of some rather extravagant claims for irony by Peter Szondi is itself I think a further attempt to distance himself from the romanticism he begins the essay by rejecting. De Man reaches a "provisional conclusion" with a lengthy citation from Schlegel's essay "Über die Unverständlichkeit"; de Man's irony is now one that is "not organic, . . . that allows for no end, for no totality" (222).

This leads to three "tempting" conclusions, two of which de Man rejects. The first would link allegory and irony "in their common discovery of a truly temporal predicament" (222). This conclusion he calls "dangerously satisfying," in that it gives "an overly coherent historical picture at the expense of stated human incoherence" (222). But why dangerous? Allegory and irony must be opposed in order to salvage human incoherence, which in terms of criticism itself apparently requires clear divisions between critical schools represented by each trope.

Here, in the midst of a conclusion he suggests we must reject, de Man distinguishes the two modes in a way that is fundamental to his essay: "More clearly even than allegory, the rhetorical mode of irony takes us back to the predicament of the conscious subject" (222). Yes. But the key concept here is not that of predicaments. De Man here restates the purpose of this essay: to establish allegory as an exegetical mode, a critical mode, while treating irony as a "rhetorical mode" related to a subject (by implication, a creative writer rather than a critic).

The second tempting conclusion is based on the leap into faith taken by former ironists, Schlegel and Kierkegaard. But the conclusion does not itself involve an analogous leap. Rather, as critics, we might distinguish texts of faith from "meta-ironical" texts that transcend irony, and call these "meta-ironical" texts allegorical. The absence of irony de Man has earlier proclaimed in Wordsworth could thus be construed as the overcoming of irony. Again, this is a temptation to be resisted: "It would be very tempting to think so, but, since the implications are far-reaching, it might be better to approach the question in a less exalted mood, by making a brief comparison of the temporal structure of allegory and irony" (223).

It is here that we fall prey to the final temptation—one that begins in a reading of Wordsworth's Lucy Gray poems. This is one temptation that we cannot resist. But there are others as well:

> Yet the two modes [allegory and irony], for all their profound distinctions in mood and structure, are the two faces of the same fundamental experience of time. One is tempted to play them off against each other and to attach value judgments to each, as if one were intrinsically superior to the other. We mentioned the temptation to confer on allegorical writers a wisdom superior to that of ironic writers; an equivalent temptation exists to consider ironists as more enlightened than their assumedly naïve counterparts, the allegorists. Both attitudes are in error. (226)

Not evaluate them? How could we not be guilty? And if we take de Man seriously, how could we possibly see either this essay, or more pointedly *Allegories of Reading,* as not succumbing to this temptation?

De Man again alters his language. After clearly establishing the priority of allegory, he rehabilitates irony at the last moment; the relation of allegory to symbol is transformed; the announced rift between irony and history is healed: "The dialectical play between the two modes, as well as their common interplay with mystified forms of language (such as symbolic or mimetic representation), which it is not in their power to eradicate, make up what is called literary history" (226).

I return to my original question. Why irony? And why an irony so repeatedly stripped of its history? De Man's romantic texts all center irony in the ironist; Schlegel's "Über die Unverständlichkeit" treats audiences largely as potential victims. But with allegory, the focus is elsewhere; in *Allegories of Reading,* de Man states directly what the earlier essay only implies about this change in focus: "Since any narrative is primarily the allegory of its own reading . . ." (76); "The allegory of reading narrates the impossibility of reading" (77). Allegories are not about allegorists; they are about exegetes.

The difference between irony and allegory for de Man does not lie in their rhetorical relations and distinctions, but rather in their accidental histories, histories that de Man only alludes to, and occasionally explicitly rejects. To privilege allegory over symbol was first of all to overturn a traditional cliché of romanticism, and to overturn with it the tenets of New Criticism associated with romanticism (represented in de Man's text and notes by Wimsatt). Moreover, allegory has an additional history, the exegetical history to which de Man only alludes. *Allegories of Reading* conflates these two histories (rhetorical and exegetical) by defining the critic as referent.

Only in American New Criticism does the word irony come close to this determined concentration on the critic. De Man's earlier claim that with irony, there is no "necessity of respecting historical chronology" (211) is ill justified in its context. Yet the association of irony and ahistoricity is almost a caricature of New Criticism. De Man seems to struggle to be freed from the (coherent) critical history that would link him with New Criticism as its extension rather than its antithesis, and freed as well from a critical concept that leads back to the creating subject of romanticism. What the romantics considered the subjectivity of irony does not constrain the artist, but it does place some implied constraints on the critical exegete. The choice of a new master trope (allegory) can dispense with New Criticism and such constraints at the same time.

De Man makes no attempt to avoid traditional critical language in this essay: we hear of ambiguities, tensions, and literature invulnerable to irony.[13] In part two of the essay, de Man goes further, focusing directly on a key New Critical term and even indulging in a concluding reading of a poem often subject to New Critical close readings. But this could be construed either as an arrogant claim of victory or a good-natured admission of defeat.

The victory over New Criticism is never complete. The relation between irony and allegory is always a close one. The New Critical monster will simply not stay dead, as witnessed by the closing sentences of de Man's "The Purloined Ribbon."[14] This passage was to become the concluding statement of *Allegories of Reading* when the essay was reprinted as its closing chapter. De Man uses a "slight extension of Friedrich Schlegel's formulation" to define irony as follows:

> the permanent parabasis of an allegory (of figure), that is to say, irony. Irony is no longer a trope but the undoing of the deconstructive allegory of all tropological cognitions, the systematic undoing, in other words, of understanding. As such, far from closing off the tropological system, irony enforces the repetition of its aberration. (46)

Whether or not that statement is true, I cannot judge. But an insistence on the position of deconstruction within the history of irony (a history de Man claims we can ignore) might well be an undoing of many of the claims now associated with deconstruction.

But that is only my version of what de Man has done. De Man, in this one essay, repeats the historical movements already found in this history of irony, while pretending that it is the history that is performing those moves for him. De Man thus takes the history of criticism and the history of irony as entwined in New Criticism a step further, by continuing the critical usurpation of literary power and authority. But to extend this history de Man must make a break with it, by freeing it from the restraints imposed by particular figures in that history (Socrates, Schlegel) and from the particular word that invokes them.

CONCLUSION

An
Alternative
History: Irony
and the
Novel

■

The relation of irony to the novel and the discontinuity between theories of irony and the literary production of (supposedly) ironic works are issues raised in passing by de Man in "The Rhetoric of Temporality" (210–11). I have not dealt with the relation of irony to specific literary genres in this study; I raise the topic here as a conclusion and as a possible basis for what I call an alternative history of irony—a history looking forward to contemporary literary production and organized as a background for that production. Irony and drama, irony and lyric—these issues remain of importance to contemporary criticism. Yet for contemporary readers, the novel, particularly the Latin American novel, is a far more vital genre, and criticism concerning its irony less insular.

The question of irony in the novel raises special problems and enjoys special advantages. If approached in a traditional manner, the topic will prove no more useful than any other literary topic. An arbitrary definition of irony can be chosen, and that definition applied to various selected novels. A glance under the heading "Irony" in any well-stocked academic library will reveal immediately the popularity of such studies. I call the initial definitions in such studies arbitrary, because I do not believe there is a significant difference between an informed and an ill-informed definition. Those readers who have followed the above study with sympathy will realize that I have not provided the basis for a safe and legitimate definition of irony at all. The study of "irony 1 in *X*" will differ from one of "irony 2 in *Y*" only on the basis of the virtuosity of the investigator.

Nonetheless, the novel has become inextricably linked to the history of the word. This is in part due to Schlegel and the early romantics, whose discussions of irony in relation to the novel created an apparent tradition beginning with Cervantes and developing through the English novel to Goethe's *Wilhelm Meister*. The topic was revived in the twentieth century, due principally to the work of Thomas Mann. Where Schlegel was considered by his contemporaries the father of irony, Mann has become for modern literature "the ironist par excellence."[1]

What kind of literary history is this?

To begin with, the history outlined above has serious gaps, and such gaps may offer more encouragement to practical studies of irony in particular novels than to studies of its history. Nineteenth-century novels have been labeled ironic, but they have been so labeled largely by twentieth-century critics attempting to fill the obvious gap between Mann with his twentieth-century progeny and Schlegel.[2] This discontinuity is further marked by discontinuity in national traditions. What Schlegel considered ironic novels were those by Cervantes, Sterne, Diderot, and Goethe; the French representative of this supposed tradition was Diderot's *Jacques le Fataliste,* ironic largely through its imitation of *Tristram Shandy.* For twentieth-century critics, a different canon of ironic novelists has developed: Flaubert and Stendhal, Dostoyevski, and, for some critics, Pushkin.[3]

Historians of the novel and its association with irony have dealt with these gaps in different ways; the works of Bakhtin and Lukács pose just two alternatives. In the lead essays in *The Dialogic Imagination,* Bakhtin maintains a fluid vocabulary and does not privilege the specific term irony. Nonetheless, his notions of "heteroglossia," multiple languages, and what in Dostoyevski he calls the "double-voiced word" are compatible with much of the twentieth-century theorizing on irony I have dealt with here.[4]

The historicity of Bakhtin's work is sporadic and at times only apparent. The polyglossia characteristic of a Rabelais or Dostoyevski responds to particular cultural conditions; for Bakhtin's readers, it becomes a model for a genre or for literature in general. Particular cultural histories become subordinate to a universal stylistics. This stylistics has great analytical power; but as we have seen, so do some of the basic forms of irony associated with medieval grammatical commentaries.[5]

I can link Bakhtin to the tradition I have been describing only through the type of sleight of hand I have objected to elsewhere: Bakhtin *says* "polyglossia" but he *means* what we mean by irony. (And since I have no Russian, I have little enough access even to what he says.) Lukács's *Theory of the Novel* is much more closely linked to the critical traditions I have discussed above. Lukács relates the modern novel directly to early romantic theories of irony. The novel is a form of maturity opposing and longing for the "Kindlichkeit" of the epic. It is the result of artistic subjectivity: "Self-knowledge and thereby the self-cancellation of subjectivity (*die Selbstaufhebung der Subjektivität*) is named irony by the first theoreticians of the novel, the early romantic aestheticians" (73). Irony is the modern writer's (romantic) awareness of maturity or belatedness, which is then turned against the novelistic hero (84). Lukács's theories of irony dovetail nicely with other descriptions of irony as a late or a self-reflective form. And since Lukács's study was published before the work of Proust, Joyce, and Mann became available, Lukács can be described as creating the critical vocabulary for a literary tradition in which the most important figures were yet to appear.[6]

But the possible history of the ironic novel that I want to see attempted is not one that arises directly from this criticism; it is one that originates in the novels themselves, with all their critical naivety. The history of the ironic novel would combine two histories: the history of irony as I have drawn it in chapters above, and the alternative history drawn from the vocabulary of the novel itself. What kind of relation would such a history have to the critical histories of Bakhtin? Lukács? or Schlegel?

Words and Things: The Ironic Novelist and the Word Irony

A history of irony and the novel involves the disparity between the language of the novel and that of the critic. The use of the word irony by the critic inevitably refers to something (vaguely or precisely defined) that is rarely named irony by the writer. Despite the presumed radical redefinitions of the word in the early nineteenth century, the use of the word by novelists and by other writers generally considered as major proponents of a new theory of irony is quite conservative.[7] I in no way claim to have conducted an exhaustive study; I invite the specialist who objects to demonstrate to me that the citations below are unrepresentative and that the true or genuine history of the ironic novel is much different from the one implied here.

Tristram Shandy is often cited by early romantic critics and by scholars of those critics as well. What does Sterne mean by irony? Nothing more than what the contemporary lexicons would suggest. Here, Tristram confronts an officious French commissary, who insists Tristram must pay for land passage:

> —But I don't go by land; said I.
> —You may if you please; replied the commissary—
> Your most obedient servant—said I, making him a low bow—
> The commissary, with all the sincerity of grave good breeding—made me one, as low again.—I never was more disconcerted with a bow in my life.
> —The devil take the serious character of these people! quoth I—

(aside) they understand no more of IRONY than this—(Vol. 7, chap. 34; published in 1765)[8]

Tristram is apparently referring to the strictly literal interpretation of his bow by the commissary—a bow that was intended to be mildly contemptuous.

In Hugo's *Notre-Dame de Paris* (1831) the same meanings are found: to deride, and to say something other than what one means. In addition, irony is a mark of superiority by virtue of its association with Greek philosophy, as suggested in Gringoire's defensive reaction to seeing his play ignored: "Gringoire, tout philosophe sceptique, tout poète ironique qu'il était . . ." (bk. 2, chap. 3) ["Gringoire, skeptical philosopher and ironic poet that he was . . ."]. Later in the same chapter, Hugo uses the word of Quasimodo, elected as King of Fools: "Et il prenait au sérieux tous ces applaudissements ironiques, tous ces respects dérisoires" ["And he took seriously all the ironic applause, all the derisory respect"]. Elsewhere, irony is a social gesture (an ironic smile) indicating contempt or superiority; this a meaning that becomes commonplace in the nineteenth-century novel.[9]

The romantic notion of "world-historical irony" can be found (itself ironized) in Balzac's *Eugénie Grandet* (1833): "Sublimité perdue! Grandet se croyait très généreux envers sa femme. Les philosophes qui rencontrent des Nanon, des madame Grandet, des Eugénie, ne sont-ils pas en droit de trouver que l'ironie est le fond du caractère de la Providence"[10] ["Lost sublimity! Grandet believed himself very generous to his wife. The philosophers who deal with these Nanons, Madame Grandets, Eugénies, are surely correct in finding that irony is the essence of the character of Providence"].

The most useful sense of the word for the novelist seems to relate to the description of social discourse and the hypocrisy of that discourse. Flaubert, in *L'Education sentimentale* (1869), speaks of a smile "plein à la fois de politesse et d'ironie" ["full of both politeness and irony"]; commonplace remarks are also subject to ironic interpretations: "sa phrase pouvait passer pour une déférence ou pour une ironie" ["her remark could pass for deference or irony"].[11] In Stendhal's *La Chartreuse de Parme* (1839), a similar sense of the word appears:

Tel est le triomphe de l'éducation jésuitique: donner l'habitude de ne pas faire attention à des choses plus claires que le jour. Un français, élevé au milieu des traits d'intérêt personnel et de l'ironie de Paris, eût pu, sans être de mauvais foi, accuser Fabrice d'hypocrisie au moment même où notre héros ouvrait son âme à Dieu avec la plus extrême sincérité et l'attendrissement le plus profond.[12]

[Such is the triumph of a Jesuit education: to instill the habit of ignoring what is as clear as day. A Frenchman, raised amid conventional personal interest and the irony of Paris, could, without bad faith, accuse Fabrice of hypocrisy at the very moment our hero opened his soul to God with the most extreme sincerity and the most profound tenderness.]

For Proust, in *Du Côté de chez Swann* (1913), for example, irony also remains linked to social discourse: "Parfois, malgré tout, il se laissait aller à émettre un jugement sur une oeuvre, sur une manière de comprendre la vie, mais il donnait alors à ses paroles un ton ironique comme s'il n'adhérait pas tout entière à ce qu'il disait" [13] ["Sometimes, in spite of everything, he would allow himself to offer a judgment on a work, or a way of understanding life, but he would then give to his words an ironic tone as if he did not adhere entirely to what he said"]. Irony is associated with critical judgment, but on the basis of the rhetorical definition. It is a form of polite talk. And in both Stendhal and Proust, the irony described (malicious in the case of Stendhal, mild in the case of Proust) is arguably the same type as that used in the description itself.

A wider range of meanings can be found in another supposedly ironic novelist, Robert Musil, but these do not seem unprecedented to me: "Es mochte ein verlegenes Lächeln sein oder ein verschlagenes, ein ironisches, heimtückisches, schmerzliches, irres, blutrünstiges, unheimliches" [14] ["It might have been an embarrassed smile or a cunning one, an ironic, malicious, grievous, mad, bloody, sinister smile"]. As in the passage from Balzac's *Eugénie Grandet* quoted above, the invocation of irony has itself a degree of irony. Traditional meanings appear elsewhere: "Er sagte das ganz ohne Ironie, denn es war seine Überzeugung; aber Diotima fühlte sich gering geschätzt" (106) ["He said that entirely without irony, for it was his conviction; but Diotima felt herself little valued"]; "Ironie des Schicksals" (330) ["irony of fate"].

None of these works shows the self-conscious development of the word found in both the critical and fictional writings of Thomas Mann. In *Doktor Faustus,* irony is related specifically to theories of distancing in artistic production: "Ganz allgemein ist mir dieser Anspruch auf ironische Distanzierung, auf eine Objektivität, der es sicherlich weniger um die Ehre der Sache als um die der freien Person zu tun ist, immer als ein Zeichen ungemeinen Hochmuts erschiene" (chap. 8) ["To me, this claim to ironic distancing, to an objectivity that has less to do with the value of the object than with the honor of the free person, has always seemed a sign of uncommon arrogance"]. Traditional meanings of the word seen in the French novel remain: "Er sprach völlig frei, distinkt, mühe- und pausenlos, druck-fertig gesetzt, in leicht ironisch gefärbten Wendungen" (chap. 13)[15] ["He spoke completely extemporaneously, distinctly, without pause or apparent difficulty, with his words composed as if ready for press, in ironically tinged formulae"].

Because of the conflation of the theory and practice of irony in Mann, a history of the ironic novel risks becoming Mann's history, with the novel as a genre functioning both as a precursor to and a development from Mann.[16] Yet Mann's importance in this tradition can certainly be acknowl-edged without viewing him as its *telos*. What the uses of the word in the novel seem to chart is a movement similar to the one we have seen already: the gradual acceptance of the term as an evaluative one, the privileging of writers over their materials, and the final characterization of the writer (Mann) as critic or perhaps as self-reflective critical parodist (Borges and John Barth).

I have several times mentioned Friedrich Schlegel's review of Goethe's *Wilhelm Meister*. Schlegel's own references to that review are of equal inter-est. For here, we see suggested all the movements in the history of irony I have charted. In a letter to his brother of 5 December 1797, Schlegel speaks of Goethe as "Meister" ("über des Meisters *alte* Lyrik"), but later in the same letter speaks of "mein *Meister,*" referring to his own review.[17] The phrase "über Meister" becomes the basis for further reevaluations: "concerning [Goethe's] *Meister*"; "over Goethe's *Meister*"; "over-master." In a letter to Schleiermacher of July 1798 Schlegel refers again to this review:

> Gott sey Dank, Du findest Ironie um Uebermeister. Das andre giebt sich. Du machst mir Lust, bald wieder ein Stück zu fertigen (denn zwey Portionen dürften es noch werden), weil Du dieses so gar sehr als Vorrede ansichtigst. Aber die Moral bleibt doch mein Meister. ([*Letters*], ed. Immerwahr, 148)
> [Thank God you find irony in " Übermeister." The rest, I can work on. Your comments encourage me to write another part soon (for there will probably still be two parts), since you view this one as only a preface. But the moral still remains *my* Meister.]

Goethe's *Meister?* Schlegel's *Meister?* His *Übermeister?* Where Schlegel could not surpass Goethe with literary fiction (that is, with *Lucinde*), he could do so through his reviews; or at least, this might have been suggested to him by the accidental ambiguities of review titles (*über* meaning either "concerning" or "super-").

The history suggests as well that the revisionist nature of modern irony—an irony Schlegel himself is said to have originated—is a fiction. Revisions were modifications only; and an unexpected continuity in the history of irony appears where its supposed practitioners are said to have most vigorously denied it. The element of contempt found in the earliest definitions has never been eliminated; it has been suppressed and modified, to emerge finally in the privileged stance of critics and metacritics over their materials.

The history of the ironic novel will be one that exhibits the same discontinuity as does a general history of irony. But such discontinuity need not be defined as being between nineteenth-century theory and practice, nor as being between something we can identify as "a full-fledged ironic consciousness" and its (inadvertent) expression in works of art.[18] For nineteenth-century French novels are not in and of themselves ironic. They are, rather, congenial to twentieth-century theories of irony in a way that German novels, from the fragmentary *Franz Sternbalds Wanderungen* of Tieck to the bourgeois novels of Fontane, are not. Discontinuities did exist: the early romantic discussions of the novel are just as difficult to relate to early romantic novels as are early romantic theories of irony (however defined) to early romantic writings (however selected). But many of the apparent discontinuities in the later nineteenth century (particularly those based on the absence of something the twentieth-century critic feels should logically be present) are perhaps illusory—the result of twentieth-century critical methodology and the ineradical influence of Mann and American New Criticism.

Throughout this study, I have treated irony not as the referent of criticism but as the discourse of criticism itself—a critical myth. That myth has served the critical community well, and in the context in which I write here, the critical community is unavoidably of more importance than the literary one. What functions such a myth will continue to serve I can only guess. But the present work seeks to define a new function for such critical mythology. Through study of such mythology, criticism can come to a better understanding of its own functions, without having to engage in a critical polemic that objectifies its own materials through questions of accuracy and error, correctness and incorrectness. There is no correct understanding of the word irony, no historically valid reading of irony; and to claim that irony has been consistently misread does not seem to me any different from assuming that every reading of irony, every invocation of irony, is legitimate. Questions as to how such critical disputes over irony can be meaningfully engaged are the ones I hope this study has raised.

NOTES

Introduction

Unless otherwise noted, all translations below are mine. I thank Josef Raab of the University of Southern California for his assistance with the translations in part 3 below.

1 Samuel Johnson, *A Dictionary of the English Language* (London: Strahan, 1755).
2 William K. Wimsatt, Jr., and Cleanth Brooks, *Literary Criticism: A Short History* (New York: Knopf, 1964), 746.
3 Anthony, Earl of Shaftesbury, *Characteristicks of Men, Manners, Opinions, Times*, 2d ed., 3 vols. (1714; reprint, Farnborough, Hants: Gregg, 1968), 1:62–71. On Hegel, see below, chap. 6.
4 Cleanth Brooks, *The Well-Wrought Urn: Studies in the Structure of Poetry* (New York: Harcourt, Brace, 1947), 209–10.
5 Because the distinctions between literary scholars, critics, and theorists vary according to the period discussed, I have kept those boundaries fluid; in most cases, I use the word critic as the general term.
6 Jacques Derrida, *Éperons: Les Styles de Nietzsche* (Paris: Flammarion, 1978).
7 J. A. K. Thomson, *Irony: An Historical Introduction* (Cambridge, Mass.: Harvard University Press, 1927), 2. The precedent for a New Critic such as Brooks is obvious.
8 Most critical discussions of irony involve, to some extent, slippage in the use of irony as a word, concept, or literary phenomenon. The distinctions themselves are not absolute ones. Because of this, I have decided against the convention of italicizing words when they are used as words; for example, when I refer specifically to irony as a word, I use the phrase "the word irony."
9 The characterization of this approach as parallactic is Jackson I. Cope's.
10 See Paul de Man, "The Rhetoric of Temporality" (1969; reprint in *Blindness and Insight: Essays in the Rhetoric of Contemporary Criticism*, 2d ed. rev., Minneapolis: University of Minnesota Press, 1983), 187–228.
11 Wayne C. Booth, *A Rhetoric of Irony* (Chicago: University of Chicago Press, 1974). I am not concerned here with simple practical studies based on arbitrary definitions, with titles such as "Irony in *X*."
12 Søren Kierkegaard, *The Concept of Irony with Constant Reference to Socrates*, trans. Lee M. Capel (Bloomington: Indiana University Press, 1965).
13 Vladimir Jankélévitch, *L'Ironie* (1936; Paris: Flammarion, 1964); titles and pagination vary, e.g., *L'Ironie ou la bonne conscience*, 2d ed. (Paris: PUF, 1950).

14 References below are to Alan Wilde, *Horizons of Assent: Modernism, Postmodernism, and the Ironic Imagination* (Baltimore: Johns Hopkins University Press, 1981). Paul A. Bové, in *Destructive Poetics: Heidegger and Modern American Poetry* (New York: Columbia University Press, 1980), claims that his own work and Wilde's respond to the ahistoricity of New Criticism (291 n. 38); see the chapter "Cleanth Brooks and Modern Irony: A Kierkegaardian Critique," 93–130.

15 The same tactic, whereby a dichotomy involving irony (irony/humor) becomes a variant of modern/postmodern, is used by Candace D. Lang in *Irony/Humor: Critical Paradigms* (Baltimore: Johns Hopkins University Press, 1988), 3, 14. I discuss Lang's work in more detail in the coda to chap. 11 below.

16 Of particular note are Ernst Behler, *Klassische Ironie, romantische Ironie, tragische Ironie: Zum Ursprung dieser Begriffe* (Darmstadt: Wissenschaftliche Buchgesellschaft, 1972); Norman Knox, *The Word "Irony" and Its Context (1500–1755)* (Durham: Duke University Press, 1961); D. C. Muecke, *The Compass of Irony* (London: Methuen, 1969); G. G. Sedgewick, *Of Irony, Especially in Drama* (Toronto: University of Toronto Press, 1935); and Thomson, *Irony: An Historical Introduction*.

17 Uwe Japp, *Theorie der Ironie* (Frankfurt am Main: Vittorio Klostermann, 1983).

18 Cf. Ingrid Strohschneider-Kohrs, *Die romantische Ironie in Theorie und Gestaltung* (1960), 2d ed. (Tübingen: Niemeyer, 1977), and the English studies that have attempted to apply it: Lilian R. Furst, *Fictions of Romantic Irony* (Cambridge, Mass.: Harvard University Press, 1984); and Anne K. Mellor, *English Romantic Irony* (Cambridge, Mass.: Harvard University Press, 1980). Furst has an excellent ten-page summary of the history of the phrase romantic irony. But this history is quickly discarded in favor of a different history altogether: Schlegel "derived his theory from the practical models he acknowledged in Socrates, Petrarch, Dante, Cervantes, Shakespeare, Sterne and Diderot" (29); or in favor of such ahistorical generalizations as "the ironist's task is the control of ambiguity, the reader's is that of rightly comprehending it" (14). See further, chap. 5 below.

19 Gary Handwerk, *Irony and Ethics in Narrative: From Schlegel to Lacan* (New Haven: Yale University Press, 1985). Despite my reservations about some of Handwerk's assumptions, his chapters on Schlegel are I think the best recent work available on Schlegel in English.

20 Such language can be found even in such critics as Edward W. Said, who describes his "oppositional criticism" as "ironic"; *The World, the Text, and the Critic* (Cambridge, Mass.: Harvard University Press, 1983), 29. For a radically different and (I find) disturbing variant, see the explicitly utopian version of the "liberal ironist" proposed by Richard Rorty in *Contingency, Irony, and Solidarity* (Cambridge: Cambridge University Press, 1989), xiii–xvi, 73–78.

Chapter 1. Socrates

1 Joseph A. Dane, *Parody: Critical Concepts vs. Literary Practices, Aristophanes to Sterne* (Norman: University of Oklahoma Press, 1988).

2 References to Plato's text are to *Platonis Opera*, ed. John Burnet (Oxford: Clarendon Press, 1910). On *agalmata*, see W. K. C. Guthrie, *A History of Greek Philosophy*, vol. 4, *Plato: The Man and his Dialogues: Earlier Period* (Cambridge: Cambridge University Press, 1975), 379. As an example of the reception of this image in modern scholarship on irony, see

Behler, *Ironie*, 26–69, and idem, "Nietzsches Auffassung der Ironie," *Nietzsche-Studien* 4 (1975): 1–35, esp. 17.

3 On the relation between irony and eroticism, see Gregory Vlastos, "Socratic Irony," *Classical Quarterly* 37 (1987): 79–97. See also Stanley Rosen, *Plato's 'Symposium'* (New Haven: Yale University Press, 1968), 186, 298, 318.

4 Cf. the metaphor used earlier, in Diotima's speech, to distinguish between grades of initiates in mystery religions (*mustēs* vs. *epoptēs*), *Sym.* 210a; on the implications of distinguishing two grades of listeners, see Joseph A. Dane, "The Defense of the Incompetent Reader," *Comparative Literature* 38 (1986): 61–62.

5 The notion of irony's pseudo-victims is discussed in Muecke, *Compass of Irony*, 34ff.

6 In *Mem.* 1.2.36 he is characterized as asking questions when he knows the answers, and in *Mem.* 4.4.9 as a mocker; W. K. C. Guthrie, *A History of Greek Philosophy*, vol. 3, *The Fifth-Century Enlightenment* (Cambridge: Cambridge University Press, 1969), 446. See also Vlastos, "Socratic Irony," 85–87.

7 References are to *Aristophanes: Clouds*, ed. K. J. Dover (Oxford: Clarendon Press, 1968); on Socrates, see xxxii–lvii. The word *eirōnikōs* appears in *Wasps* (line 174) in an aside by Sosias during a quarrel between Bdelykleon and Philokleon.

8 See Otto Ribbeck's now classic article "Ueber den Begriff des *eirōn*," *Rheinisches Museum* 31 (1876): 381–400; Ribbeck characterizes the word as "ein Schimpfwort." Ribbeck is the source for both Guthrie and Eduard Zeller, *Die Philosophie der Griechen in ihrer Geschichtlichen Entwicklung*, 5th ed., 2/1 (Leipzig: Reisland, 1922), 288. On Ribbeck's reception and for tentative modifications, see Vlastos, "Socratic Irony," and chap. 3 below.

9 Leonard Brandwood, *A Word Index to Plato* (Leeds: Maney, 1976), s.v. The references, some to be discussed below, are as follows: *eirōneia*, *Rep.* 1, 337a; *eirōneusthai*, *Soph.* 268b; *eirōneuē*, *Gorg.* 489e; *eirōneuetai*, *Crat.* 384a; *eirōneuomenos*, *Symp.* 216e; *eirōneuomenō*, *Apol.* 38a; *eirōneuou*, *Gorg.* 489e; *eirōneusoio*, *Rep.* 1, 337a; *eirōnikon*, *Soph.* 268a, *Laws* 10, 908e; *eirōnikou*, *Soph.* 268c; *eirōnikōs*, *Euth.* 302b, *Symp.* 218d, *Amat.* 133d.

10 See Stanley Rosen, *Plato's Sophist: The Drama of Original and Image* (New Haven: Yale University Press, 1983), 23–28.

11 Quoted in Erasmus, *Adagiorum Chilias Tertia*, in *Opera Omnia Desiderii Erasmi Roterodami*, 2/5, ed. Felix Heinimann and Emmanuel Kienzle (Amsterdam: North-Holland, 1981), 159–61n.

12 Reference to the *Adages* are to *Opera Omnia*, ed. Heinimann and Kienzle. Cross-references and other references to Erasmus are to the Leiden edition, *Desiderii Erasmi Roterodami Opera Omnia*, 10 vols. (1703–6; reprint, Hildesheim: Olms, 1962), abbreviated "LB."

13 Heinimann and Kienzle note a peculiarity in reception (ibid., 161n): the Italian editions include only LB 770–771d; omitted are all the lists of the various Sileni. In Italy, Erasmus's Sileni were reduced to metaphoric status throughout the sixteenth and seventeenth centuries.

14 The Silenus is also mentioned in Erasmus's preface to *Lingua* (1525): LB, vol. 4 (the preface is unpaginated).

15 *Rabelais: Oeuvres complètes*, ed. Pierre Jourda, 2 vols. (Paris: Garnier, 1962); *Oeuvres de François Rabelais*, vol. 1, *Gargantua*, ed. Abel Lefranc (Paris: Champion, 1912). References below are to Jourda's edition. On the prologue, see M. A. Screech, *Rabelais* (Ithaca: Cornell University Press, 1979), 128–30. The proverb appeared also in a contemporary collection by Charles de Bouelles.

16 See Donald M. Frame, *François Rabelais: A Study* (New York: Harcourt, Brace, Jovano-vich, 1977): "Rabelais offers us two ways of reading the book and invites us to choose the second, but without canceling the first" (32). On the problem of the "sustantificque mouelle" in Rabelais, see the debate between Abel Lefranc and Lucien Febvre; *Oeuvres de François Rabelais,* vol. 3, *Pantagruel (Prol. ch. I–XI),* ed. Lefranc, "La Pensée secrète de Rabelais," xli–xlii; Febvre, *Le Problème de l'incroyance au 16ᵉ siècle: Le Religion de Rabelais* (Paris: Michel, 1942), "Note liminaire: Le problème et la méthode," 23–29.

17 See chap. 3 below, on Cicero and Quintilian.

18 References below are to Paul Friedländer, *Plato: An Introduction* (2d ed., 1954), trans. Hans Meyerhoff (1958), 2d ed. rev. (Princeton: Princeton University Press, 1969); Guthrie's more conservative approach is heavily indebted to Zeller; see above, nn. 6, 8.

19 Friedländer, *Plato,* 363 n. 2. Friedländer is referring to "Ironie und Radikalismus," from *Betrachtungen eines Unpolitischen* (1918); see Conclusion below, n. 16.

20 See Jean Paul, *Vorschule der Ästhetik* (2d ed., 1812), *Werke,* vol. 5 (Darmstadt: Wissen-schaftliche Buchgesellschafte, 1962): "Platons Ironie . . . könnte man, wie es einen Welt-Humor gibt, eine Welt-Ironie nennen, welche nicht bloß über den Irrtümern (wie jener nicht bloß über Torheiten), sondern über allem Wissen singend und spie-lend schwebt; gleich einer Flamme frei, verzehrend und erfreuend, leicht beweglich und doch nur gen Himmel dringend" (156, sec. 38).

21 See, for example, Ulrich von Wilomowitz-Moellendorf, *Platon,* 2d ed., 2 vols. (Berlin: Weidmann, 1920), 1:572, note on the *Sophist.* Wilomowitz maintains that our use of the word, presumably influenced by romanticism, is completely different from Plato's; when used of Socrates by Plato, the word is always an insult, even in the *Symposium.*

22 Zeller, *Philosophie der Griechen,* 124–26; Zeller's reference on irony as a "Manier der Conversation" is to Hegel's *Lectures on the History of Philosophy.*

23 See below, chap. 6, specifically in reference to Hegel's review of Solger.

24 Karl R. Popper, *The Open Society and Its Enemies* (1962), 5th ed. rev., 2 vols. (Princeton: Princeton University Press, 1966). For the privileging of Socrates and consequently his irony, see esp. 1:154–55.

Chapter 2. Lexicography

1 Frédéric Godefroy, *Dictionnaire de l'ancienne langue française et de tous ses dialectes du IXᵉ au XVᵉ siècle, Complément* (1902; reprint, New York: Kraus, 1961). Adolf Tobler and Erhard Lommatzsch, in *Altfranzösisches Wörterbuch,* vol. 4 (Wiesbaden: Franz Steiner, 1960), s.v., provide only slight additions to the substance of Godefroy's entry.

2 P[ierre] Richelet, *Dictionnaire françois contenant Les Mots et Les Choses,* 2 vols. (Genève: Widerhold, 1680); Antoine Furetière, *Le Dictionnaire universel* (1690; reprint, Paris: Robert, 1978); and *Le Dictionnaire de l'Académie Françoise dedié au Roy,* 2 vols. (Paris: Coignard, 1694).

3 References are to Pierre Costar and to Nicolas Boileau.

4 This is indicated by the word "contraire" and the emphasis on pronunciation. See the definitions of Isidore (cited below, chap. 3) and Donatus (cited below, chap. 4).

5 Cf. the more extensive changes in words dealing with parody; Dane, *Parody,* 121–48.

6 *Dictionnaire de l'Académie française,* 6th ed. (Paris: Firmin-Didot, 1835). The definitions of the adjective and adverb are only grammatical variants and are essentially unchanged from 1694, e.g.: "D'une manière ironique, par ironie. Il a dit cela ironiquement."

7   *Dictionnaire de l'Académie française, Complément* (Paris: Firmin-Didot, 1862).

8   The notion of "fine irony" has precedent in Cicero, *Brut.* 292: "ego, inquit Atticus, ironiam illam, quam in Socrate dicunt fuisse . . . facetam et elegantem puto"; unless otherwise noted, references to Cicero are to *M. Tullii Ciceronis Opera quae supersunt omnia,* ed. J. G. Baiter and C. L. Kayser, 11 vols. (Leipzig: Tauchnitz, 1863).

9   E. Littré, *Dictionnaire de la langue française* (Paris: Hachette, 1863), s.v.; reference to *"Proverb* 9." See also the later humorous variation of this noted by Roland Barthes in *Sade, Fourier, Loyola* (Paris: Seuil, 1971), 100; Fourier considers the creation of the melon an example of God's irony. The notion of an irony of God has medieval precedent; see Godefroy, *Dictionnaire, Complément,* s.v.: "Dieu luy dise *erronicquement"* (à Balaam); (Fossetier, Cron. Marg. ms. Bruxelles 10509, f. 156v.) This citation, however, is still to a verbal irony.

10 The reference to the adverb also suggests a rhetorical context: " 'Vela bien dit faictement / A le prendre *ironiquement'* (Therence en franc. fo 95d Verard.)."

11 *Thesaurus Linguae Latinae* (Leipzig: Teubner, 1906–); Charles Du Cange, *Glossarium Mediae et Infimae Latinitatis* (1688) new ed. (1883–87; reprint, Graz: Akademische Druck- und Verlags-anstalt, 1954). For Du Cange, irony is a form of abuse: "Ironia, vel Injuria. *Ironicus,* Derisorius, injuriosus. Lit. remiss. ann. 1381 in Reg. 120. Charoph. reg. Ch. 322. 'Reperierunt dictum Petrum de Buillone Ironicis contendentem cum dicta Johanna matre dicti pupilli; et sic cumulando verbis Ironicis inter eos idem Petrus elevato dicto baculo, etc.' " ["They found the said Peter arguing with said Johanna, mother of the said boy; and thus as the argument between them increased with ironical words, Peter, raising the said stick, etc."]. The *Thesaurus* citations are clearly in the rhetorical tradition, e.g., "hironia inris⟨i⟩va dictio aliut dicens et aliud significans, sic laudans et eum vituperare intellegas," from the sixth-century *Glossari Ansileubi sive liber glossarium;* further citations are to Augustine, *Retractions,* 1.1.4; Fulgentius, *Myth.,* 1.praef.14.4.

12 "Ye doe likewise dissemble, when ye speake in derision or mockerie, and that may be many waies: as sometime in sport, sometime in earnest, and priuily, and apertly, and pleasantly, and bitterly: but first by the figure *Ironia,* which we call the *drye mock:* as he that said to a bragging Ruffian, that threatened he would kill and slay, no doubt you are a good man of your hands"; George Puttenham, *The Arte of English Poesie* (1589; facs. reprint, Kent: Kent State University Press, 1970), bk. 3, p. 199.

13 Sedgewick, *Of Irony, Especially in Drama,* 22. For an example of the ahistorical and uncritical use of the *OED* definitions, see Eleanor N. Hutchens, "The Identification of Irony," *ELH* 27 (1960): 352–63.

14 Littré, *Dictionnaire,* s.v.: "—Hist. 14th s. Yronie est quant l'en dit une chose par quoy l'en veult donner à entendre le contraire. Oresme, *Thèse* de Meunier."

15 See, for example, the reference listed under "ironic" to Ben Jonson, *New Inn,* act 3, scene 2: "Most Socratick lady! Or if you will, ironick!"

16 The definitions under "ironical" seem to be based on the rhetorical sense of the word. The single citation under 2.b., "Mockingly imitative," is questioned even by the editors; it associates irony with apes and is easily interpretable as a form of raillery. The verb, "ironize," appears in the early seventeenth century. The first use of "ironist" listed is by Pope, from the *Art of Sinking:* "A poet or orator would have no more to do but to send to . . . the ironist for his sarcasms, to the apothegmatist for his sentences." The *Shorter Oxford English Dictionary* adds in fine print with its citations a definition that does not appear in the *OED.* Immediately following a citation of Macaulay (1837) appears

the statement "*Dramatic or tragic irony,* use of language having an inner meaning for a privileged audience, an outer for those immediately concerned." I assume this is a reference to Thirlwall, or one at least based on Thirlwall, although there is nothing in the text to indicate that.

Chapter 3. The Development of a Definition

1   References to Chaucer are to Larry D. Benson, gen. ed., *The Riverside Chaucer* (Boston: Houghton Mifflin, 1987). For some interesting but I think often misguided speculation on the reception of this cliché, see P. B. Taylor, "Chaucer's *Cosyn to the Dede,*" *Speculum* 57 (1982): 315–27. Cf. Langland's conception of Plato, as reflected in a speech by Dame Studie: "Plato the poete, I putte hym first to boke; / Aristotle and othere mo to argue I taughte"; William Langland, *The Vision of Piers Plowman,* ed. A. V. C. Schmidt (London: Dent, 1978), B, 10.175–76; see also 11.37 and 20.275.

2   Reference is to Jerome, *Epistula adversus Jovinianum,* 1.48; see Bartlett J. Whiting, "The Wife of Bath's Prologue," in W. J. Bryan and Germaine Dempster, eds., *Sources and Analogues of Chaucer's Canterbury Tales* (1941; reprint, New York: Humanities Press, 1958), anecdote on 212. See also *Fortune,* line 17, for Chaucer's association of Socrates with Fortune.

3   On Cato's distiches and their use in Chaucer, see Aage Brusendorff, "He Knew Nat Catoun for His Wit Was Rude," in Kemp Malone and Martin B. Ruud, ed., *Studies in English Philology: A Miscellany in Honor of Frederick Klaeber* (Minneapolis: University of Minnesota Press, 1929), 320–39.

4   See above, chap. 2, n. 12. Puttenham's 1589 definition, itself a synthesis of earlier rhetorical definitions, is nearly identical to those found in the modern lexicons developed a century later.

5   Japp, *Theorie der Ironie,* 37; the statement, which is less reductive than it seems, occurs in the context of a discussion of Mann.

6   Ribbeck, "Ueber den Begriff des *eirōn,*" 381–400. See the challenge to Ribbeck by Wilhelm Büchner, "Über den Begriff der eironeia," *Hermes* 76 (1941): 339–58; and the refutation of Büchner by Leif Bergson, "Eiron und eironeia," *Hermes* 99 (1971): 409–22. See also Vlastos, "Socratic Irony." Büchner's challenge to Ribbeck argues for *Kleintun* as an original meaning; the rhetorical meanings thus arise from the imposition of self-interest (*Zweck*) and the consequent emphasis of purpose over means. Bergson finds two parallel developments in the history of the word, the everyday vs. the ideal-Socratic.

7   See also *Eudemian Ethics* 3, 1234a (contrasting the *eirōn* with the *alazōn*) and *Magna Moralia,* 1192a (quoted by Ribbeck, "Ueber den Begriff des *eirōn,*" 388 n. 1.). Valla translates the distinction as one between *dissimulatio* and *iactatio: Aristotelis Opera* (Berlin: Reimer, 1870), vol. 3; see the useful index by Bonitz in vol. 5.

8   See Ribbeck, "Ueber den Begriff des *eirōn,*" 381; cf. Bergson, who denies the possibility of discovering an original meaning beyond the connotations of Socratic/sophistic the word has in both Plato and Aristophanes ("Eiron und eironeia," 411).

9   Bergson argues that Aristotle's association is unique.

10   The same approach toward irony will be taken by Shaftesbury in *Characteristicks.* See above, Introduction, n. 2.

11   In St. Thomas's thirteenth-century commentary, the word *eirōn* (not seemingly Latin-

ized) appears, but the passage contains none of the usual language from the rhetorical tradition: "Dicit ergo *primo,* quod irones qui minus de seipsis dicunt quam sit, videntur habere mores gratiosiores quam iactatores. . . . Et dicit quod *quidam* sunt qui maxime de se negant ea quae videntur ad magnam gloriam pertinere, sicut Socrates qui negabat se esse scientam"; *S. Thomae Aquinatis In Decem Libros Ethicorum Aristotelis ad Nicomachum Expositio,* ed. Raymundi M. Spiazzi (Turin: Marietti, 1949), 232–33, sec. 846 (for "Textus Aristotelis," see 497 and 498). Elsewhere, St. Thomas defines irony in a similar manner: "per quam aliquis de se fingit minora" (*Summa theol.* 2.2.113.1 ob. 1); noted by Helmut Prang, *Die romantische Ironie* (Darmstadt: Wissenschaftliche Buchgesellschaft, 1972), 2. No mention is made of Socrates, and the language has again little relation to rhetorical tradition.

12 Herman Diels, *Theophrasti Characteres* (Oxford: Clarendon Press, 1909); Ribbeck says his own article originated in a study of Theophrastus ("Ueber den Begriff des *eirōn,*" 381).

13 See Büchner, "Über den Begriff der eironeia," 346–49.

14 Cf. Ribbeck, who argues that Theophrastus is simply a watered-down version of Aristotle ("Ueber den Begriff des *eirōn,* 390).

15 For discussion, see esp. Büchner, "Über den Begriff der eironeia," 345–46; for text, C. Hammer, ed., *Rhetores Graeci ex recognitione Leonardi Spengel,* 1/2 (Leipzig: Teubner, 1894), 8–104; section on irony is on 57–58.

16 *M. Tullius Cicero: De Officiis Quartum,* ed. C. Atzert (Leipzig: Teubner, 1971), 36 and notes. The exact text here is corrupt but close enough to Aristotle, *Nic. Eth.* 1128, to be corrected on its basis. Reference below to this edition.

17 *M. Tullius Cicero: De Oratore,* ed. Kazimierz F. Kumaniecki (Leipzig: Teubner, 1969). The same gloss appears in *Academicorum priorum,* 2.5.15: "ea dissimulatio, quam Graeci *eirōneian* vocant"; *Ciceronis Opera omnia,* ed. Baiter and Kayser, vol. 6.

18 Cf. Knox, who suggests that Cicero considers irony both a figure of speech and a habit of discourse (*The Word "Irony" and Its Context,* 6). This is valid as long as we do not assume that the habit of discourse refers to Socrates' dialectic method itself. In *De Officiis,* the point of Cicero's citation of Socrates is only to contrast his facetiousness with the gravity of Pythagoras.

19 See, for example, Rainer Warning, "Irony and the 'Order of Discourse,' in Flaubert," *New Literary History* 13 (1982): 253–86, and the discussion in Japp, *Theorie der Ironie,* "Der ironische Individualismus," 279–313.

20 References below are to *M. Fabi Quintiliani Institutionis oratoriae libri duodecim,* ed. M. Winterbottom, 2 vols. (Oxford: Clarendon Press, 1970); see also 6.3.68 for irony as a kind of joke.

21 "nam, si qua earum uerbis dissentit, apparet diuersam esse orationi uoluntatem. Quanquam in plurimis id propis accidit, ut intersit, quid de quoque dicatur, quia quod dicitur alibi uerum est. Et laudis autem simulatione detrahere et uituperationis laudare concessum est: . . ." (8.6.54–55).

22 "Est igitur tropos sermo a naturali et principali significatione translatus ad aliam ornandae orationis gratia, uel, ut plerique grammatici finiunt, dictio ab eo loco in quo propria est translata in eum, in quo propria non est: 'figura,' sicut nomine ipso patet, conformatio quaedam orationis remota a communi et primum se offerente ratione" (9.1.4).

23 *In Cat.* 1.8.19: "ad sodalem tuum virum optimum, M. Marcellum, demigrasti." Quin-

tilian's notion of an irony of two words seems equivalent to Bede's notion of an irony of a single word; I assume Quintilian is counting the word expressed (*optimum*) and the word meant (*pessimum*).

24 The bracketed *sermoni et uoci* follows the edition of Eduard Bonnell, *M. Fabii Quintiliani Institutionis oratoriae libri duodecim* (1854; Leipzig: Teubner, 1884), noted and attributed to Karl Halm (1868) in the apparatus of Winterbottom; Winterbottom's "sensus sermonis et loci" is marked as a crux.

25 Following his reference to Socrates, Quintilian adds variants of irony, those he claims have nothing to do with the trope, as when something is said through its negation (9.2.47). According to Quintilian, some call this "antiphrasis," but the examples Quintilian gives seem to relate to the familiar figure *praeteritio:* "I will not press the point that, . . ." or "I will pass over the fact that. . . ." Irony also describes a concession in the form of a command, as in Dido's "I, sequere Italiam ventis"; it can be directed against things as well as persons, and is related also to pseudo-confession and concessions.

26 "The rhetorical definition of it as saying one thing and meaning the contrary—blame-through-praise or vice versa—was passed from one rhetorician to another" (Knox, *The Word "Irony" and Its Context,* 6). According to Knox, "No one during the English classical period used the word *irony* to refer to a dialectical method, either Socrates' or anyone else's, and no one found in Socrates the irony of detachment" (21; he refers here to a peculiar formulation of Fulke Greville's).

27 See Godefroy, *Dictionnaire, Complément,* s.v., and above, chap. 2.

28 See for example Angus Fletcher, *Allegory: The Theory of a Symbolic Mode* (Ithaca: Cornell University Press, 1964), 229–30.

29 References are to *Isidori Hispalensis Episcopi Etymologiarum sive originum libri XX,* ed. W. M. Lindsay, 2 vols. (Oxford: Clarendon Press, 1911).

30 Cf. Heinrich Lausberg, *Handbuch der literarischen Rhetorik: Eine Grundlegung der Literaturwissenschaft* (1960) 2d ed., 2 vols. (Munich: Hueber, 1973), sec. 903. Lausberg distinguishes the meaning of *allo;* in irony, it has the force of the opposite (*Gegenteil*) of what is meant, not "ein Vergleichsgegenstand für des ernstlich Gemeinte."

31 The word irony also appears in the widely disseminated *Marriage of Philology and Mercury* by Martianus Capella. But the reference is a casual one and due entirely to Aquila Romanus: "Irony (*eirōneia*) is a pretense, commonly used by Cicero, and a striking figure, in which we say one thing but mean another, as in the beginning of the *Pro Ligario:* 'A new charge, Gaius Caesar . . .' " *Martianus Capella and the Seven Liberal Arts,* trans. William Harris Stahl and Richard Johnson, vol. 2 (New York: Columbia University Press, 1977), 196, 194n.

32 *Arnulfi Aurelianensis Glosule super Lucanum,* ed. Berthe M. Marti (Paris: American Academy in Rome, 1958), on *Pharsalia* 9.1108; I thank John F. Benton for this reference. On the twelfth-century Merlin prophecies, see Michael J. Curley, "A New Edition of John of Cornwall's *Prophetia Merlini,*" *Speculum* 57 (1982): 217–49, in the introductory letter on detractors: "quos magister meus Theodericus, tum vero nomine Pharaones, tum yronice fratres suos appellare consuevit" (232).

33 The basic statements on the allegorization of classical texts are by Don Cameron Allen, *Mysteriously Meant: The Rediscovery of Pagan Symbolism and Allegorical Interpretation in the Renaissance* (Baltimore: Johns Hopkins University Press, 1970); Jean Pépin, *Mythe et allégorie: Les Origines grecques et les contestations judéo-chrétiennes* (Paris: Firmin-Didot, 1958); and Jean Seznec, *La Survivance des dieux antiques* (London: Warburg Institute, 1940). On

scriptural allegory, nothing compares with Henri de Lubac, *Exégèse médiévale: Les Quatre Sens de l'écriture* (Paris: Aubier, 1959–62).

Chapter 4. The Modern Reception: Lausberg; Medieval Misprisions 1 and 2

1   *Elemente der literarischen Rhetorik: Eine Einführung für Studierende der klassischen, romanischen, englischen und deutschen Philologie* (1949) 3d ed. (Munich: Hueber, 1967); *Handbuch der literarischen Rhetorik: Eine Grundlegung der Literaturwissenschaft*, 2 vols. (1960) 2d ed. (Munich: Hueber, 1973). The 1963 edition of *Elemente* adds the examples in English and German. Both are cited below by section.

2   On irony and its relation to judgment, see below, chap. 8, on dramatic irony and Connop Thirlwall's 1833 essay on Sophocles.

3   For Tryphon (first century B.C.) see Georg Wissowa et al., *Paulys Real-encyclopädie der classischen Altertumswissenschaft*, 2/7A (Stuttgart: Metzler, 1939), 726–43. Tryphon defines the trope as follows: "eirōneia esti logos dia tou enantiou to enantion meta tinos ēthikēs hypokriseōs dēlōn" ["irony is an expression indicating its opposite meaning through some manner of hypocrisy"]. This implies that the subversion of the word does not depend on a purely verbal context. Tryphon's *to enantion* could be translated "opposite" or "contrary"; the same ambiguity appears in the Latin words *aliud* and *diversum*. Lausberg refers also to Aquila (under *simulatio*): "frequentissima apud oratores figura, ubi aliud verbis significamus, aliud re sentimus"; to Hermogenes (under *permutatio*): "permutatio est oratio aliud verbis, aliud sententia demonstrans"; and to Isidore: "ironia est, cum per simulationem diversum quam dicit intellegi cupit . . ." (*Etym.*, 2.21.41).

4   Bede, *De Schematibus et tropis*, 616.1. Lausberg reads Bede's distinction between irony and antiphrasis (somewhat unclearly I think) as an example of the distinction between his own categories of word-figure and figure of thought. The word-figure betrays its contrary through immediate verbal context; the figure of thought only through extraverbal matters such as pronunciation (but see *Elemente* 232, where one of the "context-signals" for verbal irony is pronunciation). Bede's source, not cited here by Lausberg, seems to be Donatus: "antiphrasis est unius verbi ironia." For text, see Heinrich Keil, ed., *Grammatici Latini*, 7 vols. (1857–80; reprint, Hildesheim: Olms, 1981), 4:367–402; quotation on 402.

5   References below are to Wayne C. Booth, *A Rhetoric of Irony* (Chicago: University of Chicago Press, 1974); see the excellent review by Susan Suleiman, "Interpreting Ironies," *Diacritics* 6 (Summer 1976): 15–21. Japp's *Theorie der Ironie* is analogous in its attempt to ground discussion (in this case, a historical discussion) in classical rhetorical terms.

6   Booth does not "cross that formidable chasm" into "unstable irony" until p. 240. But even here, Booth's ironies are strictly limited: "We should note that the new territory we now face is still sharply delimited by our interest in intended ironies only. In choosing this limitation, I do not mean to reject all criticism that does not; it is just that we have a great deal of it" (241 n. 7).

7   Wayne C. Booth, *Critical Understanding: The Powers and Limits of Pluralism* (Chicago: University of Chicago Press, 1979), 222.

8   See Dane, "Defense of the Incompetent Reader"; and Jonathan Culler, *Structuralist Poetics: Structuralism, Linguistics, and the Study of Literature* (Ithaca: Cornell University Press, 1975), viii. Culler seems to have changed his views since; see Jonathan Culler,

The Pursuit of Signs: Semiotics, Literature, Deconstruction (Ithaca: Cornell University Press, 1981), chap. 3: "Semiotics as a Theory of Reading," and esp. pp. 50–54, although the emphasis on teaching remains (chap. 11, "Literary Theory in the Graduate Program," 210–26).

9   This hierarchy of expression and content has been attacked in structuralist readings of Saussure's theory of the mutual dependence of the *signifiant* and *signifié*. Even in Saussure, however, referents retain a privileged position over signs in that they are prior to the signs that arbitrarily point to them; the same is not generally true of the relation between content and expression. See Ferdinand de Saussure, *Cours de linguistique générale*, ed. Charles Bally and Albert Sechehaye, ed. Tullio de Mauro (Paris: Payot, 1972), 99–103, 158–62, where signification (the relation of *Sa* to *Sé*) blurs into a relation between signs and things (referentiality).

10 See, for example, Dante, *Paradiso*, 12.137–38: "e quel Donato / ch'alla prim'arte degnò porre mano."

11 References below are to Donatus, *Ars Grammatica*, in Keil, ed., *Grammatici Latini*, 4:367–402; and Pompeius, *Commentum Artis Donati*, in Keil, ed., *Grammatici Latini*, 5:81–312. Parts of the following discussion appear also in my "The Myth of Chaucerian Irony," *Papers on Language and Literature* 24 (1988): 211–28.

12 The example is quoted also by Lausberg, *Elemente* 429.1.

13 The entire passage is as follows: "ironia est, quotienscumque re vera aliud loquimur et aliud significamus in verbis; non ita, ut diximus de allegoria, quando aliud dicimus et aliud significamus, non, sed isdem verbis potes et negare et confirmare; sola autem pronuntiatione discernitur." My tentative translation of the omitted sentence is: "The word *non* pronounced this way (*ita*), as we were saying of allegory when we say one thing and mean another, means 'no,' but. . . ." The sentence is generally read as implying instead a difference between allegory and irony ("not as we said about allegory . . ."). The phrase "non, sed" is, I think, a corruption. The combination *non sed* does not appear in any of the texts presently on the Ibycus system.

14 References below are to Alice Miskimin, *The Renaissance Chaucer* (New Haven: Yale University Press, 1975). D. H. Green, in *Irony in the Medieval Romance* (Cambridge: Cambridge University Press, 1979), also cites this passage, which I believe he interprets correctly (4, 7); see, however, my reservations on his use of such authorities, in this chapter below.

15 See Knox, *The Word "Irony" and Its Context*.

16 See Hans Robert Jauß, *Alterität und Modernitat der mittelalterlichen Literatur* (Munich: Fink, 1977); and the special issue of *New Literary History* 10 (Winter 1979).

17 D. W. Robertson, Jr., *A Preface to Chaucer: Studies in Medieval Perspectives* (Princeton: Princeton University Press, 1962). Robertson indexes under the word irony only strict uses of the word; but see 479 (unindexed) on the character of Pandarus as "a masterpiece of medieval irony" (quoted by Green, *Irony in the Medieval Romance*, 33), where the phrase "medieval irony" clearly refers to something beyond its rhetorical meaning.

18 *Sancti Aurelii Augustini De Doctrina Christiana; De Vera Religione*, ed. Joseph Martin (Turnholt: Brepols, 1962).

19 Robertson's re-romanticizing of medieval literature has often been noted; e.g., R. S. Crane, "On Hypotheses in Historical Criticism: Apropos of Certain Contemporary Medievalists," in *The Idea of the Humanities and Other Essays Critical and Historical*, 2 vols. (Chicago: University of Chicago Press, 1967), 2:236–59.

20   References below are to *Irony in the Medieval Romance*. See also an earlier essay by D. H. Green, "Irony and Medieval Romance," in D. D. R. Owen, ed., *Arthurian Romance: Seven Essays* (New York: Barnes and Noble, 1971), 49–64. The essay is a preliminary sketch of the book.

21   Jean Frappier, *Amour courtois et Table Ronde* (Geneva: Droz, 1963), 61ff, esp. 64, 66, and 92. Green (14 and 213 n. 3) also claims to be contesting Michael S. Batts, "Hartmann's *Humanitas:* A New Look at *Iwein,*" in Frithjof Andersen Raven et al., eds., *Germanic Studies in Honor of Edward Henry Sehrt* (Coral Gables: University of Miami Press, 1968); but Batts offers no arguments to support his denial to medieval romance of irony, glossed as an "ambivalence of standpoint between, say, author, narrator, and characters" (39).

22   Green's source is H. W. Fowler, *A Dictionary of Modern English Usage* (Oxford: Clarendon Press, 1926): "Irony is a form of utterance that postulates a double audience" (295). The same passage is cited by Charles Muscatine, *Chaucer and the French Tradition* (Berkeley: University of California Press, 1957), 264 n. 46; Green relies on Muscatine for his interpretation of *Troilus and Criseyde* (see below, n. 24).

23   See in particular Erich Köhler, *Ideal und Wirklichkeit in der höfischen Epik* (Tübingen: Niemeyer, 1956); idem, "Quelques observations d'ordre historico-sociologique sur les rapports entre la chanson de geste et le roman courtois," in *Chanson de geste und höfischer Roman* (Heidelberg: Carl Winter, 1963), 21–30; and idem, "Literatursoziologische Perspektiven," in Jean Frappier and Reinhold R. Grimm, eds., *Le Roman jusqu'à la fin du XIIIᵉ siècle,* Grundriß der romanischen Literaturen des Mittelalters, 4/1 (Heidelberg: Carl Winter, 1978), 82–103.

24   For example, on the characters Troilus and Pandarus in Chaucer's *Troilus and Criseyde,* "each relativises the other" (341), with reference to Muscatine; for the description of such character relations as irony, see Muscatine, *Chaucer and the French Tradition,* 137–39, 153. "Irony of Values" refers to the opposed meanings of a virtue in secular and religious contexts (*Irony in the Medieval Romance,* 287ff.).

25   Reference is to E. Talbot Donaldson, "Chaucer the Pilgrim, *PMLA* 59 (1954): 928–36.

Chapter 5. Romantic Irony: Introduction

1   Furst, in discussing Kierkegaard, avoids mention of Socrates (*Fictions of Romantic Irony,* 33–35), even though Kierkegaard's entire thesis on irony is arguably devoted to Socrates.

2   See for example the statement in the handbook of Hazard Adams, *The Interests of Criticism: An Introduction to Literary Theory* (New York: Harcourt, Brace, and World, 1969): "It appears that there is an ineradicable Romantic irony in the enterprise of criticism. Like the quest of the Byronic hero, it is endless and yet at the same time valuable—endless because its terms are finally self-defeating, and valuable because in its own inadequacy it calls attention to the greater adequacy of the poem itself" (141); quoted by Gerald Graff, *Poetic Statement and Critical Dogma* (Chicago: University of Chicago Press, 1970), 23 n. 46.

3   Kierkegaard, *Concept of Irony,* 331; also noted by Strohschneider-Kohrs, *Die romantische Ironie,* 221.

4   See Strohschneider-Kohrs, *Die romantische Ironie,* 100–112 on Novalis; and Furst, *Fictions of Romantic Irony,* 30. Reference is to *Allgemeine Brouillon,* no. 445, in *Schriften,* ed. Paul Kluckhohn and Richard Samuel (Darmstadt: Wissenschaftliche Buchgesellschaft, 1968), 3:326. *Allgemeine Brouillon* is dated 1798–99 and is less a collection of fragments than

material for a projected encyclopedia; see Hans-Joachim Mähl, "Einleitung," ibid., 237.

5   The notebooks are quoted in different form by Strohschneider-Kohrs, *Die romantische Ironie*, 1 n. 1. They have been edited twice by Hans Eichner, as *Friedrich Schlegel: Literary Notebooks, 1797–1801* (London: University of London, 1957), and most recently as *Friedrich Schlegel: Fragmente zur Poesie und Literatur*, Erster Teil, KA 16 (Paderborn: Schöningh, 1981). References to the notebooks below are to the 1981 edition.

6   *Fragmente*, ed. Eichner, fr. V, 716 (p. 146). See also, fr. 709: "Romantische Ironie ist wohl allen [rhetorischen] [Dramen] nothwendig?—" (p. 145); fr. 713: "Auch Petrarcha hat romant. [ische] *Ironie*" (p. 145).

7   Hermann Hettner, *Die romantische Schule in ihrem inneren Zusammenhange mit Goethe und Schiller* (1850), in *Schriften zur Literature* (Berlin: Aufbau-Verlag, 1959), 51–165.

8   This is partially quoted by Furst, *Fictions of Romantic Irony*, 30 (reference in notes is not accurate); Furst may be citing Prang, *Die romantische Ironie*. See also Hettner's *Geschichte der deutschen Literatur im 18. Jahrhundert* (1856ff.). Prang argues that Hettner "misunderstands" romantic irony (*Die romantische Ironie*, 85–87).

9   References below are to R. Haym, *Die romantische Schule: Ein Beitrag zur Geschichte des deutschen Geistes* (Berlin: Gaertner, 1870).

10 Heinrich Heine, "Die romantische Schule" (1835), in *Sämtliche Werke in vier Bänden* (Munich: Winkler, 1972), 3:259–394. On Heine's use of the word irony, see esp. Wolfgang Preisendanz, "Ironie bei Heine," in Albert Schaefer, ed., *Ironie und Dichtung: Sechs Essays von Beda Allemann, Ernst Zinn, Hans-Egon Hass, Wolfgang Preisendanz, Fritz Martini, Paul Böckmann* (Munich: Beck, 1970), 85–112; Preisendanz claims there is little relation to the early romantic use of the word. Roger Ayrault implies that a similar phrase was used by Jean Paul in the 1804 introduction to *Vorschule der Ästhetik* ("l'école moderne"); *La Genèse du romantisme allemand*, 4 vols. (Paris: Aubier, 1961–76), 1:44; but I cannot find the phrase to which Ayrault refers.

11 See Philippe Lacoue-Labarthe and Jean-Luc Nancy, *L'Absolu littéraire: Théorie de la littérature du romantisme allemand* (Paris: Seuil, 1978), 15, with reference to Ayrault, *Genèse du romantisme allemand;* see esp. 3:11–95 on the Jena romantics.

12 Alfred Edwin Lussky, *Tieck's Romantic Irony: With Special Emphasis Upon the Influence of Cervantes, Sterne, and Goethe* (Chapel Hill: University of North Carolina Press, 1932), 242. See also Beda Allemann, *Ironie und Dichtung* (Pfullingen: Neske, 1956), 22, for a similar strategy.

13 See Wilhelm Dilthey, *Leben Schleiermachers* (1870) in *Gesammelte Schriften*, 13/1 (Göttingen: Vandenhoeck & Ruprecht, 1970), 295; and Friedrich's letter to his brother: "Schleyermacher ist ein Mensch, in dem der Mensch begildet ist, und darum gehört er freylich für mich in eine höhere Kaste. Tieck z.B. ist doch nur ein ganz gewöhnlicher und roher Mensch, der ein seltnes und sehr ausgebildetes Talent hat"; 28 November 1797, in *Friedrich Schlegel: Briefe von und an Friedrich und Dorothea Schlegel, Die Periode des Athenäums, 25. Juli 1797–Ende August 1799*, KA 24/3, ed. Raymond Immerwahr (Paderborn: Schöningh, 1985), 45–46, hereafter *[Letters];* and in *Friedrich Schlegels Briefe an seinen Bruder August Wilhelm*, ed. Oskar F. Walzel (Berlin: Speyer and Peters, 1890), 322.

14 See Jerome J. McGann, *The Romantic Ideology: A Critical Investigation* (Chicago: University of Chicago Press, 1983), "Introduction," 1–14. On the dual creation of romanticism by romantics and romanticists, see also Tzvetan Todorov, "La Crise romantique," in *Théories du symbole* (Paris: Seuil, 1977), 179–269, esp. 200.

15 Many of Tieck's key statements on irony are secondhand, from the biography by Rudolf Köpke, *Ludwig Tieck: Erinnerungen aus dem Leben des Dichters nach dessen mündlichen und schriftlichen Mittheilungen,* 2 vols. (Leipzig: Brockhaus, 1855); see esp. 2:238–40. On its continuing influence, see Roger Paulin, *Ludwig Tieck: A Literary Biography* (Oxford: Clarendon Press, 1985), 349. And for reservations about Köpke's accuracy, see esp. Oskar Walzel, "Methode? Ironie bei Friedrich Schlegel und bei Solger," *Helicon* 1 (1938): 35–36.

16 See also Ludwig Tieck, *Schriften,* 28 vols. (Berlin: Reimer, 1828–54), 6:xxviii–xxix (quoted by Strohschneider-Kohrs, *Die romantische Ironie,* 131), where "higher irony" is that of Aristophanes, Shakespeare, Plato: "Over the whole, hovers still a higher, spiritual irony, as seen in Socrates' seeming lack of knowledge." See further, Strohschneider-Kohrs, *Die romantische Ironie,* 128–46.

17 See Marie Joachimi-Dege, *Deutsche Shakespeare-Probleme im 18. Jahrhundert und im Zeitalter der Romantik* (Leipzig: Haessel, 1907), esp. 169–71. Examples above are from Köpke, *Erinnerungen,* 2:217–23; further examples are cited by Strohschneider-Kohrs, *Die romantische Ironie,* 133.

18 References to Hegel are to *Georg Wilhelm Friedrich Hegel: Sämtliche Werke,* ed. Hermann Glockner, Jubiläumsausgabe, 20 vols. (Stuttgart: Fromann, 1927–40), hereafter JA. The phrases "d[ie] sich absolute Subjektivität" "unendliche absolute Negativität" are from his *Lectures on Aesthetics,* JA 12:104–5; see Kierkegaard, *Concept of Irony,* 271.

19 See, for example, Tieck's statements in Köpke, *Erinnerungen,* 2:238.

20 See further, Ayrault, *Genèse du romantisme allemand,* "Kant et la 'révolution dans la manière de penser': La 'Subjectivité' " (1:173ff.).

21 Raymond Immerwahr, "The Subjectivity or Objectivity of Friedrich Schlegel's Poetic Irony," *Germanic Review* 26 (1951): 173–91.

22 Walter Benjamin, *Der Begriff der Kunstkritik in der deutschen Romantik,* in *Gesammelte Schriften, unter Mitwirkung von Theodor W. Adorno und Gershom Scholem,* ed. Rolf Tiedemann and Hermann Schweppenhäuser (1974), 2d ed. (Frankfurt am Main: Suhrkamp, 1974), 1:7–122.

23 So Joachimi-Dege, *Shakespeare-Probleme,* 175: "Die Ironie ist die Objektivität, die auf der unendlichen Individualität des Dichters beruht." See Immerwahr, "Subjectivity or Objectivity," for further references. Not all scholars discussed by Immerwahr label their views with the words subjective/objective; the problems with this terminology are noted by Strohschneider-Kohrs, in *Die romantische Ironie,* 88–89.

24 *Vermischte Bemerkungen,* no. 36; *Novalis: Schriften,* ed. Richard Samuel, vol. 2, *Das philosophische Werk I* (Stuttgart: Kohlhammer, 1960), 428. The published version of this fragment edited by Schlegel for the *Athenaeum* (vol. 1, 1798), *Blüthenstaub* 29, varies slightly, and combines with this an earlier fragment on *Humor* (*Vermischte Bemerkungen,* no. 30); see introduction, 399–411.

25 Mellor, in *English Romantic Irony,* relies completely and uncritically on Strohschneider-Kohrs's *Die romantische Ironie* for Schlegel; all of Mellor's citations to Schlegel are from Minor, the edition used by Strohschneider-Kohrs, and none are to the Kritische-Ausgabe produced since 1960. For a similar method in French, see René Bourgeois, *L'Ironie romantique: Spectacle et jeu de Mme de Staël à G. de Nerval* (Grenoble: Presses Universitaires de Grenoble, 1974). Cf. the redefinition of romantic irony by David Simpson as "indeterminacy" and the resultant deconstructive readings of English works such

a definition permits; *Irony and Authority in Romantic Poetry* (Totowa, N.J.: Rowman and Littlefield, 1979), 190.

26 References below are to Kathleen M. Wheeler, *Sources, Processes, and Methods in Coleridge's "Biographia Literaria"* (Cambridge: Cambridge University Press, 1980), 59. See also Walzel, "Methode" (1938), on which Wheeler relies. Some of Walzel's arguments about the current state of scholarship are necessarily dated.

27 The result of such canon formation in English scholarship can be seen in the excellent recent anthology edited by Kathleen Wheeler, *The Romantic Ironists and Goethe* (Cambridge: Cambridge University Press, 1984), a volume in a series entitled *German Aesthetic and Literary Criticism*. We might expect a volume with such a title to be heavily weighted toward Goethe. Nonetheless, the passages from Goethe consist of some dozen pages only, and only as "an object of [the Romantic ironists'] imagination" (225). The other authors are F. Schlegel, Novalis, Tieck, Solger, Jean Paul, and A. W. Schlegel.

Chapter 6. Hegel and Solger

1 Strohschneider-Kohrs speaks of Schlegel's "hohe und positive Vorstellung der künstlerischen Ironie" (*Die romantische Ironie*, 80).

2 References below are to "Über 'Solgers nachgelassene Schriften und Briefwechsel, ed. Ludwig Tieck und Friedrich v. Haumer. (1826),' Jahrbücher f. wissensch. Kritik 1838," JA 20:132–202; *Vorlesungen über Ästhetik*, "Einleitung," JA 12:99ff.; and *Vorlesungen über die Geschichte der Philosophie*, 3 vols., JA 17–19. Hegel's passages on irony are listed in Capel's translation of Kierkegaard's *Concept of Irony*, 406 n. 7 (from the list in the 1961 German translation of Kierkegaard by E. Hirsch); they are indexed also in the *Hegel-Lexicon*, vol. 2., JA 24:1130–35.

3 "Philosophie des Sokrates," JA 18.42–121, and "Fichte's neu umgebildetes System," 19:640–41.

4 On Solger see also *Grundlinien der Philosophie des Rechts*, JA 7:217–18n. See also Jean Hyppolite, *Introduction à la philosophie de l'histoire de Hegel* (Paris: Rivière, 1948), 16–17, on *Moralität* and Hegel's *Sittlichkeit*.

5 "Die Ironie betrifft nur ein Verhalten des Gesprächs gegen Personen," *Grundlinien der Philosophie des Rechts*, JA 7:217.

6 I assume that what is presented here as a grammatical and logical slippage between *Ich, mich,* and the two meanings of *Ich* (the principle and the pronoun referring to "me") is part of Hegel's implied critique.

7 For an interesting attempt to reinterpret such "lack of character" as a virtue of ironists, see Maurice Blanchot, *L'Entretien infini* (Paris: Gallimard, 1969): "ce caractère dit romantique qui, du rest, est très attrayant, dans la mesure où lui manque précisément tout caractère . . ." (524–25).

8 The same case is still commonly made against Tieck by romanticists; see, e.g., Lussky, *Tieck's Romantic Irony*, and chap. 5 above.

9 See also Walzel, "Methode," 50, for further references (on Korner). Exceptions to this judgment of Hegel exist, most notably, Behler's in *Ironie*, 112–21.

10 Strohschneider-Kohrs rejects the particular comments of both Hegel and Kierkegaard on Schlegel and on irony generally, but concurs in their evaluation of Solger (*Die romantische Ironie*, 185–86).

11   Adam Müller, unlike Solger, explicitly relates his theories on irony to Friedrich
Schlegel; see chap. 8 below.

12   Tieck was in correspondence with the Schlegels during the *Athenaeum* period and,
although not a contributor, was an occasional subject. *Athenaeum*, vol. 2, pt. 2 (1799),
contains F. Schlegel's review of Tieck's *Don Quixote;* vol. 3, the final volume, pt. 2 (1800)
contains A. W. Schlegel's sonnet addressed to Tieck; see also [*Letters*], ed. Immerwahr,
passim (index, 487).

13   References below are to *K. W. F. Solgers Vorlesungen über Aesthetik,* ed. K. W. L. Heyse
(Leipzig: Brockhaus, 1829); Karl Wilhelm Ferdinand Solger, "Beurtheilung der Vorlesungen über dramatische Kunst und Literatur," in *Nachgelassene Schriften und Briefwechsel, ed. Ludwig Tieck und Friedrich von Raumer,* 2 vols. (1826; facs. reprint, Heidelberg:
Schneider, 1973), 493–628; and *Erwin: Vier Gespräche über das Schöne und die Kunst zusammen mit Solgers Rezension von A. W. Schlegels Vorlesungen über dramatische Kunst und Literatur,*
ed. Wolfhart Henckmann (Munich: Fink, 1970); *Erwin* is reprinted from the Berlin 1907
edition.

14   References below are to A. W. Schlegel, *Ueber dramatische Kunst und Litteratur. Vorlesungen,* 2 vols. (Heidelberg: Mohr und Zimmer, 1809–11), pt. 2, sec. 2, twelfth lecture
(in Black's translation, this is "Lecture 23"), 71–75.

15   Cf. Walzel, who claims that A. W. Schlegel's *Lectures* are merely his "exoteric" teach-
ings; his "esoteric" (and undocumented) theories of irony are the same as those of
Friedrich ("Methode," 50).

16   Solger himself defines tragic irony as the "open presence of God in the present" (515).

17   "Begeisterung und Ironie machen die künstlerische Thätigkeit, Symbol und Allegorie
des Kunstwerk aus" (*Lectures on Aesthetics,* 125).

18   René Wellek, *A History of Modern Criticism (1750–1950): The Romantic Age* (New Haven:
Yale University Press, 1955), 298; see further, 1–35, 291–302.

19   For the relation of early romantic views on irony to Schiller's essay, see esp. Dilthey,
Leben Schleiermachers, 243; see also Peter Szondi, "Friedrich Schlegel und die romantische
Ironie. Mit einem Anhang über Ludwig Tieck," *Euphorion* 48 (1954): 397–411.

Chapter 7. Friedrich Schlegel

1   "Es ist der Kern der Schlegel'schen ästhetischen Doctrin, den wir durch Klarmachung
dessen, was er unter romantischer Poesie und unter Ironie verstand, gewonnen haben"
(Haym, *Die romantische Schule,* 262). On the notion of a Schlegelian doctrine, see *Friedrich
Schlegel: Charakteristiken und Kritiken I (1796–1801),* ed. Hans Eichner, KA 2 (Munich:
Schöningh, 1967), xlvi.

2   Cf. "Über die Diotima," quoted by Eichner, *Charakteristiken und Kritiken I:* "Solange
das einzig-wahre System nicht entdeckt war, oder solange es nur noch unvollkommen
dargestellt ist, bleibt das systematische Verfahren mehr oder weniger trennend und
isolierend; das systemlos lyrische Philosophieren zerstört wenigstens das Ganze der
Wahrheit nich so sehr" (KA 2:xl).

3   "Ich kann von mir, von meinem ganzen Ich gar kein andres echantillon geben, als
so ein System von Fragmenten, weil ich selbst dergleichen bin"; *Fr. Schlegels Briefe an
seinen Bruder,* ed. Walzel, 336; [*Letters*], ed. Immerwahr, 67. Cf. Shaftesbury, *Characteristicks:* "The most ingenious way of becoming foolish, is by a system" (1:290); quoted
by Eichner in *Charakteristiken und Kritiken I,* KA 2:xxxix.

4 Quoted by Eichner in *Charakteristiken und Kritiken I, KA* 2:xliv, from *Fr. Schlegels Briefe an seinen Bruder,* ed. Walzel, 315; see [*Letters*], ed. Immerwahr, 51.

5 See, for example, K. K. Polheim, *Die Arabeske: Ansichten und Ideen aus Fr. Schlegels Poetik* (Munich: Schöningh, 1965); and Eichner's introduction on the word *Witz* (*Charakteristiken und Kritiken I, KA* 2:xxxvi–xxxviii).

6 See Strohschneider-Kohrs on the notion of "irony of love" (*Die romantische Ironie,* 80–87); and Benjamin, who (somewhat more convincingly I think) reads the Vienna lectures into Schlegel's earlier works (*Begriff der Kunstkritik*).

7 All texts available in *Charakteristiken und Kritiken I,* ed. Eichner, *KA* 2. The volumes of the *Athenaeum* are 1/2 (1798): Fragments and "Über Goethes *Meister*"; 3/1 (1800): *Ideen* and "Gespräch über die Poesie, I"; 3/2 (1800, the final volume): "Gespräch über die Poesie, II," "Über die Unverständlichkeit." Among several reprints is *Athenaeum. Eine Zeitschrift. Hrsg. von August Wilhelm Schlegel und Friedrich Schlegel,* 3 vols. (1798–1800; facs. reprint, Darmstadt: Wissenschaftliche Buchgesellschaft, 1977). For a convenient summary of the *Athenaeum* contents, see Lacoue-Labarthe and Nancy, *L'absolu littéraire,* 34–36.

8 The bulk of the essay appeared in pt. 1, along with *Ideen;* Schlegel began the essay as early as 1798; *Charakteristiken und Kritiken I,* ed. Eichner, *KA* 2:lxxxvii–lxxxviii.

9 See *Athenaeum* fr. 51 and 121, discussed in this chapter below.

10 See "Gespräch über die Poesie"; Lothario glosses this as meaning that all plays of art are imitations of the "eternal play of the world, the self-fashioning artwork"; Ludoviko: "Mit andern Worten: alle Schönheit ist Allegorie" (324). See further, chap. 12 below, n. 6.

11 See also "Gespräch über die Poesie" with reference to Gozzi: "Auch der 'Triumph der Empfindsamkeit' geht sehr weit ab vom Gozzi, und in Rücksicht der Ironie weit über ihn hinaus" (344). For Gozzi's relation to Germany, see Strohschneider–Kohrs, *Die romantische Ironie,* 77; and Jean Starobinski, "Ironie et melancolie (I): Le théâtre de Carlo Gozzi," *Critique* 22 (1966): 291–308.

12 The word *schweben* and its translations, here "hover," become part of the standard vocabulary of irony; see Allemann, *Ironie und Dichtung,* 13–14.

13 "Ironie ist klares Bewußtsein der ewigen Agilität ⟨,⟩ des unendlich vollen Chaos" (*Ideen,* 69) ["Irony is the clear consciousness of eternal agility ⟨,⟩ of infinitely full chaos"]. The editorial comma is symptomatic of the ambiguity of this fragment.

14 *Friedrich Schlegel: Philosophische Lehrjahre (1796–1806) nebst philosophischen Manuscripten aus den Jahren 1796–1828,* Erster Teil, ed. Ernst Behler, *KA* 18 (Munich: Schöningh, 1963), fr. II, 668 (p. 85). Some of the fragments were available in *Friedrich Schlegel's Philosophische Vorlesungen aus den jahren 1804 bis 1806; nebst Fragmenten vorzüglich philosophisch-theologischen Inhalts,* ed. C. J. Windischmann, 2 vols. (Bonn: Eduard Weber, 1837), 2:403–27; these do not bear specifically on the problem of irony.

15 Strohschneider-Kohrs, *Die romantische Ironie,* 35–37; see also Behler, *Ironie,* 79–80.

16 See above, chap. 5, n. 5. Fragments are quoted from *Schlegel: Fragmente,* ed. Eichner (1981) *KA* 16; cross-references, abbreviated "LN," are to *Schlegel: Literary Notebooks,* ed. Eichner (1957).

17 "Absicht bis zur Ironie, und mit willkürlichem Schein von Selbstvernichtung ist ebensowohl naiv, als Instinkt bis zur Ironie" (*Athenaeum* fr. 305). Irony here seems to indicate a negative limit.

18   Cf. *Schlegel: Fragmente,* ed. Eichner, fr. V, 409 (p. 119), and 783 (p. 152): "Ironie = Selbstparodie?"

19   Not discussed in detail below is fr. 7, where Schlegel criticizes his own history of Greek literature for "its complete lack of indispensable irony" ("der gänzliche Mangel der unentbehrlichen Ironie").

20   The interpretation of this as a reference to the artistic and dramatic breaking of illusion characteristic of Tieck's drama has not been accepted by all romanticists; see Immerwahr, "Subjectivity or Objectivity," 190.

21   Wellek, *History: The Romantic Age,* 1.

22   Marshall Brown, *The Shape of German Romanticism* (Ithaca: Cornell University Press, 1979), 101; Furst, *Fictions of Romantic Irony,* 23–28; Mellor, *English Romantic Irony,* 7, 13; Prang, *Die romantische Ironie,* 13–15. Schlegel's comments are found in a letter to Dorothy: "Der alte Essay über die Unverständlichkeit ist in dieser Fuge von Ironie so ziemlich in Kochstückchen zerhackt, wie Du leicht seyn wirst"; Ludwig Jonas and Wilhelm Dilthey, *Aus Schleiermacher's Leben, In Briefen,* 3 vols. (Berlin: Reimer, 1861), 3:191n. The final essay was reworked from an earlier version of 1799; see *Charakteristiken und Kritiken I,* ed. Eichner, KA 2:xcvii.

23   *Fr. Schlegels Briefe an seinen Bruder,* ed. Walzel, 299, 301; quoted also by Eichner, *Charakteristiken und Kritiken I,* KA 2:xlii, Martin Walser, *Selbstbewußtsein und Ironie* (Frankfurt am Main: Suhrkamp, 1981), 21; text from [*Letters*], ed. Immerwahr, 31.

24   See, for example, *Ideen* 131; and esp. Lacoue-Labarthe and Nancy, *L'absolu littéraire,* "La religion dans les limites de l'art," 181–205.

Chapter 8. Dramatic Irony

1   JA 18:64; the reference has nothing to do with the theater. In Schlegel's "Über die Unverständlichkeit," "dramatic irony" refers somewhat whimsically to the difference between boxes and parterre.

2   Froma L. Zeitlin, "Playing the Other: Theater, Theatricality, and the Feminine in Greek Drama," *Representations* 11 (1985): 75. See also Germaine Dempster, *Dramatic Irony in Chaucer* (Stanford: Stanford University Press, 1932), for strictly metaphorical uses.

3   Alex Preminger, ed., *Princeton Encyclopedia of Poetry and Poetics,* enlarged ed. (Princeton: Princeton University Press, 1974), 407. The definition continues: "(b) the character reacts in a way contrary to that which is appropriate or wise; (c) characters or situations are compared or contrasted for ironic effects, such as parody; (d) there is marked contrast between what the character understands about his acts and what the play demonstrates about them." Definition (d) seems a close variant of (a). Definitions (b) and (c) seem merely versions of "[possible] irony in drama."

4   The *Oxford English Dictionary,* s.v., uses Thirlwall's phrase "tragic irony" to support a figurative definition, irony of fate; see above, chap. 2.

5   Ernst Robert Curtius, "Friedrich Schlegel und Frankreich," in *Kritische Essays zur europäischen Literatur* (Bern: Francke, 1950), 86.

6   References below are to Adam Müller, *Kritische-ästhetische und philosophische Schriften,* ed. Walter Schroeder and Werner Sieber, 2 vols. (Neuwied: Luchterhand, 1967), 1:233–48. On the reception of Müller, see 2:311–95. The essay was written as a lecture in 1806–7 and published in 1808; see notes, 2:441.

7 See esp. Strohschneider-Kohrs, *Die romantische Ironie*, 162–85.

8 Müller later provides a historical basis for this: since only the stage speaks in tragedy, tragedy is of a monologic, monarchical nature; in comedy, both the stage and the public represented on stage speak; comedy is thus of a more dialogic, democratic nature. The difference corresponds to what Müller claims is the development of democracy in Athens from the earlier aristocracy (244). The similarity of certain modern critical terminology to such romantic statements need hardly be pointed out.

9 The phrase is used also by Japp in *Theorie der Ironie*, with reference to irony in Solger, Müller, and the late work of Friedrich Schlegel (191 n. 19).

10 Müller, *Schriften*, 2:153–87; see esp. 2:173–75, where Müller expands on Fichte for a concept of irony and the artist; the active (and "higher") artist is characterized in the dialectic as *Antigegensatz:* "Ein göttlicher Richter und Mittler schwebe er geflügelt und leicht über beiden . . . [the real and the ideal]" (2:175).

11 References below are to Connop Thirlwall, "On the Irony of Sophocles," *Philological Museum* 1–2 (1833): 483–537.

12 Alan Reynolds Thompson, *The Dry Mock: A Study of Irony in Drama* (Berkeley: University of California Press, 1948), 143–48.

13 See Sedgewick, *Of Irony, Especially in Drama*, 23; D. C. Muecke in *Irony* (London: Methuen, 1970), suggests, not quite accurately I think, that Thirlwall's phrase "tragic irony" refers to the special sense of dramatic irony defined in Preminger (21–23).

14 See Hegel's discussion of Socratic irony as a form of midwifery in *Lectures on the History of Philosophy*, JA 18:61–62, and his distinction between Socrates' particular irony and his "tragische Ironie" (64).

15 See Hutchens, "Identification of Irony," 355–58.

16 Thirlwall admits that "the irony we have been illustrating [in *Oedipus Rex* and *Oedipus at Colonnus*] is not equally conspicuous in all the plays of Sophocles" (503). Nor, one would assume, in other drama.

17 See Japp, *Theorie der Ironie*, 60–64.

18 Sedgewick, *Of Irony, Especially in Drama*, 34–37.

19 A. C. Bradley, *Shakespearean Tragedy* (1904), 2d ed. (1905; reprint, New York: Macmillan, 1955), 338–39. See further, Muecke, *Compass of Irony*, 8, on Bradley and Sedgewick.

20 So William Empson, *Seven Types of Ambiguity* (1930), 2d ed. (London: Chatto and Windus, 1947): "Dramatic irony is an interesting device for my purpose, because it gives an intelligible way in which the reader can be reminded of the rest of a play while he is reading a single part of it" (44).

21 Lewis Campbell, ed., *Sophocles, edited with English Notes and Introductions*, 2d ed. rev., 2 vols. (Oxford: Clarendon Press, 1879); Lewis Campbell, *Tragic Drama in Aeschylus, Sophocles, and Shakespeare: An Essay* (New York: Longmans, 1904).

22 The notion of dramatic irony is less prominent in French dramatic criticism than in English; classical French theory requires that the spectators be deceived by the stage action (they interpret it as true), and this forecloses discussions of audience superiority.

23 See Sedgewick, *Of Irony, Especially in Drama*, on the *Oxford English Dictionary* (23).

Chapter 9. The Myth of Chaucerian Irony: Medieval Misprisions 3

1 A version of the present chapter appears as "The Myth of Chaucerian Irony," *Papers on Language and Literature* 24 (1988): 211–28.

2   Thomas Warton, in *Observations on the Faerie Queene of Spenser* (London: Dodsley, 1754), notes Chaucer's "true humour," "pathos," and "sublimity" (141), but does not mention irony; see also *The History of English Poetry from the Close of the Eleventh to the Commencement of the Eighteenth Century,* 4 vols. (London: Dodsley, 1774–), 1:341–68. On Tyrwhitt, see below, n. 8.

3   Peter Elbow, *Oppositions in Chaucer* (Middleton, Conn.: Wesleyan University Press, 1973), 14.

4   "Chaucer the Pilgrim" (1954), reprint, *Speaking of Chaucer* (New York: Norton, 1970), 3.

5   Donald R. Howard, *The Idea of the Canterbury Tales* (Berkeley: University of California Press, 1976).

6   Charles Muscatine, *Poetry and Crisis in the Age of Chaucer* (Notre Dame: University of Notre Dame Press, 1972), chap. 4, "Irony and Its Alternatives," 111ff.; quotations on 32 and 111.

7   Robertson, *Preface to Chaucer,* 288; although Robertson is consistent in his definition of irony, he is less consistent in his use of the word; see chap. 4, n. 17, above.

8   *The Canterbury Tales of Chaucer,* [ed. Thomas Tyrwhitt], 5 vols. (London: Payne, 1775–78) 4:276, v. 7514 (comment on SumT, line 1932). The references to Tyrwhitt by Earle Birney, in "Is Chaucer's Irony a Modern Discovery?" *JEGP* 41 (1942), are misleading (317 and n. 62), and the word irony does not appear in the other passages he cites.

9   See Leigh Hunt, *Wit and Humor, selected from the English Poets, with an illustrative essay and critical comments* (London: Smith, Elder, and Co., 1846), introduction, esp. 18–21. See also Alexander Smith (1863) on William Dunbar, quoted by Caroline F. E. Spurgeon, *Five Hundred Years of Chaucer Criticism and Allusion (1357–1900)* 5 pts. (1908–17; reprint [3 vols.] New York: Russell and Russell, 1960), 3:71; and Isaac d'Israeli, *Amenities of Literature* (1841), quoted by Spurgeon, ibid. 2:231. References to *Chaucer Criticism* are to part and page.

10   Adolphus William Ward, *Chaucer* (London: Macmillan, 1888), 145, 147; quoted in part by Spurgeon, *Chaucer Criticism,* 3:123.

11   John W. Hales, "Chaucer and Shakespeare," *Quarterly Review* (1873): 225–55; quotations below from the reprint, *Notes and Essays on Shakespeare* (London: Bell, 1884), 56–104. Other passages are quoted by Spurgeon, *Chaucer Criticism,* 3:115–17.

12   Cf. A. W. Schlegel, *Vorlesungen,* lecture 12. See also Matthew Arnold, *The Study of Poetry* (1880); Chaucer's lack of "high seriousness" is in part a failure of "freedom": "[Burns's] view is large, free, shrewd, benignant,—truly poetic. The freedom of Chaucer is heightened in Burns, by a fiery, reckless energy; the benignity of Chaucer deepens, in Burns, into an overwhelming sense of the pathos of things" (quoted by Spurgeon, *Chaucer Criticism,* 4:128–30).

13   Walter W. Skeat, ed., *The Complete Works of Geoffrey Chaucer* (1894) 2d ed., 7 vols. (Oxford: Clarendon Press, 1900), 5:354.

14   George Lyman Kittredge, *Chaucer and His Poetry* (Cambridge, Mass.: Harvard University Press, 1915); George Saintsbury, "Chaucer," in Cambridge History of English Literature (Cambridge: Cambridge University Press, 1908), 2:183–224; Frederick Tupper, "Chaucer and the Seven Deadly Sins," *PMLA* 19 (1914): 93–128; John Livingston Lowes, "Chaucer and the Seven Deadly Sins," *PMLA* 30 (1915): 237–371. Thomas Raynsford Lounsbury, in *Studies in Chaucer, His Life and Writings* (New York: Harper, 1892), associates Chaucer's "understatement" with his "exquisite urbanity" (3:442)—a phrase normally used of Socratic irony. For Lowes, see his "Simple and Coy: A Note on

Fourteenth-Century Poetic Diction," *Anglia* 33 (1910), where he speaks of Chaucer's "delicate irony, . . . [the] perfect merging of artistic detachment with humorously sympathetic comprehension" (440).

15 Cf. the contemporary rejection by Campbell of the concept of irony because of its exclusion of sympathy (*Sophocles,* 1:126–28).

16 Dempster, *Dramatic Irony in Chaucer* (1932).

17 Earle Birney, "The Beginnings of Chaucer's Irony," *PMLA* 54 (1939): 637–55; idem, "Is Chaucer's Irony a Modern Discovery?" These, and several other Birney essays, are reprinted in Beryl Rowland, ed., *Earle Birney: Essays on Chaucerian Irony* (Toronto: University of Toronto Press, 1985).

18 Wimsatt and Beardsley, *The Verbal Icon* (1954; the articles collected here appeared somewhat earlier). Muscatine is aware of the implications of using New Critical language, and after citing Brooks he continues: "Our own generation has necessarily its peculiar sensibility. To use such terms as 'irony,' 'ambiguity,' 'tension,' and 'paradox' in describing Chaucer's poetry is to bring to the subject our typical mid-century feeling for an unresolved dialectic" (*Chaucer and the French Tradition,* 9–10); see also Muscatine, "Chaucer: Irony and Its Alternatives," chap. 4 of *Poetry and Crisis* (1972), a book dedicated to Wimsatt.

19 See, for example, R. A. Shoaf, *Dante, Chaucer, and the Currency of the Word: Money, Images, and Reference in Late Medieval Poetry* (Norman: University of Oklahoma Press, 1983): "And this because of Chaucer, the other voice if not the voice of Other. I am not here invoking tale-teller irony, that old if not wearied dogma of Chaucer criticism. I am speaking rather to the phenomenon of a text which revels in disclosure, which plays with the profoundest of all paradoxes of mediation, or the concealment simultaneous with every revelation" (209).

20 Donaldson, "Chaucer the Pilgrim," 2–3. The relation between Donaldson's notion of a narrative persona and irony has been noted by Muecke, *The Compass of Irony,* 34. The relation of persona and romantic theories of irony are clearly shown in Henry Lüdeke, *Die Funktionen des Erzählers in Chaucers epischer Dichtung* (Halle: Niemeyer, 1928), 110, 119.

21 For a variant, see the "four levels of fictionalization" discussed by James Dean, "Dismantling the Canterbury Book," *PMLA* 100 (1985): 747.

22 Even critics of Donaldson's system do not always avoid the authoritative figure of Donaldson's Chaucer the Poet; see, for example, H. Marshall Leicester, Jr., "The Art of Impersonation: A General Prologue to the *Canterbury Tales,*" *PMLA* 95 (1980): "The proper method is to ascribe the entire narration in all its details to a *single* speaker . . . and to use it as evidence in constructing that speaker's consciousness" (218). The New Critical roots of this theory are shown on the same page: "The poet is the creation rather than the creator of his poem." Leicester's solution is the same as Bronson's of 1960: "We are not involved in *them* [his characters], but in *him* [Chaucer.] For he is almost the only figure in his 'drama' who is fully realized psychologically, and who truly matters to us"; Bertrand H. Bronson, *In Search of Chaucer* (Toronto: University of Toronto Press, 1960), 67. For similar attempts to avoid the word persona through the concept of voices, see Barbara Nolan, "'A Poet Ther was': Chaucer's Voices in the General Prologue to the *Canterbury Tales,*" *PMLA* 101 (1986): 154–69; and Jesse Gellrich, *The Idea of the Book in the Middle Ages: Language Theory, Mythology, and Fiction* (Ithaca: Cornell University Press, 1985), 154–69.

23   Edmund Reiss, "Chaucer and Medieval Irony," *Studies in the Age of Chaucer* 1 (1979): 69, 82.

24   See Judson B. Allen, "The Old Way and the Parson's Way: An Ironic Reading of the Parson's Tale," *Journal of Medieval and Renaissance Studies* 3 (1973): 255–71; and Lisa J. Kiser, *Telling Classical Tales: Chaucer and the "Legend of Good Women"* (Ithaca: Cornell University Press, 1983), on "self-consciously bad art" (97). See also, the revisionist conception of the Knight by Terry Jones, *Chaucer's Knight: The Portrait of a Medieval Mercenary* (Baton Rouge: Louisiana State University Press, 1980).

Chapter 10. Cleanth Brooks and New Critical Irony

1   Examples are the articles by Birney on Chaucer, noted above, chap. 9, n. 17.

2   See, for example, Gerald Graff, *Professing Literature: An Institutional History* (Chicago: University of Chicago Press, 1987), 183–243.

3   For Brooks's ambivalence toward the ordinary modern reader (one both sophisticated and "corrupted by Hollywood and the Book of the Month Club"), see "Irony as a Principle of Structure" (from 1948) in Morton Dawen Zabel, ed., *Literary Opinion in America: Essays Illustrating the Status, Methods, and Problems of Criticism in the United States in the Twentieth Century,* 2d ed. rev., 2 vols. (1951; reissued, New York: Harper and Row, 1962), 2:738 (quoted below). On dehistoricization, see also the more vigorous manifestos by W. K. Wimsatt, Jr., and Monroe C. Beardsley in *The Verbal Icon: Studies in the Meaning of Poetry* (Louisville: University of Kentucky Press, 1954), e.g., "The Intentional Fallacy," 3–16.

4   See Friedrich Schlegel, *Philosophische Vorlesungen [1800–1807],* ed. Jean-Jacques Anstett, KA 12–13, 2 vols. (Munich: Schöningh, 1964), 1:xxi–xxxii.

5   Antoine Compagnon, *La Troisième République des lettres: De Flaubert à Proust* (Paris: Seuil, 1983), 130–37. See also Graff, *Professing Literature,* 65–80. Cf. the history of English as a discipline constructed by Terry Eagleton, *Literary Theory: An Introduction* (Minneapolis: University of Minnesota Press, 1983), 17–53.

6   Daniel O'Hara, review of Derrida, *Of Grammatology,* in *Journal of Aesthetics and Art Criticism* 36 (1977), 362, quoted by Wilde, *Horizons of Assent,* 6.

7   Elbow, *Oppositions in Chaucer,* 14.

8   See Paul A. Bové, "Cleanth Brooks and Modern Irony," *Destructive Poetics,* 93–120.

9   Zabel, ed. *Literary Opinion,* 2:729–41; the article was adapted from "Irony and 'Ironic' Poetry," *College English* 9 (1948): 231–37.

10   See I. A. Richards, *Principles of Literary Criticism* (1924; New York: Harcourt, Brace and Co., 1938), on the difference between the nonpoetic and the imaginative and poetic: "A poem of the first group ["Rose Aylmer," "Love's Philosophy"] is built out of sets of impulses which run parallel, which have the same direction. In a poem of the second group ["Ode to the Nightingale," "Nocturnal upon S. Lucie's Day"] the most obvious feature is the extraordinarily [*sic*] heterogeneity of the distinguishable impulses. But they are more than heterogeneous, they are opposed. . . . The difference comes out clearly if we consider how comparatively unstable poems of the first kind are. They will not bear an ironical contemplation. . . . Irony in this sense consists in the bringing in of the opposite, the complementary impulses; that is why poetry which is exposed

to it is not of the highest order, and why irony itself is so constantly a characteristic of poetry which is" (250).

11　See the ill-tempered contemporary critique of Brooks by R. S. Crane, "Cleanth Brooks; or, the Bankruptcy of Critical Monism," *Modern Philology* 45 (1948): 226–45. Brooks is taken to task for not accepting the neo-Aristotelian language of the Chicago School (236); Crane's most legitimate criticism, however, is based on Brooks's definition of irony and his distinction between literature and science, a critique that leads to Crane's often-quoted remark that $E=mc^2$ meets all of Brooks's criteria for irony (243).

12　Cf. de Man's flat denial of irony in Wordsworth; "Rhetoric of Temporality," 208.

13　Cf. Brooks's earlier formulation in an article often cited in histories of irony, "The Language of Paradox" (in *The Language of Poetry* [1942]), reprint, Mark Schorer, Josephine Miles, Gordon McKenzie, eds., *Criticism: The Foundations of Modern Literary Judgment* (New York: Harcourt, Brace, and Co., 1948), 358–66. In this essay, Brooks uses the word irony only casually, for example in analyzing a passage from Pope's "Essay on Man": "Here, it is true, the paradoxes insist on the irony, rather than on the wonder" (360). The key term is "paradox" in its relation to metaphor: "All metaphor, of course, involves some element of paradox" (361 n. 1).

14　Gerald Graff, *Poetic Statement*, 108–9.

15　See above, in chap. 4, "Pompeius on Donatus."

16　Robert Penn Warren, "Pure and Impure Poetry," (*Kenyon Review,* 1943), often reprinted; references below are to Schorer et al., eds., *Criticism*, 366–78.

17　Brooks's failure to distinguish between poetry and poems is one of the charges Crane levels in "Cleanth Brooks," 229.

18　New Critics are ambivalent about the religious dimension of poetry; see, e.g., Wimsatt, who reiterates Brooks's flat statement from "A Burden for Critics" (1949) that poetry is not a surrogate for religion (*The Verbal Icon,* 276). The language of *Literary Criticism* (1957) seems to contradict this (746). Similar points were raised by Paul Alpers in "Donne's Heroism," at Directions in Renaissance Literary Criticism: A Colloquium, University of Southern California, 13 February 1988.

19　See Paul A. Bové, *Intellectuals in Power: A Genealogy of Critical Humanism* (New York: Columbia University Press, 1986).

20　See, for example, Warren's personification of poems and poetry in "Pure and Impure Poetry": "Poetry wants to be pure, but poems do not" (267).

Chapter 11. Viconian Ironies

1　References are to *Scienza Nuova*, from *Giambattista Vico: Opere*, ed. Fausto Nicolini (Milan: Ricciardi, [1953]); *Institutiones Oratoriae*, from *Opere di G. B. Vico,* 8 vols. in 11 (Bari: Laterza, 1911–41), 8:101ff.; quoted by Michael Mooney in *Vico in the Tradition of Rhetoric* (Princeton: Princeton University Press, 1985), 79.

2　References below are to Hayden White, *Tropics of Discourse: Essays in Cultural Criticism* (Baltimore: Johns Hopkins University Press, 1978), chap. 9: "The Tropics of History: The Deep Structure of the *New Science,*" 196–217.

3　References below are to Hayden White, *Metahistory: The Historical Imagination in Nineteenth-Century Europe* (Baltimore: Johns Hopkins University Press, 1973). White often reads his theories into his subject matter: "In the eighteenth century, thinkers conventionally distinguished among three kinds of historiography: fabulous, true, and satirical" (*Metahistory*, 49). The citations to Bayle and Voltaire in no way support this statement.

4 White, *Metahistory*, 32n; see also Mooney, *Vico in the Tradition of Rhetoric:* "Grouping the tropes under four primary types was an idea of Peter Ramus and likely came to Vico through the work of Gerard Jan Voss" (80 and n.). The reference for both is Andrea Battistini, "Tradizione e innovazione nella tassonomia tropologica vichiana," *Bollettino del Centro di Studi vichiani* 3 (1973): 67–81.

5 *Tropics of Discourse*, 72–73; Kenneth Burke, *A Grammar of Motives* (Berkeley: University of California Press, 1969), appendix D: "Four Master Tropes," 503–17. Burke is also cited in *Metahistory*, 37, within the quotation above. Aristotle reference noted by Mooney, *Vico in the Tradition of Rhetoric*, 80.

6 See, for example, the 1847 and 1868 prefaces to Jules Michelet's *Histoire de la Révolution française*, ed. Claude Mettra, 2 vols. (Paris: Laffont, 1979), 1:31–50; and for one of many statements in the text itself in which Michelet emphasizes experienced history, see 1:758.

7 The classic statement of this position in the social sciences is Claude Lévi-Strauss, *Le Cru et le cuit* (Paris: Plon, 1964), "Ouverture," 21.

8 See also "Foucault Decoded: Notes from Underground," in *Tropics of Discourse*, 254–55, and 260 n. 3 for an attempt to include Foucault within this scheme.

9 "Interpretation in History," *Tropics of Discourse*, 51–80; cf. White's rejection of Frye's distinction between "(undisplaced) myths, fiction, and . . . historiography" (*Tropics of Discourse*, 61).

10 References below are to Northrop Frye, *Anatomy of Criticism: Four Essays* (Princeton: Princeton University Press, 1957). For the four modes of emplotment, romance, tragedy, comedy, and satire see *Metahistory*, 7.

11 Cf. Wimsatt and Brooks, *Literary Criticism*, 746.

12 Kierkegaard quotes Hegel's *Lectures on the History of Philosophy*, JA 18:62: "All dialectic accepts as valid what shall become valid as if it were valid, and allows the internal destruction to develop within it. Such is the universal irony of the world" (*Concept of Irony*, 279); see also 283–84 and Capel's note, 296 n. 11.

13 Both of these definitions are glossed and indexed separately by Frye in *Anatomy of Criticism*, s.v. Irony, Mythos, 366–67, 375.

14 A phase, for Frye, also has two definitions (*Anatomy of Criticism*, 367). It is one of "five contexts in which the narrative and meaning of a work of literature may be considered, classified as literal, descriptive, formal, archetypal, and anagogic and . . . one of six distinguishable stages of a mythos (sense 2)." The present discussion involves sense 2.

15 On the six phases, see the discussion in *Anatomy of Criticism*, 219–22; the six phases of tragedy ("mythos of autumn"), as an example, are: (1) birth, (2) youth, (3) quest, (4) fall, (5) ironic, (6) shock and horror (198–202). For comic phases, see 177–88; romance phases, 198–202; ironic, 225–38. These six phases are introduced on 158–60 with "five structures of meaning" and "seven categories of images."

16 The popularity of the word irony in New Historicism could be subjected to a similar critique; the formalist bases of New Historicism are being explored by Alan Liu; see "The Power of Formalism: The New Historicism," *ELH* 56 (1989): 721–71.

17 Lang, *Humor/Irony*, chap. 2, "Irony/Humor," 37–69 and notes. Less useful is chap. 6, devoted specifically to Barthes, "Barthes: *Écrire le Corps*," 167–92.

18 References are to Roland Barthes, *Critique et Vérité* (Paris: Seuil, 1966); *S/Z* (Paris: Seuil,

1970); *Sade, Fourier, Loyola* (1971); *Le Plaisir du texte* (Paris: Seuil, 1973). Many of the passages cited here are also cited by Lang, with the exception of those from *Sade, Fourier, Loyola*.

19 Cited also by Lang, *Irony/Humor*, 57. Other passages that support Lang's thesis more clearly are *S/Z*, 51–52, 145–46, and 212, where irony is more clearly delimited as a classical code: irony is the "classical remedy" of "superimposing a second code over the vomited-up first one" (52); see Lang, *Irony/Humor*, 58–59.

20 Barthes equates irony and humor only in a note on "l'ironie du critique" in relation to studies on the novel (74 n. 1). This irony is equivalent to "that irony or humor" involved in the distance between the novelists' consciousness and that of their heroes (references to Goldmann, Girard, and Lukács).

21 "Thus Barthesian *ironie*, as a negative assertion of Authority or difference, is equivalent to Kierkegaardian romantic irony. Indeed, Barthes's ironist *is* the romantic ironist, the subject who clings to the illusion of his ipseity and autonomy and perceives his being in the world as a tragic one or a fallen condition. . . . Barthes's *autre ironie*— which I shall henceforth designate as *humor*—is not Kierkegaard's irony as a mastered moment" (*Irony/Humor*, 60). The emphasis on *is* seems to me a dead giveaway that no such identity can be reasonably maintained.

22 Barthes concludes the preface with the statement that "This excess has the name *écriture*"; cf. the association of (non-classical) irony with excess in *Critique et vérité* (75), and the definition of "écrire" as "a certain manner of fracturing the world (the book) and remaking it" (76).

23 "The term *ironie* occurs often enough in Derrida, in a sense closely related to that of *le jeu*"; Lang, *Irony/Humor*, 207 n. 30, citing Wilde, *Horizons of Assent*, 6. But the only supporting passage, offered on 203 n. 25, from "La Pharmacie de Platon," is not very interesting: "when Plato . . . pushes irony—and the serious—to the rehabilitation of a certain game (*jeu*)"; in *La Dissémination* (Paris: Seuil, 1972), 178. Derrida is talking about "l'écriture ludique," of which irony (as well as seriousness) can be a part. But irony no more *is* this game than seriousness *is* this game. Another reference to irony I find in Derrida's essay is in the phrase "le bon remède, l'ironie socratique" (146; cf. 75). Certainly, a different irony is meant here, but again, not a particularly Derridean one.

Chapter 12. Paul de Man

1 The original essay appears in Charles S. Singleton, ed., *Interpretation: Theory and Practice* (Baltimore: Johns Hopkins University Press, 1969), 173–209. I cite the reprinted essay in *Blindness and Insight* (1983), 187–228.

2 De Man's close association with New Criticism is often noted; see de Man's own essay "Form and Intent in the American New Criticism," *Blindness and Insight*, 20–35, and its easy adoption of New Critical vocabulary—"ambiguity and irony" (32); "a discontinuous world of reflective irony and ambiguity" (28). See also Paul A. Bové, "Variations on Authority: Some Deconstructive Transformations of the New Criticism," in Jonathan Arac, Wlad Godzich, and Wallace Martin, eds., *The Yale Critics: Deconstruction in America* (Minneapolis: University of Minnesota Press, 1983), 3–19. Said, in *World, Text, Critic*, refers to the "so-called Yale School" as "new New Criticism" (157).

3   For example, Paul de Man, *Allegories of Reading: Figural Language in Rousseau, Nietzsche, Rilke, and Proust* (New Haven: Yale University Press, 1979).

4   De Man quotes from Fletcher, *Allegory*, but the same passage can be found in Wimsatt and Brooks, *Literary Criticism*, 400 n. 3.

5   For Goethe's texts from *Maximen und Reflexionen*, see Bengt Algot Sörensen, *Allegorie und Symbol: Texte zur Theorie des dichterischen Bildes im 18. und frühen 19. Jahrhundert* (Frankfurt am Main: Athenäum, 1972), 34–35: the symbol transforms the appearance into idea, the idea into a picture; allegory transforms the appearance into a concept into a picture, with the result that the concept is both contained and perfectly expressed in the picture. Again, Goethe is thinking of personification (for example, the representation, in art or literature, of Virtue).

6   Schlegel, "Gespräch über die Poesie," in *Charakteristiken und Kritiken I*, ed. Eichner: "alle Schönheit ist Allegorie. Das Höchste kann man eben weil es unaussprechlich ist, nur allegorisch [var. symbolisch] sagen" (KA 2:324). De Man's reference is to Eichner's introduction, xci n. 2. Eichner seems to mean only that we might just as well read (conceptually) *Symbol* for *Allegorie*, since in the later text Schlegel obviously does not intend a distinction between *Allegorie* and *symbolisch;* the later change in the text acknowledges that by 1832 the word *symbolisch* is used to describe this higher form of allegory.

7   See "Nachricht von den poetischen Werken des Johannes Boccaccio" (1801), distinguishing an "elevated sense" of allegory from a vulgar one involving the "delivery of mere moral instruction through sensory images" ("den sinnbildlichen Vortrag des bloß moralischer Lehrer"); *Charakteristiken und Kritiken I*, ed. Eichner, KA 2:387. See also "Nachricht von den Gemälden in Paris" (1802), where Schlegel denies that he is speaking of ordinary allegory, allegory that "does not point out the infinite, but rather translates particular abstract and therefore definite and limited concepts into sensory images (*Sinnbilden*)"; in *Friedrich Schlegel: Ansichten und Ideen von der christlichen Kunst*, ed. Hans Eichner, KA 4 (Munich: Schöningh, 1959), 23–24.

8   De Man criticizes Wimsatt for maintaining the distinction de Man is attempting to erase (205); the quotation de Man cites from Wimsatt is clearly confined to personification allegory. A further example of how de Man slips from personification to exegetical allegory can be seen in his summary of a statement by Gadamer: "Allegory appears as dryly rational and dogmatic in its reference to a meaning it does not itself constitute" (189). In the preceding quotation, Gadamer clearly refers to personification allegory in art; but de Man's paraphrase is equivocal, in fact revising Gadamer's statement that allegory is finished "as soon as its meaning is reached" to mean that "allegory does not itself constitute" this meaning. The two texts are not incompatible, but only de Man's paraphrase could properly apply to exegetical allegory, which involves teasing out meanings constituted in another text.

9   Such assertions are discussed by Frank Lentricchia, *After the New Criticism* (Chicago: University of Chicago Press, 1980), chap. 8, "Paul de Man: The Rhetoric of Authority," 281–317.

10   Among these writers are Schlegel, E. T. A. Hoffmann, Kierkegaard, and Solger. De Man's somewhat breezy reference to Solger's description of symbol and allegory as a dialectic of identity and difference gives no page numbers in the citation to *Erwin* (209 n. 49; for "Friedrich," read "Karl" or "K. W. F." and so in de Man's text); this

particular discussion, I believe, is on 218–29 in *Erwin;* translation of this passage is available in Wheeler, ed., *German Criticism,* 128–35.

11 Dominick LaCapra, *Soundings in Critical Theory* (Ithaca: Cornell University Press, 1989), 118.

12 De Man cites only one other Baudelaire essay, "Quelques caricaturistes français," but does not imply that it is about irony, which it is not. The gap in logic is filled to some extent by Lang, who cites many of the passages de Man may well have in mind, although the word irony does not occur in all of them (*Irony/Humor,* 100–103). Most of these passages are from Baudelaire's poetry. In Baudelaire's prose, I am unconvinced that any notions of irony worthy of de Man's discussion develop. Many seem perfectly compatible with earlier romantic definitions. See "Du Vin et du hachish" (1851), *Charles Baudelaire: Oeuvres complètes,* ed. Y.-G. Le Dantec (Paris: Gallimard, 1961), 325–43, for what may well be a parodic version of romantic irony. Here, Baudelaire relates irony to a drug-induced self-assurance, and the way in which a sober (or straight) person appears to one who is not: "La sagesse de ce malheureux vous réjouit outre mesure, son sang-froid vous pousse aux dernières limites de l'*ironie;* il vous paraît le plus fou et le plus ridicule de tous les hommes. . . . Dès lors, l'idée de supériorité point l'horizon de votre intellect" (336).

13 See "Rhetoric of Temporality" on the "curiously ambiguous" (though unironic!) lines in Wordsworth as well as the reference to a speaker "no longer vulnerable to irony" (224). Cf. the language of Brooks in "Irony as a Principle of Structure" (737). Brooks here also speaks of his battle with a critical "temptation" (to call the poem ironic).

14 *Glyph* 1 (1977): 28–49; reprinted as "Excuses: (*Confessions*)," in *Allegories of Reading,* 278–301.

Conclusion. An Alternative History: Irony and the Novel

1 The conventional description of Schlegel as the "father of irony" is found even in Hegel, "Über Solgers nachgelassene Schriften," JA 20:161; Mann is described as "der Ironi-ker der modernen Literatur par excellence" in Japp's *Theorie der Ironie,* 277. Muecke feels Schlegel's praise of *Wilhelm Meister* is more appropriate to Mann's *Magic Mountain* (*Compass of Irony,* 185). Muecke refers here to the discussion in Erich Heller, *The Ironic German: A Study of Thomas Mann* (Boston: Little, Brown, 1958), 204. Heller's book is explicitly written as a tribute; see Heller's introduction, 11.

2 An example is Handwerk's use of George Meredith to fill the historical gap between Schlegel and Lacan; *Irony and Ethics,* chap. 3, 91ff.

3 Irony in French fiction is variously defined, depending on its object text, e.g., Flaubert (Warning, Richards), Stendhal (de Man, Genette), or even the New Novelists. See de Man, "Rhetoric of Temporality," 110–11; Rainer Warning, "Irony and the 'Order of Discourse' in Flaubert," *New Literary History* 13 (1982): 253–86; Richards, *Principles of Literary Criticism,* 210; Robert Weimann, "Structure and History in Narrative Perspec-tive: The Problem of Point of View Reconsidered" (1973), in *Structure and Society in Literary History: Studies in the History and Theory of Historical Criticism,* expanded ed. (Balti-more: Johns Hopkins University Press, 1984), 234–66; Gérard Genette, *Nouveau discours du récit* (Paris: Seuil, 1983), 100 (on the relation of irony to Stendhal's "happy few"). For the German tradition, see Japp, *Theorie der Ironie,* 288–99.

4   See Mikhail Bakhtin, *Problems of Dostoevsky's Poetics* (1929), trans. R. W. Rotsel, 2d ed. (Ann Arbor: Ardis, 1973), 160–64, on "double-voiced words"; M. M. Bakhtin, *The Dialogic Imagination: Four Essays by M. M. Bakhtin,* ed. Michael Holquist, trans. Caryl Emerson and Michael Holquist (Austin: University of Texas Press, 1981), esp. "Epic and Novel: Toward a Methodology for the Study of the Novel," 3–40; on the relation between irony, laughter, and multiple languages, see 24ff.

5   Long before Bakhtin's work became popular, Ian Watt warned against the proliferation of such readings of the novel as Bakhtin's work supports: ironic readings are both ahistorical and misrepresentative (Watt's targets include Coleridge, Virginia Woolf, and Dobrée); Ian Watt, *The Rise of the Novel: Studies in Defoe, Richardson, and Fielding* (Berkeley: University of California Press, 1957), 129–30. In reference to Defoe's *Moll Flanders,* Watt objects to "convert[ing] the extreme cases of his narrative *gaucherie* into irony" (120). Watt's language shows that he accepts the New Critical and romantic understanding of irony as an evaluative term.

6   Georg Lukács, *Die Theorie des Romans: Ein geschichtsphilosophischer Versuch über die Formen der großen Epik* (1920), 2d ed. (Neuwied: Luchterhand, 1963), esp. 69–93. On Lukács's subsequent renunciation of this theory, see de Man, *Blindness and Insight,* chap. 4, "Georg Lukács's *Theory of the Novel,*" 51–59. See also the reading by Michael Holzman, *Lukács's Road to God: The Early Criticism Against Its Pre-Marxist Background* (Washington, D.C.: Center for Advanced Research in Phenomenology, 1985), 117–61.

7   The disparity between Nietzsche's conception of irony and the irony attributed to him is noted by Ernst Behler in "Nietzsches Auffassung der Ironie," *Nietzsche-Studien* 4 (1975): 1–35; see, by way of contrast, Daniel O'Hara, "The Genius of Irony: Nietzsche in Bloom," in Arac et al., ed., *The Yale Critics,* 109–32. Nietzsche himself does not use the word irony as a self-description: in *Jenseits von Gut und Böse* (1886), sec. 260, irony refers to the aristocratic contempt of selflessness; see also *Der Antichrist* (1895), sec. 31, which argues against Renan's characterization of Christ as "le grant maître en ironie" (sec. 36 speaks of "an ironic divinity controlling world-historical irony"). See also *Ecce Homo. Wie man wird, was man ist,* on *Der Fall Wagner,* sec. 4: "*amor fati* ist meine innerste Natur. Dies schließt aber nicht aus, daß ich die Ironie liebe, sogar die welthistorische Ironie"; Karl Schlechta, *Friedrich Nietzsche: Werke in drei Bänden* (Munich: Carl Hanser, 1954–56).

8   Laurence Sterne, *The Life and Opinions of Tristram Shandy, Gentleman,* ed. Ian Watt (Boston: Houghton Mifflin, 1965).

9   Victor Hugo, *Notre-Dame de Paris 1482,* ed. Jacques Seebacher (Paris: Gallimard, 1975). For the social use of ironic smiles: "le rictus ironique que la présence de Jacques Coictier avait fait éclore sur son visage morose s'évanouit peu à peu comme le crépuscule à un horizon de nuit" (bk. 5, chap. 1, on Claude Frollo, who is now taking Coictier's friend Tourangeau more seriously). See also bk. 7, chap. 1, on the catty remarks of "ces belles filles, avec leurs langues envenimées et irritées" and their uneasy superiority to Esmeralda: "Elles étaient cruelles et gracieuses. Elles fouillaient, elles furetaient malignement de la parole dans sa pauvre et folle toilette de paillettes et d'oripeaux. C'étaient des rires, des ironies, des humiliations sans fin."

10 Honoré de Balzac, *La Comédie humaine, III,* ed. Pierre Georges Castex (Paris: Gallimard, 1976), 1046. The phrase "world-historical irony" appears also in Nietzsche; see n. 7 above.

11   *Oeuvres de Flaubert,* ed. A. Thibaudet and R. Dumesnil, 2 vols. (Paris: Gallimard, 1952), 2:220, 392.

12   Stendhal, *Romans et nouvelles,* ed. Henri Martineau, 2 vols. (Paris: Gallimard, 1948), chap. 12, 2:212.

13   Marcel Proust, *A la recherche du temps perdu,* ed. Pierre Clarac and André Ferré, 3 vols. (Paris: Gallimard, 1954), 1:210–11.

14   Robert Musil, *Der Mann ohne Eigenschaften,* ed. Adolf Frisé, 2 vols. (Reinbek bei Hamburg: Rowohlt, 1978), 1:68; see also 301 for an ironic, contemptuous, laugh. In his notes, Musil speaks of a "constructive" irony, involving in part the empathy of the author and his characters, an irony he claims is unknown in Germany, where irony is considered mere raillery ("Spott u Bespötteln"; ibid. 2:1939).

15   Thomas Mann, *Doktor Faustus: Das Leben des deutschen Tonsetzers Adrian Leverkühn erzählt von einem Freunde* (Frankfurt am Main: Fischer, 1967), 70, 101.

16   See Mann's frequent but inconsistent statements on irony, esp. "Ironie und Radicalismus," in *Betrachtungen eines Unpolitischen* (1918), ed. Peter de Mendelssohn (Frankfurt am Main: Fischer, 1983): "Was ist Konservativismus? Die erotische Ironie des Geistes" (570); cf. Mann's later "[Humor und Ironie: Beitrag zu einer Rundfunkdiskussion]" (this first appeared in 1953 under the title "Sprache und Humor in der Literatur"), in *Gesammelte Werke in Dreizehn Bänden,* vol. 11 (Frankfurt am Main: Fischer, 1960), 801–5; here Mann attempts to distance himself from the theories of irony within which he has been received.

17   *[Letters],* ed. Immerwahr, 55; see also a letter to Caroline of the following week, ibid., 60.

18   De Man, "Rhetoric of Temporality," 210.

WORKS CITED

Adams, Hazard. *The Interests of Criticism: An Introduction to Literary Theory.* New York: Harcourt, Brace, and World, 1969.

Allemann, Beda. "Ironie als literarisches Prinzip." In *Ironie und Dichtung: Sechs Essays von Bede Allemann, Ernst Zinn, Hans-Egon Hass, Wolfgang Preisendanz, Fritz Martini und Paul Böckmann,* ed. Albert Schaefer, 11–37. Munich: Beck, 1970.

————. *Ironie und Dichtung.* Pfullingen: Neske, 1956.

Allen, Don Cameron. *Mysteriously Meant: The Rediscovery of Pagan Symbolism and Allegorical Interpretation in the Renaissance.* Baltimore: Johns Hopkins University Press, 1970.

Allen, Judson B. "The Old Way and the Parson's Way: An Ironic Reading of the Parson's Tale." *Journal of Medieval and Renaissance Studies* 3 (1973): 255–71.

Alpers, Paul. "Donne's Heroism." Paper presented at Directions in Renaissance Literary Criticism: A Colloquium, University of Southern California, 13 February 1988.

Aquinas, Thomas. *S. Thomae Aquinatis In Decem Libros Ethicorum Aristotelis ad Nicomachum Expositio.* Ed. Raymundi M. Spiazzi. Turin: Marietti, 1949.

Aristophanes. *Clouds.* Ed. K. J. Dover. Oxford: Clarendon Press, 1968.

Arac, Jonathan, Wlad Gozich, and Wallace Martin, ed. *The Yale Critics: Deconstruction in America.* Minneapolis: University of Minnesota Press, 1983.

Aristotle. *Aristotelis Opera.* 5 vols. Berlin: Reimer, 1831–70.

Arnulf of Orleans. *Arnulfi Aurelianensis Glosule super Lucanum.* Ed. Berthe M. Marti. Paris: American Academy in Rome, 1958.

Athenaeum. Eine Zeitschrift. Hrsg. von August Wilhelm Schlegel und Friedrich Schlegel. 3 vols., 1798–1800. Facs. reprint. Darmstadt: Wissenschaftliche Buchgesellschaft, 1977.

Augustine. *Sancti Aurelii Augustini De Doctrina Christiana; De Vera Religione.* Ed. Joseph Martin. Turnholt: Brepols, 1962.

Ayrault, Roger. *La Genèse du romantisme allemand.* 4 vols. Paris: Aubier, 1961–76.

Bakhtin, Mikhail M. *The Dialogic Imagination: Four Essays by M. M. Bakhtin.* Ed. and trans. Michael Holquist and Caryl Emerson. Austin: University of Texas Press, 1981.

————. *Problems of Dostoevsky's Poetics* (1929). Trans. R. W. Rotsel. 2d ed. Ann Arbor: Ardis, 1973.

Balzac, Honoré de. *La Comédie humaine, III.* Ed. Pierre Georges Castex. Paris: Gallimard, 1976.

Barthes, Roland. *Critique et Vérité.* Paris: Seuil, 1966.

————. *Le Plaisir du texte.* Paris: Seuil, 1973.

————. *S/Z.* Paris: Seuil, 1970.

————. *Sade, Fourier, Loyola*. Paris: Seuil, 1971.

Battistini, Andrea. "Tradizione e innovazione nella tassonomia tropologica vichiana." *Bollettino del Centro di Studi vichiani* 3 (1973): 67–81.

Batts, Michael S. "Hartmann's *Humanitas*: A New Look at *Iwein*." In *Germanic Studies in Honor of Edward Henry Sehrt*, ed. Frithjof Andersen Raven et al., 33–51. Coral Gables: University of Miami Press, 1968.

Baudelaire, Charles. *Oeuvres complètes*. Ed. Y.-G. Le Dantec. Paris: Gallimard, 1961.

Behler, Ernst. *Klassische Ironie, romantische Ironie, tragische Ironie: Zum Ursprung dieser Begriffe*. Darmstadt: Wissenschaftliche Buchgesellschaft, 1972.

————. "Nietzsches Auffassung der Ironie." *Nietzsche-Studien* 4 (1975): 1–35.

Benjamin, Walter. *Der Begriff der Kunstkritik in der deutschen Romantik*. In *Gesammelte Schriften, unter Mitwirkung von Theodor W. Adorno und Gershom Scholem*, ed. Rolf Tiedemann and Hermann Schweppenhäuser, 1:7–122. 2d ed. Frankfurt am Main: Suhrkamp, 1974.

Bergson, Leif. "Eiron und eironeia." *Hermes* 99 (1971): 409–22.

Birney, Earle. "The Beginnings of Chaucer's Irony." *PMLA* 54 (1939): 637–55.

————. *Essays on Chaucerian Irony*. Ed. Beryl Rowland. Toronto: University of Toronto Press, 1985.

————. "Is Chaucer's Irony a Modern Discovery?" *Journal of English and Germanic Philology* 41 (1942): 303–19.

Blanchot, Maurice. *L'Entretien infini*. Paris: Gallimard, 1969.

Booth, Wayne C. *Critical Understanding: The Powers and Limits of Pluralism*. Chicago: University of Chicago Press, 1979.

————. *A Rhetoric of Irony*. Chicago: University of Chicago Press, 1974.

Bourgeois, René. *L'Ironie romantique: Spectacle et jeu de Mme de Staël à G. de Nerval*. Grenoble: Presses Universitaires de Grenoble, 1974.

Bové, Paul A. *Destructive Poetics: Heidegger and Modern American Poetry*. New York: Columbia University Press, 1980.

————. *Intellectuals in Power: A Genealogy of Critical Humanism*. New York: Columbia University Press, 1986.

————. "Variations on Authority: Some Deconstructive Transformations of the New Criticism." In *The Yale Critics: Deconstruction in America*, ed. Jonathan Arac, Wlad Gozich, and Wallace Martin, 3–19. Minneapolis: University of Minnesota Press, 1983.

Bradley, A. C. *Shakespearean Tragedy*. 2d ed., 1905. Reprint. New York: Macmillan, 1949.

Brandwood, Leonard. *A Word Index to Plato*. Leeds: Maney, 1976.

Bronson, Bertrand H. *In Search of Chaucer*. Toronto: University of Toronto Press, 1960.

Brooks, Cleanth. "Irony as a Principle of Structure." In *Literary Opinion in America: Essays Illustrating the Status, Methods, and Problems of Criticism in the United States in the Twentieth Century*, ed. Morton Dawen Zabel, 2:729–41. 2d ed. rev. 1951. Reissue. New York: Harper and Row, 1962.

————. "Irony and 'Ironic' Poetry." *College English* 9 (1948): 231–37.

————. "The Language of Paradox." 1942. Reprint, in *Criticism: The Foundations of Modern Literary Judgment*, ed. Mark Schorer, Josephine Miles, and Gordon McKenzie, 358–66. New York: Harcourt, Brace, and Co., 1948.

————. *The Well-Wrought Urn: Studies in the Structure of Poetry*. New York: Harcourt, Brace, 1947.

Brusendorff, Aage. "He Knew Nat Catoun for His Wit Was Rude." In *Studies in English*

Philology: A Miscellany in Honor of Frederick Klaeber, ed. Kemp Malone and Martin B. Ruud, 320–39. Minneapolis: University of Minnesota Press, 1929.

Büchner, Wilhelm. "Über den Begriff der eironeia." *Hermes* 76 (1941): 339–58.

Burke, Kenneth. *A Grammar of Motives.* Berkeley: University of California Press, 1969.

Campbell, Lewis. *Tragic Drama in Aeschylus, Sophocles, and Shakespeare: An Essay.* New York: Longmans, 1904.

———, ed. *Sophocles, edited with English Notes and Introductions.* 2d ed. rev. 2 vols. Oxford: Clarendon Press, 1879.

Chaucer, Geoffrey. *The Canterbury Tales of Chaucer.* [Ed. Thomas Tyrwhitt]. 5 vols. London: Payne, 1775–78.

———. *The Complete Works of Geoffrey Chaucer.* Ed. Walter W. Skeat. 2d ed. 7 vols. Oxford: Clarendon Press, 1900.

———. *The Riverside Chaucer.* Gen. ed. Larry D. Benson. Boston: Houghton Mifflin, 1987.

Cicero. *M. Tullii Ciceronis Opera quae supersunt omnia.* Ed. J. G. Baiter and C. L. Kayser. 11 vols. Leipzig: Tauchnitz, 1860–69.

———. *M. Tullius Cicero: De Officiis Quartum.* Ed. C. Atzert. Leipzig: Teubner, 1971.

———. *M. Tullius Cicero: De Oratore.* Ed. Kazimierz F. Kumaniecki. Leipzig: Teubner, 1969.

Compagnon, Antoine. *La Troisième République des lettres: De Flaubert à Proust.* Paris: Seuil, 1983.

Crane, R. S. "Cleanth Brooks; or, the Bankruptcy of Critical Monism." *Modern Philology* 45 (1948): 226–45.

———. "On Hypotheses in Historical Criticism: Apropos of Certain Contemporary Medievalists." In *The Idea of the Humanities and Other Essays Critical and Historical.* 2 vols. Chicago: University of Chicago Press, 1967.

Culler, Jonathan. *The Pursuit of Signs: Semiotics, Literature, Deconstruction.* Ithaca: Cornell University Press, 1981.

———. *Structuralist Poetics: Structuralism, Linguistics, and the Study of Literature.* Ithaca: Cornell University Press, 1975.

Curley, Michael J. "A New Edition of John of Cornwall's *Prophetia Merlini.*" *Speculum* 57 (1982): 217–49.

Curtius, Ernst Robert. "Friedrich Schlegel und Frankreich." In *Kritische Essays zur europäischen Literatur,* 78–94. Bern: Francke, 1950.

Dane, Joseph A. "The Defense of the Incompetent Reader." *Comparative Literature* 38 (1986): 53–72.

———. "The Myth of Chaucerian Irony." *Papers on Language and Literature* 24 (1988): 115–33.

———. *Parody: Critical Concepts vs. Literary Practices, Aristophanes to Sterne.* Norman: University of Oklahoma Press, 1988.

Dean, James. "Dismantling the Canterbury Book." *PMLA* 100 (1985): 746–62.

De Man, Paul. *Allegories of Reading.* New Haven: Yale University Press, 1979.

———. *Blindness and Insight: Essays in the Rhetoric of Contemporary Criticism.* 2d ed. rev. Minneapolis: University of Minnesota, 1983.

———. "The Rhetoric of Temporality." 1969. Reprint in *Blindness and Insight,* 187–228.

Dempster, Germaine. *Dramatic Irony in Chaucer.* Stanford: Stanford University Press, 1932.

Derrida, Jacques. *La Dissémination.* Paris: Seuil, 1972.

———. *Éperons: Les Styles de Nietzsche.* Paris: Flammarion, 1978.

Le Dictionnaire de l'Académie Françoise dedié au Roy. 2 vols. Paris: Coignard, 1694.

Dictionnaire de l'Académie française. 6th ed. Paris: Firmin-Didot, 1835.

Dictionnaire de l'Académie française, Complément. Paris: Firmin-Didot, 1862.

Dilthey, Wilhelm. *Leben Schleiermachers* (1870). In *Gesammelte Schriften,* vol. 13. Göttingen: Vandenhoeck and Ruprecht, 1970.

Donaldson, E. Talbot. "Chaucer the Pilgrim." *PMLA* 59 (1954): 928–36. Reprint in *Speaking of Chaucer.* New York: Norton, 1970.

Du Cange, Charles. *Glossarium Mediae et Infimae Latinitatis.* 1688. New ed. 1883–87. Rpt. Graz: Akademische Druck– und Verlags-anstalt, 1954.

Eagleton, Terry. *Literary Theory: An Introduction.* Minneapolis: University of Minnesota Press, 1983.

Eichner, Hans, ed. See Schlegel, Friedrich.

Elbow, Peter. *Oppositions in Chaucer.* Middleton, Conn.: Wesleyan University Press, 1973.

Empson, William. *Seven Types of Ambiguity.* 1930. 2d ed. London: Chatto and Windus, 1947.

Erasmus. *Adagiorum Chilias Tertia.* Ed. Felix Heinimann and Emmanuel Kienzle. *Opera Omnia Desiderii Erasmi Roterodami,* 2/5. Amsterdam: North-Holland, 1981.

———. *Desiderii Erasmi Roterodami Opera Omnia.* 10 vols. 1703–6. Reprint. Hildesheim: Olms, 1962.

Febvre, Lucien. *Le Problème de l'incroyance au 16ᵉ siècle: Le Religion de Rabelais.* Paris: Michel, 1942.

Flaubert, Gustave. *Oeuvres de Flaubert.* Ed. A. Thibaudet and R. Dumesnil. 2 vols. Paris: Gallimard, 1952.

Fletcher, Angus. *Allegory: The Theory of a Symbolic Mode.* Ithaca: Cornell University Press, 1964.

Fowler, H. W. *A Dictionary of Modern English Usage.* Oxford: Clarendon Press, 1926.

Frame, Donald M. *François Rabelais: A Study.* New York: Harcourt, Brace, Jovanovich, 1977.

Frappier, Jean. *Amour courtois et Table Ronde.* Geneva: Droz, 1963.

Friedländer, Paul. *Plato: An Introduction.* 2d ed. 1954; trans. Hans Meyerhoff, 1958. 2d ed. rev. Princeton: Princeton University Press, 1969.

Frye, Northrop. *Anatomy of Criticism: Four Essays.* Princeton: Princeton University Press, 1957.

Furetière, Antoine. *Le Dictionnaire universel.* 1690. Reprint. Paris: Robert, 1978.

Furst, Lilian R. *Fictions of Romantic Irony.* Cambridge: Harvard University Press, 1984.

Gellrich, Jesse M. *The Idea of the Book in the Middle Ages: Language Theory, Mythology, and Fiction.* Ithaca: Cornell University Press, 1985.

Genette, Gérard. *Nouveau discours du récit.* Paris: Seuil, 1983.

Godefroy, Frédéric. *Dictionnaire de l'ancienne langue française et de tous ses dialectes du IXᵉ au XVᵉ siècle.* 10 vols. 1881–1902. Reprint. New York: Kraus, 1961.

Graff, Gerald. *Poetic Statement and Critical Dogma.* Chicago: University of Chicago Press, 1970.

———. *Professing Literature: An Institutional History.* Chicago: University of Chicago Press, 1987.

Green, D. H. "Irony and Medieval Romance." In *Arthurian Romance: Seven Essays,* ed. D. D. R. Owen, 49–64. New York: Barnes and Noble, 1971.

———. *Irony in the Medieval Romance.* Cambridge: Cambridge University Press, 1979.

Guthrie, W. K. C. *A History of Greek Philosophy.* Vol. 3, *The Fifth-Century Enlightenment.* Vol. 4, *Plato: The Man and his Dialogues: Earlier Period.* Cambridge: Cambridge University Press, 1969–75.

Hales, John W. "Chaucer and Shakespeare." *Quarterly Review* (1873): 225–55. Reprint in *Notes and Essays on Shakespeare,* 56–104. London: Bell, 1884.

Hammer, C., ed. *Rhetores Graeci ex recognitione Leonardi Spengel,* 1/2. Leipzig: Teubner, 1894.

Handwerk, Gary. *Irony and Ethics in Narrative: From Schlegel to Lacan.* New Haven: Yale University Press, 1985.

Hardenberg, Friedrich von. See Novalis.

Haym, R. *Die romantische Schule: Ein Beitrag zur Geschichte des deutschen Geistes.* Berlin: Gaertner, 1870.

Hegel, Georg Wilhelm Friedrich. *Sämtliche Werke.* Ed. Hermann Glockner. Jubiläumsausgabe, 20 vols. Stuttgart: Fromann, 1927–40.

Heine, Heinrich Heine. "Die romantische Schule." 1835. In *Sämtliche Werke in vier Bänden,* 3:259–394. Munich: Winkler, 1972.

Heller, Erich. *The Ironic German: A Study of Thomas Mann.* Boston: Little, Brown, 1958.

Hettner, Hermann. *Die romantische Schule in ihrem inneren Zusammenhange mit Goethe und Schiller.* 1850. In *Schriften zur Literatur,* 51–165. Berlin: Aufbau-Verlag, 1959.

Holzman, Michael. *Lukács's Road to God: The Early Criticism Against Its Pre-Marxist Background.* Washington, D.C.: Center for Advanced Research in Phenomenology, 1985.

Howard, Donald R. *The Idea of the Canterbury Tales.* Berkeley: University of California Press, 1976.

Hugo, Victor. *Notre-Dame de Paris 1482.* Ed. Jacques Seebacher. Paris: Gallimard, 1975.

Hunt, Leigh. *Wit and Humor, selected from the English Poets, with an illustrative essay and critical comments.* London: Smith, Elder, and Co., 1846.

Hutchens, Eleanor N. "The Identification of Irony." *ELH* 27 (1960): 352–63.

Hyppolite, Jean. *Introduction à la philosophie de l'histoire de Hegel.* Paris: Rivière, 1948.

Immerwahr, Raymond. "The Subjectivity or Objectivity of Friedrich Schlegel's Poetic Irony." *Germanic Review* 26 (1951): 173–91.

————, ed. See Schlegel, Friedrich.

Isidore of Seville. *Isidori Hispalensis Episcopi Etymologiarum sive originum libri XX.* Ed. W. M. Lindsay. 2 vols. Oxford: Clarendon Press, 1911.

Jankélévitch, Vladimir. *L'Ironie.* 1936. Paris: Flammarion, 1964.

Japp, Uwe. *Theorie der Ironie.* Frankfurt am Main: Vittorio Klostermann, 1983.

Jauß, Hans Robert. *Alterität und Modernität der mittelalterlichen Literatur.* Munich: Fink, 1977.

Jean Paul [Friedrich Richter]. *Vorschule der Ästhetik.* 2d ed., 1812. *Werke,* vol. 5. Darmstadt: Wissenschaftliche Buchgesellschaft, 1962.

Joachimi-Dege, Marie. *Deutsche Shakespeare-Probleme im 18. Jahrhundert und im Zeitalter der Romantik.* Leipzig: Haessel, 1907.

Johnson, Samuel. *A Dictionary of the English Language.* London: Strahan, 1755.

Jonas, Ludwig, and Wilhelm Dilthey. *Aus Schleiermacher's Leben. In Briefen.* 3 vols. Berlin: Reimer, 1861.

Jones, Terry. *Chaucer's Knight: The Portrait of a Medieval Mercenary.* Baton Rouge: Louisiana State University Press, 1980.

Keil, Heinrich, ed. *Grammatici Latini.* 7 vols. 1857–80. Reprint. Hildesheim: Olms, 1981.

Kierkegaard, Søren. *The Concept of Irony with Constant Reference to Socrates.* Trans. Lee M. Capel. Bloomington: Indiana University Press, 1965.

Kiser, Lisa J. *Telling Classical Tales: Chaucer and the "Legend of Good Women."* Ithaca: Cornell University Press, 1983.

Kittredge, George Lyman. *Chaucer and His Poetry.* Cambridge, Mass.: Harvard University Press, 1915.

Knox, Norman. *The Word "Irony" and Its Context (1500–1755).* Durham: Duke University Press, 1961.

Köhler, Erich. *Ideal und Wirklichkeit in der höfischen Epik*. Tübingen: Niemeyer, 1956.

––––––. "Literatursoziologische Perspektiven." In *Le Roman jusqu'à la fin du XIIIe siècle*, ed. Jean Frappier and Reinhold R. Grimm. Grundriß der romanischen Literaturen des Mittelalters, 4/1. Heidelberg: Carl Winter, 1978.

––––––. "Quelques observations d'ordre historico-sociologique sur les rapports entre la chanson de geste et le roman courtois." In *Chanson de geste und höfischer Roman*. Heidelberg: Carl Winter, 1963.

Köpke, Rudolf. *Ludwig Tieck: Erinnerungen aus dem Leben des Dichters nach dessen mündlichen und schriftlichen Mittheilungen*. 2 vols. Leipzig: Brockhaus, 1855.

LaCapra, Dominick. *Soundings in Critical Theory*. Ithaca: Cornell University Press, 1989.

Lacoue-Labarthe, Philippe, and Jean-Luc Nancy. *L'Absolu littéraire: Théorie de la littérature du romantisme allemand*. Paris: Seuil, 1978.

Lang, Candace. *Irony/Humor: Critical Paradigms*. Baltimore: Johns Hopkins University Press, 1988.

Langland, William. *The Vision of Piers Plowman*. Ed. A. V. C. Schmidt. London: Dent, 1978.

Lausberg, Heinrich. *Elemente der literarischen Rhetorik: Eine Einführung für Studierende der klassischen, romanischen, englischen und deutschen Philologie*. 1949. 3d ed. Munich: Hueber, 1967.

––––––. *Handbuch der literarischen Rhetorik: Eine Grundlegung der Literaturwissenschaft*. 1960. 2d ed. 2 vols. Munich: Hueber, 1973.

Leicester, H. Marshall, Jr. "The Art of Impersonation: A General Prologue to the *Canterbury Tales*." *PMLA* 95 (1980): 213–24.

Lentricchia, Frank. *After the New Criticism*. Chicago: University of Chicago Press, 1980.

Lévi-Strauss, Claude. *Le Cru et le cuit*. Paris: Plon, 1964.

Littré, E. *Dictionnaire de la Langue française*. Paris: Hachette, 1863.

Liu, Alan. "The Power of Formalism: The New Historicism." *ELH* 56 (1989): 721–71.

Lounsbury, Thomas Raynsford. *Studies in Chaucer, His Life and Writings*. 3 vols. New York: Harper, 1892.

Lowes, John Livingston. "Chaucer and the Seven Deadly Sins." *PMLA* 30 (1915): 237–371.

––––––. "Simple and Coy: A Note on Fourteenth-Century Poetic Diction." *Anglia* 33 (1910): 440–51.

Lubac, Henri de. *Exégèse médiévale: Les Quatre Sens de l'écriture*. Paris: Aubier, 1959–62.

Lüdeke, Henry. *Die Funktionen des Erzählers in Chaucers epischer Dichtung*. Halle: Niemeyer, 1928.

Lukács, Georg. *Die Theorie des Romans: Ein geschichtsphilosophischer Versuch über die Formen der großen Epik*. 1920. 2d ed. Neuwied: Luchterhand, 1963.

Lussky, Alfred Edwin. *Tieck's Romantic Irony: With Special Emphasis Upon the Influence of Cervantes, Sterne, and Goethe*. Chapel Hill: University of North Carolina Press, 1932.

McGann, Jerome J. *The Romantic Ideology: A Critical Investigation*. Chicago: University of Chicago Press, 1983.

Mann, Thomas. *Betrachtungen eines Unpolitischen*. 1918. Ed. Peter de Mendelssohn. Frankfurt am Main: Fischer, 1983.

––––––. *Doktor Faustus: Das Leben des deutschen Tonsetzers Adrian Leverkühn erzählt von einem Freunde*. 1947. Frankfurt am Main: Fischer, 1967.

––––––. "[Humor und Ironie: Beitrag zu einer Rundfunkdiskussion]." 1953. *Gesammelte Werke in Dreizehn Band*, 11:801–5. Frankfurt am Main: Fischer, 1960.

Martianus Capella. *Martianus Capella and the Seven Liberal Arts*. Trans. William Harris Stahl and Richard Johnson. 2 vols. New York: Columbia University Press, 1977.

Mellor, Anne K. *English Romantic Irony*. Cambridge, Mass.: Harvard University Press, 1980.

Michelet, Jules. *Histoire de la Révolution française.* Ed. Claude Mettra. 2 vols. Paris: Laffont, 1979.

Miskimin, Alice. *The Renaissance Chaucer.* New Haven: Yale University Press, 1975.

Mooney, Michael. *Vico in the Tradition of Rhetoric.* Princeton: Princeton University Press, 1985.

Muecke, D. C. *The Compass of Irony.* London: Methuen, 1969.

————. *Irony.* London: Methuen, 1970.

Müller, Adam. *Kritische-ästhetische und philosophische Schriften.* Ed. Walter Schroeder and Werner Sieber. 2 vols. Neuwied: Luchterhand, 1967.

Muscatine, Charles. *Chaucer and the French Tradition.* Berkeley: University of California Press, 1957.

————. *Poetry and Crisis in the Age of Chaucer.* Notre Dame: University of Notre Dame Press, 1972.

Musil, Robert. *Der Mann ohne Eigenschaften.* Ed. Adolf Frisé. 2 vols. Reinbek bei Hamburg: Rowohlt, 1978.

Nietzsche, Friedrich. *Werke in drei Bänden.* Ed. Karl Schlechta. Munich: Carl Hanser, 1954–56.

Nolan, Barbara. " 'A Poet Ther was': Chaucer's Voices in the General Prologue to the *Canterbury Tales.*" *PMLA* 101 (1986): 154–69.

Novalis [Friedrich von Hardenberg]. *Schriften.* Ed. Paul Kluckhorn and Richard Samuel. 4 vols. Stuttgart: Kohlhammer, 1960–75.

O'Hara, Daniel. "The Genius of Irony: Nietzsche in Bloom." In *The Yale Critics: Deconstruction in America,* ed. Jonathan Arac, Wlad Gozich, and Wallace Martin. Minneapolis: University of Minnesota Press, 1983.

Paulin, Roger. *Ludwig Tieck: A Literary Biography.* Oxford: Clarendon Press, 1985.

Pépin, Jean. *Mythe et allégorie: Les Origines grecques et les contestations judéo-chrétiennes.* Paris: Firmin-Didot, 1958.

Plato. *Platonis Opera.* Ed. John Burnet. Oxford: Clarendon, 1910.

Polheim, Karl Konrad. *Die Arabeske: Ansichten und Ideen aus Fr. Schlegels Poetik.* Munich: Schöningh, 1965.

Popper, Karl R. *The Open Society and Its Enemies.* 1962. 5th ed. rev. 2 vols. Princeton: Princeton University Press, 1966.

Prang, Helmut. *Die romantische Ironie.* Darmstadt: Wissenschaftliche Buchgesellschaft, 1972.

Preisendanz, Wolfgang. "Ironie bei Heine." In *Ironie und Dichtung: Sechs Essays von Beda Allemann, Ernst Zinn, Hans-Egon Hass, Wolfgang Preisendanz, Fritz Martini, Paul Böckmann,* ed. Albert Schaefer, 85–112. Munich: Beck, 1970.

Preminger, Alex, ed. *Princeton Encyclopedia of Poetry and Poetics.* Enlarged ed. Princeton: Princeton University Press, 1974.

Proust, Marcel. *A la recherche du temps perdu.* Ed. Pierre Clarac and André Ferré. 3 vols. Paris: Gallimard, 1954.

Puttenham, George. *The Arte of English Poesie.* 1589. Facs. reprint. Kent: Kent State University Press, 1970.

Quintilian. *M. Fabii Quintiliani Institutionis oratoriae libri duodecim.* Ed. Eduard Bonnell. 2 vols. Leipzig: Teubner, 1883.

————. *M. Fabi Quintiliani Institutionis oratoriae libri duodecim.* Ed. M. Winterbottom. 2 vols. Oxford: Clarendon Press, 1970.

Rabelais, François. *Oeuvres complètes.* Ed. Pierre Jourda. 2 vols. Paris: Garnier, 1962.

————. *Oeuvres de François Rabelais.* Ed. Abel Lefranc. Vol. 1, *Gargantua.* Vol. 3, *Pantagruel* *(Prol. ch. I–XI).* Paris: Champion, 1913–22.

Reiss, Edmund. "Chaucer and Medieval Irony." *Studies in the Age of Chaucer* 1 (1979): 67–82.

Ribbeck, Otto. "Ueber den Begriff des *eirōn*." *Rheinisches Museum* 31 (1876): 381–400.

Richards, I. A. *Principles of Literary Criticism*. 1924. New York: Harcourt, Brace and Co., 1938.

Richelet, P[ierre]. *Dictionnaire françois contenant Les Mots et Les Choses*. 2 vols. Geneva: Widerhold, 1680.

Richter, Jean Paul Friedrich. See Jean Paul.

Robertson, D. W., Jr. *A Preface to Chaucer: Studies in Medieval Perspectives*. Princeton: Princeton University Press, 1962.

Rorty, Richard. *Contingency, Irony, and Solidarity*. Cambridge: Cambridge University Press, 1989.

Rosen, Stanley. *Plato's Sophist: The Drama of Original and Image*. New Haven: Yale University Press, 1983.

————. *Plato's Symposium*. New Haven: Yale University Press, 1968.

Said, Edward W. *The World, the Text, and the Critic*. Cambridge, Mass.: Harvard University Press, 1983.

Saintsbury, George. "Chaucer." In *Cambridge History of English Literature*, 2:183–224. Cambridge: Cambridge University Press, 1908.

Saussure, Ferdinand de. *Cours de linguistique générale*, ed. Charles Bally and Albert Sechehàye. Ed. Tullio de Mauro. Paris: Payot, 1972.

Schlegel, A. W. *Ueber dramatische Kunst und Litteratur. Vorlesungen*. 2 vols. Heidelberg: Mohr und Zimmer, 1809–11.

Schlegel, Friedrich. *Ansichten und Ideen von der christlichen Kunst*. Ed. Hans Eichner. Kritische Friedrich-Schlegel-Ausgabe, 4. Munich: Schöningh, 1959.

————. *Briefe von und an Friedrich und Dorothea Schlegel. Die Periode des Athenäums, 25. Juli 1797–Ende August 1799*. Ed. Raymond Immerwahr. Kritische Friedrich-Schlegel-Ausgabe, 24/3. Paderborn: Schöningh, 1985.

————. *Charakteristiken und Kritiken I (1796–1801)*. Ed. Hans Eichner. Kritische Friedrich-Schlegel-Ausgabe, 2. Munich: Schöningh, 1967.

————. *Fragmente zur Poesie und Literatur. Erster Teil*. Ed. Hans Eichner. Kritische Friedrich-Schlegel-Ausgabe, 16. Paderborn: Schöningh, 1981.

————. *Friedrich Schlegels Briefe an seinen Bruder August Wilhelm*. Ed. Oskar F. Walzel. Berlin: Speyer and Peters, 1890.

————. *Literary Notebooks, 1797–1801*. Ed. Hans Eichner. London: Athlone Press, 1957.

————. *Philosophische Lehrjahre (1796–1806) nebst philosophischen Manuscripten aus den Jahren 1796–1828. Erster Teil*. Ed. Ernst Behler. Kritische Friedrich-Schlegel-Ausgabe, 18. Munich: Schöningh, 1963.

————. *Philosophische Vorlesungen [1800–1807]*. Ed. Jean-Jacques Anstett. Kritische Friedrich-Schlegel-Ausgabe, 12–13. Munich: Schöningh, 1964.

Screech, M. A. *Rabelais*. Ithaca: Cornell University Press, 1979.

Sedgewick, G. G. *Of Irony, Especially in Drama*. Toronto: University of Toronto Press, 1935.

Seznec, Jean. *La Survivance des dieux antiques*. London: Warburg Institute, 1940.

Shaftesbury, Anthony, Earl of. *Characteristicks of Men, Manners, Opinions, Times*. 2d ed., 1714. 3 vols. Reprint. Farnborough, Hants: Gregg, 1968.

Shoaf, R. A. *Dante, Chaucer, and the Currency of the Word: Money, Images, and Reference in Late Medieval Poetry*. Norman: University of Oklahoma Press, 1983.

Simpson, David. *Irony and Authority in Romantic Poetry*. Totowa, N.J.: Rowman and Littlefield, 1979.

Skeat, Walter W., ed. See Chaucer.

Solger, Karl Wilhelm Ferdinand. *Erwin: Vier Gespräche über das Schöne und die Kunst zusammen mit Solgers Rezension von A. W. Schlegels Vorlesungen über dramatische Kunst und Literatur.* Ed. Wolfhart Henckmann. Munich: Fink, 1970.

———. *Nachgelassene Schriften und Briefwechsel.* Ed. Ludwig Tieck und Friedrich von Raumer. 1826. 2 vols. Facs. reprint. Heidelberg: Schneider, 1973.

———. *Vorlesungen über Aesthetik.* Ed. K. W. L. Heyse Leipzig: Brockhaus, 1829.

Spurgeon, Caroline F. E. *Five Hundred Years of Chaucer Criticism and Allusion (1357–1900).* 1908–17. 5 pts. Reprint. 3 vols. New York: Russell and Russell, 1960.

Starobinski, Jean. "Ironie et melancolie (I): Le théâtre de Carlo Gozzi." *Critique* 22 (1966): 291–308.

Stendhal [Henri Beyle]. *Romans et nouvelles.* Ed. Henri Martineau. 2 vols. Paris: Gallimard, 1948.

Sterne, Laurence. *The Life and Opinions of Tristram Shandy, Gentleman.* Ed. Ian Watt. Boston: Houghton Mifflin, 1965.

Strohschneider-Kohrs, Ingrid. *Die romantische Ironie in Theorie und Gestaltung.* 1960. 2d ed. Tübingen: Niemeyer, 1977.

Suleiman, Susan. "Interpreting Ironies." *Diacritics* 6 (Summer 1976): 15–21.

Szondi, Peter. "Friedrich Schlegel und die romantische Ironie. Mit einem Anhang über Ludwig Tieck." *Euphorion* 48 (1954): 397–411.

Taylor, P. B. "Chaucer's *Cosyn to the Dede.*" *Speculum* 57 (1982): 315–27.

Theophrastus. *Theophrasti Characteres.* Ed. Herman Diels. Oxford: Clarendon Press, 1909.

Thesaurus Linguae Latinae. Leipzig: Teubner, 1906–.

Thirlwall, Connop. "On the Irony of Sophocles." *Philological Museum* 1–2 (1833): 483–537.

Thompson, Alan Reynolds. *The Dry Mock: A Study of Irony in Drama.* Berkeley: University of California Press, 1948.

Thomson, J. A. K. *Irony: An Historical Introduction.* Cambridge, Mass.: Harvard University Press, 1927.

Tieck, Ludwig. *Schriften.* 28 vols. Berlin: Reimer, 1828–54.

Tobler, Adolf, and Erhard Lommatzsch. *Altfranzösisches Wörterbuch,* vol. 4. Wiesbaden: Franz Steiner, 1960.

Todorov, Tzvetan. *Théories du symbole.* Paris: Seuil, 1977.

Tupper, Frederick. "Chaucer and the Seven Deadly Sins." *PMLA* 19 (1914): 93–128.

Tyrwhitt, Thomas, ed. See Chaucer.

Vico, Giambattista. *Opere.* Ed. Fausto Nicolini. Milan: Ricciardi, [1953].

———. *Opere di G. B. Vico.* 8 vols. Bari: Laterza, 1911–41.

Vlastos, Gregory. "Socratic Irony." *Classical Quarterly* 37 (1987): 79–97.

Walser, Martin. *Selbstbewußtsein und Ironie.* Frankfurt am Main: Suhrkamp, 1981.

Walzel, Oskar. "Methode? Ironie bei Friedrich Schlegel und bei Solger." *Helicon* 1 (1938): 33–50.

———, ed. See Schlegel, Friedrich.

Ward, Adolphus William. *Chaucer.* London: Macmillan, 1888.

Warning, Rainer. "Irony and the 'Order of Discourse' in Flaubert." *New Literary History* 13 (1982): 253–86.

Warren, Robert Penn. "Pure and Impure Poetry." 1943. Reprint in *Criticism: The Foundations of Modern Literary Judgment,* ed. Mark Schorer, Josephine Miles, and Gordon McKenzie, 366–78. New York: Harcourt, Brace, and Co., 1948.

Warton, Thomas. *The History of English Poetry from the Close of the Eleventh to the Commencement of the Eighteenth Century.* 3 vols. London: Dodsley, 1774–81.

————. *Observations on the Faerie Queene of Spenser.* London: Dodsley, 1754.

Watt, Ian. *The Rise of the Novel: Studies in Defoe, Richardson, and Fielding.* Berkeley: University of California Press, 1957.

Weimann, Robert. *Structure and Society in Literary History: Studies in the History and Theory of Historical Criticism.* Expanded ed. Baltimore: Johns Hopkins University Press, 1984.

Wellek, René. *A History of Modern Criticism (1750–1950): The Romantic Age.* New Haven: Yale University Press, 1955.

Wheeler, Kathleen M. *Sources, Processes, and Methods in Coleridge's "Biographia Literaria."* Cambridge: Cambridge University Press, 1980.

————, ed. *German Aesthetic and Literary Criticism: The Romantic Ironists and Goethe.* Cambridge: Cambridge University Press, 1984.

White, Hayden. *Metahistory: The Historical Imagination in Nineteenth-Century Europe.* Baltimore: Johns Hopkins University Press, 1973.

————. *Tropics of Discourse: Essays in Cultural Criticism.* Baltimore: Johns Hopkins University Press, 1978.

Whiting, Bartlett J. "The Wife of Bath's Prologue." In *Sources and Analogues of Chaucer's Canterbury Tales,* ed. W. J. Bryan and Germaine Dempster. 1941. Reprint. New York: Humanities Press, 1958.

Wilde, Alan. *Horizons of Assent: Modernism, Postmodernism, and the Ironic Imagination.* Baltimore: Johns Hopkins University Press, 1981.

Wilomowitz-Moellendorf, Ulrich von. *Platon.* 2d ed. 2 vols. Berlin: Weidmann, 1920.

Wimsatt, W. K., Jr., and Monroe C. Beardsley. *The Verbal Icon: Studies in the Meaning of Poetry.* Louisville: University of Kentucky Press, 1954.

Wimsatt, William K., Jr., and Cleanth Brooks. *Literary Criticism: A Short History.* New York: Knopf, 1964.

Wissowa, Georg et al. *Paulys Real-Encyclopädie der classischen Altertumswissenschaft,* 2/7A. Stuttgart: Metzler, 1939.

Zeitlin, Froma L. "Playing the Other: Theater, Theatricality, and the Feminine in Greek Drama." *Representations* 11 (1985): 63–94.

Zeller, Eduard. *Die Philosophie der Griechen in ihrer Geschichtlichen Entwicklung.* 5th ed. Leipzig: Reisland, 1922.

INDEX